handwritten: 7/6/02 — For Cathy O... A ... in thanksgiving for all your work for the church! God Bless you! Denis Nolan

MEDJUGORJE

AND THE

CHURCH

Denis Nolan

Queenship

PUBLISHING COMPANY
P.O. Box 220 • Goleta, CA 93116
(800) 647-9882 • (805) 692-0043 • Fax: (805) 967-5133
www.queenship.org

NIHIL OBSTAT
Most Rev. Sylvester W. Treinen
Retired Bishop of Boise
March 1, 1995

Copyright © 1995 by Denis Nolan

4th Edition: June, 2007

Library of Congress Number # 2007929459

Published by:
   Queenship Publishing
   P.O. Box 220
   Goleta, CA 93116
   (800) 647-9882 • (805) 692-0043 • Fax: (805) 967-5133
   www.queenship.org

Printed in the United States of America

ISBN: 1-57918-330-1

When it all began 25 years ago, nobody could possibly imagine anything ahead of time ... The people of the village responded to the invitations of the young visionaries, and many believed with all their heart that the Queen of Peace was with them. The very deep and straightforward message was, and remains: Peace, through prayer, fasting, penance, sacramental life and strong faith. Those tools nourish our on-going conversion which is never completed. In the messages given to the parish, we find a school of a simple and deep spiritual life:

"Dear children! Today I bless you in a special way with my motherly blessing and I am interceding for you before God that He gives you the gift of conversion of the heart. For years I am calling you and exhorting you to a deep spiritual life in simplicity, but you are so cold. Therefore, little children, I ask you to accept and live the messages with seriousness, so that your soul will not be sad when I will no longer be with you, and when I will no longer lead you like insecure children in their first steps. Therefore, little children, every day read the messages that I have given you and transform them into life. I love you and therefore I am calling you all to the way of salvation with God. Thank you for having responded to my call." (12/25/89).

The simplicity – yet the depth of this way of life – has been unaltered. Every pilgrim responds in his very own way. My personal experience is that Our Lady wishes us to live with the true and living God – our God who wishes to embrace our whole existence, and bring us back to him fully through the woman he chose, Mary. The graces are so numerous and abundant, that nobody will ever know how much humanity has received in these 25 years.

Many pilgrims chose to completely change their lives. Out of those choices grew a new way to discover marriage within the Catholic Church, and many wonderful families were born. Many men received the call to the priesthood. Many men and women chose religious life. Prayer groups came into life all over the world. Communities were born, and many different styles of service came along with the civilization of love – and all that in the heart of the Church – so close to the Holy Father. Pilgrims came from many backgrounds, some had faith and some had none.

Nobody is excluded, everybody welcome. How many times did I translate the most wonderful encounters and exchanges Father Slavko had with all sorts of pilgrims! Some kept in touch, many did not. We know what to do; pray for everybody, like our dear visionaries tell us so often.

We need to make the world and the Church alive by means of our transformed life wherever we are, mature and peaceful... In her message of May, 2006, she clarifies it again, what her coming means:

"Dear children! Also today I call you to put into practice and to live my messages that I am giving you. Decide for holiness, little children, and think of heaven. Only in this way, will you have peace in your heart that no one will be able to destroy. Peace is a gift, which God gives you in prayer. Little children, seek and work with all your strength for peace to win in your hearts and in the world. Thank you for having responded to my call." (5/25/06)

All will go according to Our God's timing. He began it, He watches over it, and if we are personally faithful, God's plan will be fulfilled."*

Milona de Rambures

For many years Milona von Hapsburg was the secretary to Fr. Slavko Barbaric, OFM, spiritual director to the visionaries. Fr. Slavko died on November 24, 2000.

---

* The Mother of Jesus began appearing in Medjugorje on the Feast of John the Baptist, June 24, 1981, though she would later request that June 25th be the day celebrating her coming, explaining that was the first day the visionaries remained to speak with her. **"I have come to call the world to conversion for the last time. Afterwards, I will not appear any more on this earth"** (May 2, 1982). She would eventually ask the parish to gather together before Jesus in the Blessed Sacrament in the church every Thursday evening, at which time she would give a message **"as it has never been done in history from the beginning of the world"** (4/4/85). She also requested that everyone read each Thursday, along with her message, Matthew 6: 24 - 34. Later, after stating that a certain part of her Son's plan had been fullfilled, she said she would be giving her messages on the 25th of each month. And so it continues to this day (her messages are posted on the parish's web page: <medjugorje.hr>). In her first monthly message, given

Fr. Marek Kosciolek, of Warsaw, Poland, sent the third English edition of this book to Cardinal Stanislaw Dziwisz, at the time personal secretary to Pope John Paul II.

Fr. Kosciolek wrote on January 5, 2004, "Congratulations! Your book has reached the Vatican. Mons. Stanislaw Dziwisz, the personal secretary to His Holiness Pope John Paul II has informed me about it." In a letter Fr. Kosciolek received from Vatican City, dated November 26, 2004, Mons. Dziwicz thanked him, writing: "I have received your mail. Thank you for your letter and the materials enclosed, answering the question of Medjugorje."

---

on January 25, 1987, Gospa ("Our Lady") said: **"Dear children, I want you to comprehend that God has chosen each one of you, in order to use you in a great plan for the salvation of mankind. You are not able to comprehend how great your role is in God's plan. Therefore, dear children, pray so that through prayer you may comprehend God's plan through you. I am with you so that you can realize it completely."** In her January 25, 1997, message she told us, **"This time is my time!"**

This book is dedicated to the memory of

Pope John Paul II

The Pope of the Secret of Fatima
May 18, 1920 - April 2, 2005
(who every day went to Medjugorje as a pilgrim in his prayer, see p. 15)

(who every day went to Medjugorje as a pilgrim in his prayer, see p. 15)

"...If victory comes it will be brought by Mary. *Christ will conquer through her, because He wants the Church's victories now and in the future to be linked to her.'* " Mary appeared to the three children at Fatima in Portugal and spoke to them words that now, at the end of this century, seem to be close to their fulfillment."

Pope John Paul II, *Crossing The Threshold of Hope*, 1994, p. 221

"Medjugorje is the continuation and fullfillment of Fatima!"
Pope John Paul II, March 25, 1984

"Victory, when it will come, will be a victory through Maria!"
written by Pope John Paul II in his will [1]

[1] Speaking on Polish television in October, 2005, Pope Benedict XVI said that John Paul II left us "a rich patrimony that has not yet been assimilated by the Church. My personal mission is not to issue many new documents, but to ensure that his documents are assimilated, because they are a rich treasure, they are the authentic interpretation of Vatican II. We know that the Pope was a man of the Council, that he internalized the spirit and the word of the Council. Through these writings he helps us understand what the Council wanted and what it didn't. This helps us to be the Church of our times and of the future."

On April 2, 2007 Pope Benedict XVI presided at a Eucharistic concelebration in St. Peter's Square in order, he said, to give thanks to God for John Paul II, "for 27 years ... father and sure guide in the faith, zealous pastor and courageous prophet of hope, tireless witness and passionate servant of God's love. Servant of God, this is what he was and this is what we call him now in the Church, while the process of his beatification continues apace. ... Servant of God, a particularly appropriate title for him. The Lord called him to His service on the path of the priesthood and little by little opened ever vaster horizons before him: from his diocese to the Universal Church. This universal dimension reached its greatest extent at the moment of his death, an event that the entire world experienced with a level of participation never before seen in history." (VIS 070403 - 630)

Having brought this statue (preceding page) from Fatima, Bishop Paolo Hnilica presented it to Pope John Paul II on August 22, 1981, after his release from Gemelli Hospital following the May 13, 1981, assassination attempt in St. Peter's Square. The Holy Father had a small chapel built in Poland, in a forest bordering Russia, where he placed Our Lady's statue gazing towards Russia.

After that assassination attempt, "as he was being rushed to the hospital, John Paul II said, more and more feebly as the moments passed, only Our Lady's name, Mary, and none of the things the newspapers attributed to him." [1] The following month she began appearing in the little village of Medjugorje in communist Yugoslavia.

Perceiving the hand of Providence – the attempt on his life having taken place on the anniversary of Our Lady's apparition at Fatima [2] – the Holy Father asked Bishop Hnilica to bring to him, while he was convalescing in the hospital, all the materials he could gather on Fatima.

The Pope asked bishops throughout the world to join him in his March 25, 1984, Act of Consecration to Our Lady that he did in response to her request at Fatima. Bishop Hnilica, traveling to Moscow and secretly slipping into the Kremlin, consecrated Russia while saying Mass behind an issure of the communist newspaper *Pravda* Returning to Rome the following day he arrived in St. Peter's Square just as the Pope was beginning to recite the words of Consecration.[3] The Holy Father was overjoyed hearing Bishop Hnilica's account of his trip. They spent four hours together that day in the Pope's private apartment. Taking from his shelf Fr. Rene Laurentin's first book on

---

[1] Andre Fróssard, *Portrait of John Paul II*, p. 55.

[2] "Could I forget that the event in St. Peter's Square took place on the day and at the hour when the first appearance of the Mother of Christ to the poor little peasants has been remembered for over sixty years at Fatima in Portugal? For, in everything that happened to me on that day, I felt that extraordinary motherly protection and care, which turned out to be stronger than the deadly bullet." *Memory and Identity*, Pope John Paul II, p. 163. [Pope Benedict XVI would later declare:"Everyone was quite aware of the presence of the Virgin Mary as Mother and Queen of the Church during his spirituality and his untiring ministry...this presence was most obvious during the attack on his life in St. Peter's Square on May 13, 1981." (Vatican AGI, 3/25/05)]

[3] The Holy Father said Bishops could do the Consecration on March 24th (as Bishop Hnilica did) or on March 25th. In a book of her writings published after her death, Sr. Lucia confirmed Our Lady had accepted it in response to her Fatima request.

Medjugorje (written with Fr. Ljudevit Rupcic) *Is the Virgin Mary Appearing in Medjugorje?*, the Pope read to him several sections out loud, asking, "Didn't you stop in Medjugorje on your way back to Rome?" In response to the Bishop's reply, 'No, your Holiness, I have been advised against it!,'' with a wave of his hand the Holy Father told him, "Go to Medjugorje! Medjugorje is the fulfillment and continuation of Fatima!" [4]

Sr. Lucia had also confirmed this in a February 12, 1992, letter sent to the author by Fr. John De Marchi, I.M.C., "Yes, the consecration of the world is well established." Furthermore, a June 4, 2007 CNA report from Rome, headlined, **"Cardinal Bertone shows original letter containing third secret of Fatima on TV"** is worth noting: "Vatican Secretary of State, Cardinal Tarcisio Bertone, showed the original letter from Sister Lucia containing the third secret of Fatima, which the Vatican revealed in 2000, for the first time on television. During the program *Porta a Porta* on the RAI Uno network, the cardinal first opened an orange envelope with a translation in Italian of the letter, and then he opened a white envelope and showed the original letter written in 1944. The cardinal read the phrase that appears on the outside of the envelope: 'Through express order of Our Lady, this envelope can be opened in 1960.' Inside is the letter in which Sister Lucia revealed the third secret of the Fatima apparitions of 1917. In 2000 Pope John Paul II decided to reveal the secret, which did not refer to any world-wide catastrophe, but rather to the attempt on his life on May 13, 1981."

[4] On two separate occasions Bishop Hnilica gave this testimony — to the author.

"All Bishops should visit Medjugorje and personally witness what is happening there, so that they could then bring a decision that will be based not only on reading reports and hearing witnesses but on our own experience."[1]

Bishop Franjo Komarica,
President of the Commission

Bishop Komarica presented this decision of the Bishops Conference during a homily in Medjugorje on November 21, 1990.

x

"The theology of Medjugorje rings true. I am convinced of its truth. Everything concerning Medjugorje is authentic from the Catholic point of view. All that happens there is so evident, so convincing! ...There is only one danger alone for Medjugorje – that people will pass it by!"

Cardinal Hans Urs von Balthasar[1]

"Medjugorje is a world phenomenon that has outgrown the limits of the local diocese. Responsibility for the judgment of the Medjugorje phenomenon must rest with the Holy See."

Bishop Franjo Komarica[2]

---

1 Interview with Fr. Richard Foley, S.J., November, 1985. His work *The Glory of the Lord* is viewed by many as the "Summa Christiana" of modern times. Fr. Henry de Lubac, S.J., said of von Balthasar, who was widely recognized as Pope John Paul II's favorite theologian, "he is the greatest Christian thinker of our era."

2 April 25, 2006, statement by Bishop Komarica, President of the Church's Commission investigating Our Lady's apparitions in Medjugorje.

Table of Contents

Appendix

1. The Church's Unprecedented Stand on Medjugorje

Medjugorje is unique in the history of apparitions of the Blessed Virgin Mary in many respects. For instance, no apparition has attracted as many pilgrims* – over 30 million – in so short a period of time. No apparition other than Guadalupe has caused conversions on such a scale within so compressed a time frame. No apparition has attracted as many religious, tens of thousands of priests and hundreds of cardinals and bishops, while the phenomenon is still in progress.

Medjugorje is also unique in terms of the Church's response to it. For the first time in Church history, the authority for investigating and pronouncing on an apparition was specifically removed from the jurisdiction of the bishop of the diocese in which it took place by a direct action of the Vatican. Henceforth, as confirmed repeatedly by the Vatican, all pronouncements on the apparition by the Bishop of Mostar, to whose diocese Medjugorje belongs, are to be considered simply "his personal opinion" with no bearing on the validity of the apparition itself. Officially, responsibility for investigating the phenomenon that is Medjugorje has rested with the Bishops Conference of Bosnia-Hercegovina, with the head of the commission now declaring "Medjugorje has become a world phenomenon and responsibility for judgment must rest with the Holy See"! (see p. 180). This unprecedented act bears witness to the Church's recognition of the universal significance of Medjugorje. The sequence of events that led to this dramatic development is well known.

---

* Parish records from 1986 through February, 2007 list more than 444,376 registered concelebrants who celebrated Mass in Medjugorje. The Shrine reports that during this time, pilgrimage groups came from more than 83 countries, including: Argentina, Malta, Australia, Austria, Belgium, Romania, Bosnia and Hercegovina, Brazil, Czech Republic, Denmark, Egypt, England, Philippines, Finland, France, Gibraltar, Malawi, Greece, Croatia, India, Indonesia, Ireland, Italy, Israel, Japan, South African Republic, Canada, China, Bulgaria, Martinique, Korea, La Reunion, Latvia, Lebanon, Luxemburg, Hungary, Macedonia, Malaysia, Mexico, New Zealand, the Netherlands, Liechtenstein, Germany, Panama, Poland, Portugal, Russia, USA, Singapore, Slovakia, Slovenia, Serbia and Montenegro, Scotland, Spain, Honduras, Hungary, Puerto Rico, Sri Lanka, Switzerland, Sweden, Turkey, Tahiti, Ukraine, Vietnam, Curacao, Aruba, Chile, El Salvador, Cameroon, Congo, Ethiopia, Guatemala, Hong Kong, Kosovo, Lithuania, Palestine, Peru, Zambia and Wales. (See: <www.medjugorje.hr>)

The public expects us to say something about the events in the parish of Medjugorje, where six children claim the Madonna appears to them... It is certain that the children have not been "talked into" anything, and have not – certainly not by the Church – been encouraged to speak falsehoods. Everything indicates that the children are not lying... When the Jews tried to silence the Apostles, according to the Acts of the Apostles, a teacher of the Law, highly regarded by all the people, Gamaliel, said to the Jewish assembly: "If their purpose or activity is human in its origins, they will destroy themselves. If, on the other hand, what they say comes from God, you will not be able to destroy them. You might even be found opposing God!" (Acts 5:38-39).

This is our stand at present.

Bishop Pavao Zanic
Bishop of Mostar

(*Glas Koncila,** August 16, 1981, p. 1)

* *Glas Koncila* (*"Voice of the Council"*) is the official newspaper of the Croatian Bishops Conference.

After having given his support to the testimony of the six visionaries at the beginning of the apparitions ("It is certain that the children have not been talked into anything... Everything indicates that the children are not lying," *Glas Koncila*, August 16, 1981), Bishop Zanic, the Bishop of Mostar, changed his mind and denied their authenticity.[1] Entrusted by Rome with the Commission of Inquiry as local bishop, he submitted a negative judgment to Cardinal Joseph Ratzinger, Prefect for the Congregation of the Doctrine of the Faith, in 1986. This judgment was printed in various newspapers and many Christians, even among the clergy, did not pursue the matter any further.

But **Cardinal Ratzinger** (presently **Pope Benedict XVI) rejected these negative conclusions.** And — an event without precedent in the history of apparitions — the local bishop (Bishop Zanic) was relieved of the dossier. This fact was not widely reported. Rome dissolved Bishop Zanic's commission and then put the matter in the hands of the Yugoslavian Episcopal Conference. A new commission was subsequently appointed under the presidency of Bishop Komarica (of Banja Luka, Bosnia-Hercegovina).

Reiterating its position that the apparition does not fall under the Bishop of Mostar's jurisdiction the Vatican responded with an implicit rebuke of the present Bishop's widely publicized June 15, 2006, condemnation of Medjugorje when Cardinal Vinko Puljic, president of the Bosnia and Hercegovina Bishops Conference and Archbishop of Sarajevo, announced on July 15, 2006: "The Catholic Church is starting a new commission that will look into the Medjugorje events." The Cardinal said he was waiting for the Congregation for the Doctrine of the Faith to give to him the names of the members of the new worldwide commission. Cardinal Puljic was, in fact, noticeably displeased by the June 15th statement of the Bishop of Mostar.

In 1984 - 1985, Professor Henri Joyeux, of world renown, conducted scientific tests on the visionaries during states of ecstasy.

Professor Joyeux, of world renown, conducted scientific tests...	His research, presented with Fr. René Laurentin in *Scientific and Medical Studies on the Apparitions at Medjugorje*, (Dublin, Veritas, 1987) discarded definitively the thesis of deceit on the part of the visionaries, as well as that of their psychical dis-

equilibrium. These findings were confirmed in 1998 by tests carried out on the visionaries by 14 doctors from various parts of Europe.[2] Further extensive scientific tests on the visionaries reported in the 2001 edition of England's "Journal of Scientific Exploration" once again confirmed these same findings (Vol. 15, No.2, pp. 229 - 239).[3]

Now, the results of hundreds of tests conducted from June 2005 through June 2006 by a new team of scientists have been sent to the Vati-	*"Twenty years later our conclusion is the same!"* Dr. Henri Joyeux

can and Pope Benedict XVI: "What is happening in Medjugorje is serious and should be taken seriously," reported Dr. Henri Joyeux. "Twenty years later our conclusion is the same!"

As with every other place of apparitions that have been neither condemned nor recognized by the Church, private pilgrimages (organized by laity regardless of size) are permitted, and official diocesan pilgrimages (organized by bishops) are not permitted. Bishops and priests are, of course, permitted to participate in private pilgrimages.

According to the number of consecrated hosts distributed each day, Medjugorje is one of the foremost places of pilgrimage in the world. By 2006 Medjugorje had received more than 30 million pilgrims. Parish records state that over 70,000 priests, including several hundred bishops, have visited, many with encouragement from Pope John Paul II. In 2006, for the 25th anniversary of the apparitions, the Vatican's official travel agency for pilgrimages, *Opera Romana Pelligrini*, organized about 14 pilgrimages to Medjugorje by bus and 24 by plane.

On the 21st of November, 1990, **Bishop Franjo Komarica** (President of the Commission) came in person to celebrate the pilgrimage Mass and to announce that other bishops on the Commission would follow, and this happened up until the war. According to the customs of the Church, this is the equivalent of a recognition of the devotion and of the pilgrimage. In his homily he acknowledged the good fruits of prayer and conversion at Medjugorje: "The Commission recognizes these fruits." Bishop Komarica further clarified that the BYC had decided that **"all bishops should visit Medjugorje and personally witness what is happening there, so that they could then bring a decision that will be based not only on reading reports and hearing witnesses but on our own experience."**[4] Many have done so. (Note testimonies, pp. 46 - 111.)

On November 28, 1990, a text was sent to Rome: "On the basis of the research conducted so far, the supernatural character of the apparitions and revelations has not been established..." This text was private and pertained to a certain context, and the bishops of the Commission had not intended it for the public since it was not definitive. It was published through an indiscretion, sowing great confusion.[5]

On the 11th of April, 1991, at Zadar, the Episcopal Conference responsible for the Commission accepted Medjugorje as a place of prayer. This was not yet a final "Yes" on the part of the Church but it was a big "Yes." It was in any case an explicit encouragement for the making of pilgrimages and for priests to come and administer

> *The May 31, 1991, edition of "L'Osservatore Romano" reported the Yugoslavian Bishops Conference's pastoral and liturgical guidelines for the pilgrim shrine of Medjugorje.*

the sacraments there. The German edition of the May 31, 1991, issue of *L'Osservatore Romano* reported the Yugoslavian Bishops Conference's pastoral and liturgical guidelines for the pilgrim shrine of Medjugorje.

On the 17th of June, 1991, the Commission formed a "Pastoral and Liturgical Conference" to assist the Franciscans in safeguarding Catholic doctrine in the Sanctuary. To this day, the Commission has demanded no modification to local pastoral practice. This Commission was composed of two bishops and two theologians.

Bishop Ratko Peric, just after being named Bishop of Mostar, came to Medjugorje on June 6, 1993, to confirm 150 children there. In his homily, he recalled the most important points made by the Commission on the 11th of April, 1991, on the subject of Medjugorje, namely:

– Medjugorje is officially accepted as a place of prayer and worship.
– A liturgical and pastoral team is responsible for ensuring the rightful status of the Virgin in the offices of the Parish.
– The Commission has declared a **"non constat de supernaturalitate."** (See Declaration, p. 175).

This Latin phrase signifies that at the present stage of investigation, it is not yet possible to declare the supernatural reality of the phenomena, but that such a possibility remains open for the future.

There exists another canonical phrase – "constat de non supernaturalitate"– which the Commission has not employed. It signifies that the phenomena have been declared false definitively. Few people know of these canonical subtleties, which is why the rumor has circulated – even among the clergy – that the Commission had made a negative declaration and that, therefore, pilgrimages to Medjugorje are either not advised or forbidden. This is not the case at all. On the contrary, there is every reason to hope that the supernatural authenticity of the apparitions will be declared in the future. At the same time, we ought to be patient, because waiting for this declaration may take as much as half a century! In fact, has there been a single case where the Church has recognized apparitions while they were still occurring? How many years after the last apparition did the Church wait before recognizing Lourdes or Fatima?

Well, at Medjugorje, according to Mirjana Dragicevic, Ivanka Elez and Jakov Colo, Our Lady has promised that She will appear to them until their deaths. This promise was made to them when they received their 10th secret and stopped seeing the Virgin daily as previously (on the 25th of December, 1982, for Mirjana; the 5th of May, 1985, for Ivanka; and the 12th of September, 1998, for Jakov). It is possible the Virgin will promise the same thing to the three other visionaries when they receive their 10th secret. They still have only nine and they are all relatively young. If the Church were to wait only ten years after the death of the last one...many among us will have already passed on to our eternal reward!

With the responsibility and authority as President of the Bishops Conference, the late **Cardinal Franjo Kuharic** had said with regard to the Declaration of Zadar: "After three years of study

> *"We bishops have accepted Medjugorje as a place of prayer, as a sanctuary..."*
> Cardinal Kuharic

conducted by the appropriate Commission, we Bishops have accepted Medjugorje as a place of prayer, as a sanctuary... With regard to the supernatural factor of the apparitions, we have said that for now we cannot affirm that it exists... We therefore leave this aspect for further investigation. The Church is in no hurry," *(Glas Koncila,* August, 1993).

On January 27 - 29, 1995, the Episcopal Conference of Bosnia - Hercegovina met for the first time in history. Their meeting took place in Mostar. They made no mention of Medjugorje in their subsequent statement (declaration). Their time was taken up in dealing with the tragic results of "ethnic cleansing" in their dioceses.

One might add that since the Commission appointed by Rome represents the official court of first process with respect to Medjugorje, it does not pertain to the authority of bishops or priests to forbid pilgrimages to Medjugorje. Advice of a personal nature can be offered on their part, but every believer visiting Medjugorje remains in total communion with the Church. (On November 15, 1966, Pope Paul VI approved a decree by the Congregation for the Doctrine of the Faith, *Post Editam Notificationem,* allowing the organization of talks about apparitions and the publishing of new revelations, prophecies, messages, etc., without an imprimatur.)

On August 21, 1996, **Dr. Joaquin Navarro-Valls,** spokesman for the Holy See, instructed the Catholic News Service; "You cannot say people cannot go [to Medjugorje] until it has been proven false. This has not been said, so anyone can go if they want." "In addition," clarified a CNS report issued later that day, "when Catholic faithful go anywhere, they are entitled to spiritual care, so the church does not forbid priests to accompany lay-organized trips to Medjugorje in Bosnia-Hercegovina. Navarro-Valls insisted 'nothing has changed' regarding the Vatican's position on Medjugorje... 'Has the church or the Vatican said no (to Catholics visiting Medjugorje)? No!'"(CNS News Release, August 21, 1996).

On January 15, 1992, (seven months after the outbreak of the war), **Cardinal Franjo Kuharic**, Primate of Croatia, solemnly consecrated his country to the Immaculate Heart of Mary, and (a fact much noted at the time) chose the title "Queen of Peace" to implore the Virgin's help.[6] Just before the prayer of consecration, in community with the members of the Croatian Bishops Conference and 10,000 of the faithful, **Cardinal Kuharic** said:

"Many in the world believe that the Mother of God has established herself also in the highlands of Hercegovina and as Queen of Peace has called in Medjugorje for conversion and peace..."

> *"...the Mother of God has established herself also in the highlands of Hercegovina and as Queen of Peace has called in Medjugorje for conversion and peace."*
>
> Cardinal Kuharic
> Primate of Croatia

"In a society brutalized by a scorn for God reaching even

8

to the destruction of human beings ... God reveals the power of the motherly heart! He is sending the Most Holy Virgin Mary right into such a time and such a world to draw people anew to the only Redeemer..."

"In her messages in the Church and in the world the Blessed Virgin Mary calls Jesus' call to awareness: 'The time is fulfilled, and the kingdom of God is at hand; repent and believe in the gospel.' (Mk. 1:15)..."

"Whoever entrusts himself to her will surely find the Redeemer! She leads each one with her motherly hand on the way of salvation! With this confidence we now want to entrust, devote and consecrate ourselves to her, the Queen of Peace!"

On September 27, 1992, **Cardinal Kuharic** stated for the publication, *Gebetsaktion:* "People who believe and are convinced in conscience that with these messages [from Our Lady in Medjugorje] they can stimulate people to the good – to conversion, to peace – they should do it. This is a matter of conscience." When asked by a journalist to give his opinion about Medjugorje, without hesitation, Cardinal Kuharic answered, "If I use the biblical criterion of the fruits, then Medjugorje is authentic!"[7] In 1983 he had told his friend, Rev. David du Plessis: "How can I doubt that Medjugorje is God's doing?... Do you know that half a million young people have surrendered to Christ? The Lord is stirring this country! They need fifty to sixty priests every weekend, just to hear confessions and to counsel these young people! And it's all because [of] this apparition!" The late Rev. Du Plessis, founder of the modern day Pentecostal Movement, quoted the Cardinal's testimony in his final book, *Simple and Profound* (Paraclete Press, 1985, [USA] p. 198).

> *"If I use the Biblical criterion of the fruits, then Medjugorje is authentic!"*
> Cardinal Kuharic
> Primate of Croatia

In an April, 1992, interview published in *Medjugorje Gebetsaktion*, **Cardinal Kuharic** was asked: "Do you believe that we have

9

neglected to listen to this call, this voice of peace from the Queen of Peace in Medjugorje – and if it would have been recognized that the Mother of God comes, maybe the graces would have been spread over the people in a much greater measure?" The cardinal responded: "This will remain an open question."

During a November 19, 1994, interview with Dr. Max Domej, **Bishop Franjo Komarica** (President of the commission at the time) stated: "Medjugorje is a phenomenon of itself, and the Church has not yet spoken the final word about it. As you know, there was an explanation by the Yugoslavian Bishops Conference,[8] where, according to the investigations up until that point – this means that the investigations are not yet concluded, because unfortunately war broke out in the meantime – it is stated that we should consider Medjugorje as a phenomenon. There is of course also, from what I know, good fruit everywhere in the world, but there are still some things to be clarified and the decision of the Pope or of the Church's Magisterium is to be awaited," (*Medjugorje Gebetsaktion*, 4th Quarter, 1994).

> *"There is of course also, from what I know, good fruit everywhere in the world ... the decision of the Pope or of the Church's Magisterium is to be awaited."*
>
> Bishop Komarica

At the present time, as noted earlier, the Medjugorje phenomenon continues to be studied by the Church with the President of the Catholic Bishops Conference of Bosnia and Hercegovina declaring on July 15, 2006, "The Catholic Church is starting a new commission that will look into the Medjugorje events." Furthermore, a representative of the commission made a very significant statement that appeared in the following September 6, 2006, news report from the Catholic Wire Service (CWS): "Church leaders in Bosnia-Hercegovina plan to assemble a commission to study the effects of pilgrimages to Medjugorje. Msgr. Mato Zovkic, the vicar general of the Sarajevo archdiocese, confirmed the plans for a study commission during a September 5 conversation with the I Media News Service in Rome. He said that the bishops' plans had been discussed that summer with

Archbishop Alessandro D'Errico, the Apostolic Nuncio in Bosnia-Hercegovina. The steady influx of pilgrims to Medjugorje is 'a phenomenon that must be taken seriously,' Msgr. Zovkic said. 'The faithful who come to Medjugorje to receive the sacraments deserve proper pastoral attention from the local priests and bishops, and the many reports from pilgrims who experienced a spiritual renewal there should be taken into account,' he said. '**The Church is not likely to make any final conclusion on the authenticity of the reported Marian apparitions at Medjugorje,'** Msgr. Zovkic said, **'until the "seers" report that those apparitions have ended.'** To date the seers have continued to say that the Virgin Mary appears to them daily, 25 years after the first such reports."

> *"The church is not likely to make any final conclusion on the authenticity of the reported Marian apparitions at Medjugorje until the 'seers' report that those apparitions have ended."*

In response to many questions from priests and bishops about Medjugorje, this compendium of information has been assembled regarding its standing within the Church. During the war in Bosnia-Hercegovina, radio, television and non-Christian periodicals began presenting reports on this exceptional village.[9] It is hoped that this modest summary will help dispel any confusion in people's minds as to the Church's position on Medjugorje. Retracing the history of the apparitions has not been attempted here – that has already been competently related in numerous books. Nor has there been an attempt to be exhaustive, but rather to awaken interest and provide some points of departure from which each person can undertake a more comprehensive study.

Chapter 1 End Notes

1. *(text on p. 3)* On March 22, 1995, Archbishop Frane Franic, Ordinary of the Metropolitan See in 1981 that included Medjugorje, informed the author that at a meeting of the BYC (Bishops' Conference of Yugoslavia) held soon after Bishop Zanic had changed his mind, Mons. Zanic explained before the Bishops Conference why he had done so. "Through one of the children Our Lady sent me an admonition, and the Blessed Mother would never admonish a bishop!" The Conference granted Bishop Zanic's request. and Archbishop Franic's response, "But in the Book of the Apocalypse the Holy Spirit admonishes seven bishops," was not recorded in the minutes of their meeting.

Diocesan and parish records confirm that in 1981, Vicka Ivankovic, one of the visionaries in Medjugorje, relayed this to the Bishop in regard to his treatment of two Franciscan priests, Fr. Vego and Fr. Prusina, who had appealed their case to Our Lady through the visionaries:

"The Gospa wants it said to the bishop that he has made a premature decision. Let him reflect again, and listen well to both parties. He must be just and patient. She says that both priests are not guilty," *(Parish Chronicle*, p. 43. The bishop had severely disciplined the priests for having administered the sacraments to Catholics who had chosen to attend Mass in their Franciscan chapel in Mostar instead of the church in Mostar he had taken from the Franciscans and given to the secular clergy as part of his Cathedral parish). "This support given against the authority of the Church," Bishop Zanic declared at that time, "proves that it is not the Virgin!"

On March 27, 1993 – more than 10 years later – the highest tribunal of the Holy See (the Apostolic Signatura Tribunal) rendered the Church's verdict: in case No. 17907/86CA Bishop Zanic had acted prematurely. His expulsion of the priests and his declaration of "ad statem laicalem" against them was declared unjust and illegal *(Mir i Dobro*, No. 2, 1993). In 1991 Fr. Michael O'Carroll had written in *Is Medjugorje Approved?* "The Bishop's displeasure at what is attributed to Our Lady about the condemnation of the young friars is understandable. But does he not push his indignation too far? Is Our Lady forbidden to find fault with an episcopal ruling, one also in this case supported by the Order? Of course Our Lady does not oppose lawful Church authority, but to point to an error in a particular case is something very different. A priest who, in his sermons in a Nazi-occupied country, denounced the evils of the forced regime, was censured by his Bishop, eventually cast into prison by the Nazis where he died. After the war he was glorified as a hero, the bishop joining in the ceremonies! It was a bishop who condemned Joan of Arc to be burned at the stake as a witch. And presumably all the English bishops who supported Henry VIII against the Pope disapproved of the one who was faithful, St. John Fisher. The entire French hierarchy accepted the Gallican Articles of Louis XIV in 1683!" *(Veritas*, pp. 57, 58*)*.

2. *(text on p. 4)* Regarding Medjugorje, Roy Varghese notes in *God Sent – A*

History of Accredited Apparitions of Mary, "It is entirely possible that if the intrepid psychiatrists who conducted such elaborate tests on the visionaries were to study some of the critics they might end up detecting some of the pathologies and neuroses they failed to find in the visionaries!" (see next note).

3. *(text on p. 4)* When Professor Joyeux through Cardinal Decourtay delivered the results of scientific tests to the CDF, Cardinal Ratzinger replied to the cardinal in a letter dated July 27, 1988: "This Congregation eagerly recommends that these results be relayed with the mediation of your Eminence to Cardinal Kuharic who will submit them to the Commission." But the Commission wasn't interested. "In June 1984 a member of the Bishops Commission, Nicolas Bulat, Professor of Dogma at the University of Split, had applied the medieval test of prodding an ecstatic. He twice inserted a large unsterilized needle into Vicka's left shoulder-blade, but provoked no reaction (though when the apparition was over and Vicka got up to leave a blood-stain marked the spot where the needle had penetrated her blouse). This was the only test known to have been carried out by the Bishop's Commission," *(Spark From Heaven,* Craig, pp. 125 & 131 - 142; and *Once Again the Truth About Medjugorje,* Dr. Ljudevit Rupcic, pp. 244 - 248). Rupcic also reports (pp. 244-248) during the first days of the apparitions the Communist government organized a commission of 12 members (doctors, professors, psychologists and psychiatrists) and obliged the commission to question the visionaries and pronounce them mad. After two hours of questioning, the president of the commission told the children to go home stating, "You are not mad, but they who brought you here are!"

4. *(text on p. 5)* During a meeting in Mostar in March of 1994, Bishop Peric, the Ordinary of the diocese, informed Bishop Paolo Hnilica and Bishop Nicholas D'Antonio, in the presence of the author, "Anyone coming to Medjugorje is doing so in disobedience to the Church." (On March 17, 1987, in response to a question about pilgrimages to Medjugorje, the Prefect for the Congregation of the Clergy, Cardinal Silvio Oddi, wrote: "It remains true that pilgrims go there and obtain grace. Why prevent this? There is not a question of devotion and praying to an imaginary 'Being,' but to the Mother of God")! See also endnote #1 on p 183.

5. *(text on p. 5)* Note the last paragraph of endnote #1, p. 183.

6. *(text on p. 8)* Cardinal Kuharic's words were reported in the January 26, 1992, issue of the Croatian Catholic weekly, *Glas Koncila* and the February 7, 1992, German edition of *L'Osservatore Romano.*

7. *(text on p. 9) Is Medjugorje a Spiritual Movement in the Church?* Fr. D. Grothues, 1998. In a May, 2003, interview with Fr. Dario Dodig, Fr. Rene Laurentin disclosed that Cardinal Kuharic had told him that he was present during an apparition with Vicka that had taken place in his living room.

8. *(text on p. 10)* Fr. Michael O'Carroll, C.S.Sp, (respected for his scholarly

works, for example, *Theotokos*, an encyclopedia on the Blessed Mother) states in *Is Medjugorje Approved?*, "I have refrained from value judgments on the sequence of events involving the national episcopal conference. Dr. Franic has been quoted as saying that the episcopal conference did not want to humiliate Dr. Zanic. But is not their primary duty to consider first the dignity of the Blessed Virgin Mary? Can they risk offending her dignity as an intermediary conveying God's message of light, mercy and encouragement to a world drifting towards darkness, hardship and despair? What historians will say is always guesswork; the guess of many would not be flattering to the Yugoslav bishops." (*Veritas*, 1991, p. 41)

During a lecture at the University of Notre Dame on March 28, 1990, Fr. Michael O'Carroll stated: "The good fruits of Medjugorje are unparalleled in the history of the Church!"

9. *(text on p. 11)* For example, a front - page headline in the November 9, 1992 *Wall Street Journal:* "Forward Into Battle? Not Here Where the Virgin Reigns." Several further examples of the media's attention to Medjugorje: *Life Magazine* (July, 1991 & December, 1996); *US News and World Report* (March 12, 1990); *NBC Inside Edition* (September, 1990); *The Oprah Winfrey Show* (November 23, 1988); *ABC 20/20* (June 17, 1988); *NBC Dateline* (May 18, 2005); *Livre Belgiue* (January 9, 1984); *The Guardian* (September 17, 1984); *The Readers Digest* (February, 1986); *The Internation Herald Tribune* (July 21, 1987); *The Times of London* (July 27, 1987); *The New York Times* (November 18, 1985); *Newsweek* (July 29, 1987, August 25, 1997, January 17, 2000); *Time Magazine* (July 7, 1986); *The Boston Globe* (March 31, 2000); *The Chicago Sun Times* (October 9, 1988); *The Washington Times* (June 22, 1996, October 27, 1996, December 23, 1996, August 30, 1997, August 1, 2001, September 12, 2004); *The Daily Mail* (December 23, 1996, July 10, 2004); *Le Figaro* (June 24, 1998, January 3, 2002, August 15, 2006); *The Mirror* (April 20, 1998, March 24, 2005 July 21, 2005, April 10, 2006); *Daily Record* (November 28, 2005); *Evening Chronicle* (May 15, 2004); *Daily Herald* (January 19, 2006): *New Statesman* (December 18, 1998); *The Advocate* (September 14, 1999); *The Nation* (October 18, 1999); *Free Inquiry* (Spring, 1994); *Historical Studies* (2001, 2004); *Journal of Ecumenical Studies* (1999); *Cross Currents* (Fall, 2004); *Wailes On Sunday* (October 31, 2004) *The People* (August 31, 1997); *Oxford University Press* (1995, 1997, 1998, 2002, 2003); *University of Pennsylvania Press* (1995); *Manchester University Press* (2002); *Duke University Press* (1990, 1991, 1998); *University of North Carolina Press* (1989); *University of California Press* (2004); *State University of New York Press* (1989); *University Press of Mississippi* (2003); *East European Quarterly* (Vol. 33, 1999); *Journal of Ecumenical Studies* (1999); *International Journal on World Peace* (Vol. 21, 2004); *BBC Documentary* (1986); *Review of Religious Research* (Vol. 39, 1998); *Journal of Social History* (Vol. 37, 2003); *The Stockton Record* (January 13, 1999), etc., etc. (Regarding the Catholic media's response, see p. 35.)

2. Personal Comments on Medjugorje from Pope John Paul II

"I thank Sophia for everything concerning Medjugorje. I, too, go there every day as a pilgrim in my prayers: I unite in my prayers with all those who pray there or receive a calling for prayer from there. Today we have understood this call better. I rejoice that our time does not lack people of prayer and apostles." *

Pope John Paul II

* The letter containg the paragraph above, written in Pope John Paul II's own hand, can be found it its entirety on p. 152. Upon pubishing in Poland letters he had been receiving from the Holy Father, John Paul II: I Send You Greetings and Bless You; the Pope's Private Letters, Marek Skwarnicki gave the author permission to include several making reference to Medjugorje in this book (see Appendix 1, p. 151).

3. Blessed Mother Teresa of Calcutta on Medjugorje

MISSIONARIES OF CHARITY
54A ACHARYA J. CHANDRA BOSE
CALCUTTA 700016, INDIA

J.M.J.   8/4/92

Dear Mr. Denis Nolan,

Thank you for your kind letter of 4-4-92. I am afraid I will not be able to come for the National Conference, due to my health – though I will be with you with my prayer. We are all praying our Hail Mary before Holy Mass to Our Lady of Medjugorje asking Her to give us the medicine for Aids patients – up to now we have nothing – ask Our Lady to answer our prayers.

Try to have one hour of Adoration during the Conference.

Please keep praying for our Society, our Poor and for me.

God bless you
Sr. Teresa MC

Blessed Mother Teresa was scheduled to give her personal testimony regarding Our Lady's apparitions in Medjugorje at the 1992 National Conference on Medjugorje at the University of Notre Dame. Due to poor health, however, she was not able to attend.

4. Cardinal Ratzinger's Comments on Medjugoje

In September, 1991, during a conference in Vienna, **Joseph Cardinal Ratzinger** (who was Prefect for the Congregation of the Doctrine of the Fatih before becoming **Pope Benedict XVI**) declared that no definitive position had been taken by the Church as yet. "We are open. The Commission on Medjugorje proceeds with its work. One must continue to wait and pray." On August 28, 1991, at a theological conference in Aigen, Austria, **Cardinal Ratzinger** stated that the Bishops of Yugoslavia had said, "We want to be concerned that this place, which has become a place of prayer and faith, remain and come to be even more in the most interior unity with the entire Church," (*Gebetsaktion, #22,* 1992, p. 4).

> *"We want to be concerned that this place, which has become a place of prayer and faith, remain and come to be even more in the most interior unity with the entire Church."*
>
> Cardinal Ratzinger

5. The Official Vatican Statement on Medjugorje

A CLARIFICATION FROM THE VATICAN
ON MEDJUGORJE

Eight years ago a page turned in regard to the "question of Medjugorje." Faithful Catholics should know the position of the Church.[1] On May 26, 1998, the Vatican issued the clearest directive on the subject since the apparitions began.

Bishop Denis Aubry wrote in January, 1998, to Cardinal Ratzinger requesting that the Congregation for the Doctrine of the Faith submit to him some fundamental questions concerning the pastoral attitude to adopt toward Medjugorje. Note the Congregation's response on page 19. One can know that:

– the Ordinary of Mostar has not been in charge of the file (question) since 1986.

– the Church refers us to the Declaration of Zadar (1991).

– all faithful may travel to Medjugorje on private pilgrimages.

– the Church has not issued a definitive judgment and remains open to more ample studies.

– the Bishop of Mostar's judgment concerning these events, "is and remains his personal opinion."

The following page contains the Vatican's response:

---

1   *An important clarification:* "I want to mention the importance of stressing the freedom the Church gives to accept an apparition after prudent and conscious examination, making sure that the message content is not against the teaching of the Church. But often times, you will hear a response that a person is not an obedient Catholic to the magisterium unless he awaits the final decision of the Church. And the proper response to that is: that is *not* Church teaching. The Church teaching and precedence itself is that, after prudent and cautious examination, they have the freedom to personally incorporate not only belief in the message, but to incorporate the message itself. We have that, for example, in Fatima. In 1917, the apparitions took place where the local episcopal authorities prohibited all priests from visiting Fatima. And then in 1931, those same episcopal authorities led the first pilgrimage to Fatima. And when the approval for Fatima came 13 years later, the cathedral was already half built. So clearly Lucia, Francesco and Jacinta were not disobedient Catholics when they accepted the message of Our Lady of the Rosary in 1917." (Dr. Mark Miravalle, *Spirit of Medjugorje,* June, 2006, Vol. 19, No. 6)

00120 Città del Vaticano
Palazzo del S. Uffizio

May 26, 1998

CONGREGATIO
PRO DOCTRINA FIDEI
Pr. No 154/81-06419

To His Excellency Mons. Gilbert Aubry,
Bishop of Saint-Denis de la Reunion

Excellency:

In your letter of January 1, 1998, you submitted to this Dicastery several questions about the position of the Holy See and of the Bishop of Mostar in regard to the so called apparitions of Medjugorje, private pilgrimages and the pastoral care of the faithful who go there.

In regard to this matter, I think it is impossible to reply to each of the questions posed by Your Excellency. The main thing I would like to point out is that the Holy See does not ordinarily take a position of its own regarding supposed supernatural phenomena as a court of first instance. As for the credibility of the "apparitions" in question, this Dicastery respects what was decided by the bishops of the former Yugoslavia in the Declaration of Zadar, April 10, 1991: "On the basis of the investigation so far, it can not be affirmed that one is dealing with supernatural apparitions and revelations." Since the division of Yugoslavia into different independent nations it would now pertain to the members of the Episcopal Conference of Bosnia-Hercegovina to eventually reopen the examination of this case, and to make any new pronouncements that might be called for.

What Bishop Peric said in his letter to the Secretary General of "Famille Chretienne," declaring: "My conviction and my position is not only 'non constat de supernaturalitate,' but likewise, ''constat de non supernaturali tate' of the apparitions or revelations in Medjugorje," should be considered the expression of the personal conviction of the Bishop of Mostar which he has the right to express as Ordinary of the place, but which **is and remains his personal opinion.**

Finally, as regards pilgrimages to Medjugorje, which are conducted privately, this Congregation points out that they are permitted on condition that they are not regarded as an authenitcation of events still taking place and which still call for an examination by the Church.

I hope that I have replied satisfactorily at least to the principal questions that you have presented to this Dicastery and I beg Your Excellency to accept the expression of my devoted sentiments.

Archbishop Tarcisio Bertone
(Secretary to the "Congregation" at the time presided over by Cardinal Ratzinger)[2]

To summarize:

1 The declarations of the Bishop of Mostar only reflect his personal opinion. Consequently, they are not an official and definitive judgement requiring assent and obedience.[3]

2 One is directed to the declaration of Zadar, which leaves the door open to future investigations. In the meanwhile private pilgrimages with pastoral accompaniment for the faithful are permitted.

3 A new commission will carry on the investigation.

4 In the meanwhile, all pilgrims may go to Medjugorje in complete obedience to the Church.

---

2   On January 12, 1999, Archbishop Bertone, at the time Secreatary to CDF (presently the Vatican Secretary of State) instructed the leaders of the Beatitudes Community that the Church needed their community's presence in Medjugorje in order to help serve the needs of pilgrims. On that occasion the Secretary for the Congregation of the Doctrine of the Faith stated: "For the moment one should consider Medjugorje as a Sanctuary, a Marian Shrine, in the same way as Czestochowa."

3   This important clarification from the Congregation for the Doctrine of the Faith has not been widely reported in the Catholic media. For example, seven months after being made public, this directive was published in the January/ February, 2000, issue of *Our Sunday Visitor's The Catholic Answer*, but the phrase, "but which is and remains his personal opinion," was deleted.

6. Cardinal Schönborn's Comments on the Vatican's Medjugorje Statement

Cardinal Christoph Schönborn, the Archbishop of Vienna, who gave the Holy Father and his Papal Household their 1998 Lenten Retreat, and who was the main author of the *Catechism of the Catholic Church,* gave the following testimony in Lourdes on July 18, 1998. The Cardinal's testimony was published in "Medjugorje Gebetsakion", #50, and "Stella Maris," #343, pp. 19, 20. (This English translation is being published here with the Cardinal's permission.)

Cardinal Schönborn comments:

The letter of Archbishop Bertone to the Bishop of Le Reunion sufficiently makes clear what has always been the official position of the hierarchy during recent years concerning Medjugorje: namely, that it knowingly leaves the matter undecided. The supernatural character is not established; such were the words used by the former conference of bishops of Yugoslavia in Zadar in 1991. It really is a matter of wording, which knowingly leaves the matter pending. It has not been said that the supernatural character is substantially established. Furthermore, it has not been denied or discounted that the phenomena may be of a supernatural nature. There is no doubt that the magisterium of the Church does not make a definite declaration while the extraordinary phenomena are going on in the form of apparitions or other means. Indeed it is the mission of the shepherds to promote what is growing, to encourage the fruits which are appearing, to protect them, if need be, from the dangers which are obviously everywhere.

It is also necessary at Lourdes to see to it that the original gift of Lourdes not be stifled by unfortunate developments. Neither is Medjugorje invulnerable. That is why **it is and will be so important that bishops also publicly take under their protection the pastoral pronouncement of Medjugorje so that the obvious fruits that are in that place might be protected** from any possible unfortunate developments.

21

I believe that the words of Mary at Cana: "Do whatever He tells you," make up the substance of what She says throughout the centuries. Mary helps us to hear Jesus and She desires with her whole heart and with all her strength that we do what He tells us.

This is what I wish for all the communities of prayer which were formed from Medjugorje; this is what I wish for our diocese and for the Church.

Personally, I have not yet gone to Medjugorje; but in a way I have gone there through the people I know or those I have met who, themselves, have gone to Medjugorje. And I see good fruits in their lives. I should be lying if I denied that these fruits exist.

These fruits are tangible, evident. And in our diocese and in many other places, I observe graces of conversion, graces of a life of supernatural faith, of vocations, of healings, of a rediscovering of the sacraments, of confession. These are all things which do not mislead.

This is the reason why I can only say that it is these fruits which enable me, as bishop, to pass a moral judgment. And if as Jesus said, we must judge the tree by its fruits, I am obliged to say that the tree is good.

7. Authorities on the Supernatural Speak about Medjugorje

Normally, when it comes to assessing supernatural phenomena (on which the Church has not yet pronounced, as is the case with Medjugorje), one should consider judgments made by Catholics who are universally acclaimed for their spiritual discernment. On this score, the three greatest such Catholics over the last 25 years who had an opportunity to analyze the apparitions were unanimous in their hearty commendation. They are the late Pope John Paul II, Blessed Mother Teresa and Fr. Gabriel Amorth, the world's dean of exorcists.

Pope John Paul II many times expressed his faith in Medjugorje. The late **Cardinal Tomasek** had made public the Holy Father's remark in his presence,

> *"If I were not the Pope, I would be in Medjugorje already."*
>
> Pope John Paul II

"If he were not Pope he would like to go to Medjugorje to help at the work with the pilgrims." The Holy Father had invited numerous priests and bishops to go there. He had received several of the Medjugorje visionaries,[1] among them Mirjana Dragicevic. Upon visiting Rome in 1987 he spoke for 20 minutes with her in private. The visionary states that she will reveal nothing about this conversation for the time being, apart from these words of the Holy Father: "If I were not the Pope, I would be in Medjugorje already." (In March, 2004, she received an invitation from Pope John Paul II to come to the Vatican to meet with him again. His declining health, however, prevented the meeting from taking place).

As the Holy Father was being introduced to 310 disabled from the Balkan War during his March 2, 1995, General Audience, he recognized the Medjugorje visionary, Vicka, when she presented him with a rosary that had been blessed by Our Lady specifically for him. The Pope said to her, "Pray for me and I will pray for you!" She then accompanied him, helping to introduce the most severe cases as he visited each one, (Press Bulletin 10, April 12, 1995)[2].

Here are some of the things **Pope John Paul II** had said, (verifiable by the witnesses cited):[3]

To **Bishop Paolo Hnilica** on August 1, 1989: "Today the world has lost the supernatural. Many people sought it and found it in Medjugorje through prayer, fasting

> *"Medjugorje is the fulfillment and continuation of Fatima."*
>
> Pope John Paul II

and through confession," and on March 25, 1984, "Medjugorje is the fulfillment and continuation of Fatima."

The **Archbishop of Kzangju**'s conversation with the Holy Father was recorded in the February 3, 1991 issue of *L'Homme Nouveau*: "In Korea, in the city of Nadju, there is a statue of Our Lady that weeps." The Pope replied to him: "And there are some bishops, as in Yugoslavia, who are against ... But you must consider the response of the people, the many conversions... All this is in line with the Gospel. All these facts must be studied seriously."

Archbishop Patrick Flores of San Antonio, Texas (USA) shared in August, 1989: "When I met with the Pope, I asked him, 'What do we do about the many people going to Medjugorje?' The Holy Father said, 'Let them go – they're going there to pray. When you get there, you pray for me.' Sometimes the people follow the bishops. Sometimes the bishops follow the people," (*Message de Paix,* Montreal, 11/12/89).

To Father Jozo Zovko, parish priest to the visionaries (1981), during a visit to Rome, June 17, 1992, the Pope said: "I give you my blessing. Take courage, I am with you. Tell Medjugorje I am with you. Protect Medjugorje. Protect Our Lady's messages!" [4]

Bishop Jean Chabbert of Perpignan, France, states: "Medjugorje is the actual answer to the serious problems of today's world... I do know that the Pope is truly convinced of the authenticity of the apparitions" *(Nasa Ognjista,* November, 1994).

24

In autumn, 1994, several Centers for Peace were preparing an apostolic tour for Fr. Slavko of Medjugorje to South America, for January/February, 1995. The **Archbishop of Asuncion**, Paraguay, **Msgr. Felipe Santiago Benitez**, hesitated. He wasn't sure that he should allow gatherings about Medjugorje in the churches. He therefore requested letters of recommendation about Fr. Slavko from the Provincial of the Franciscans and from the Bishop of Mostar. As he was in Rome in November, 1994, he asked the Pope whether or not it was appropriate to give permission for these meetings in the spirit of Medjugorje to take place – particularly with a priest from Medjugorje. The Holy Father answered him with these words: **"Authorize everything that concerns Medjugorje!"** Archbishop Benitez then considered it unnecessary to receive any other recommendations. He called the Center for Peace and gave them permission, for the Pope himself had said to do so!

The news that the Pope had said, *"Authorize...,"* spread like wildfire all over South America, which resulted in the eight countries visited by Fr. Slavko opening wide the doors of their churches and cathedrals to the message of Medjugorje!

> *"Authorize everything that concerns Medjugorje!"*
>
> Pope John Paul II

Words of encouragement by the Holy Father to bishops and priests to go to Medjugorje and pray there are countless. What is more, the Holy Father would read each month the message given by the Virgin at Medjugorje, as well as news of the village, in the *Echo of Medjugorje*.

In February, 1995, a number of Croatian Bishops met with the Holy Father in Rome. Archbishop Franic reports that during the meeting, Bishop Zanic (the retired Bishop of Mostar) asked the Holy Father, "Your Holiness, when are you coming to Sarajevo?" John Paul II replied, "Oh, I thought you were going to ask me: 'When are you coming to Medjugorje?'"

On April 6, 1995, a Croatian delegation made an official visit to the Holy Father. The delegation included Croatia's Vice President Jure Radic (representing President Tudjman) and Cardinal Kuharic. After reading his official statement,

> *"I want to go to Medjugorje!"*
> Pope John Paul II

Pope John Paul II said: "I want to go to Split, to Maria Bistrica and to Medjugorje!" (*Slobodna Dalmacija*, April 8, 1995, p. 3).

A February 6, 1997 CNS release sent out from Rome quoted that day's issue of *Il Messaggero*: "A statue of Our Lady of Medjugorje that cried tears of blood on 14 occasions in early 1995 after being brought from the Marian Sanctuary of Medjugorje to the Italian port city of Civitavecchia was judged 'supernatural' by a panel of Italian theological experts, who had spent nearly two years studying the controversy." At the time

> *Bishop Grillo decreed that a statue of Our Lady of Medjugorje weeping in Civitavecchia is a miracle!*

of the miracle, the April 6, 1995, issue of Italy's main news daily, *La Stampa*, reported: "Bishop Grillo has disclosed to the press without any further reservation that the Blessed Virgin Mary's weeping is a miracle!" With two hundred priests concelebrating, **Bishop Grillo** asked Fr. Jozo to address 3,000 people present at Mass on June 17, 1995, the Feast of the Body and Blood of Christ, to enthrone the statue of Our Lady of Medjugorje in his diocese for public veneration.[5] During his homily the bishop said: **"This grace is granted to us through Medjugorje!"**

In a February 10, 2005, Zenit report Bishop Grillo declared the shrine had become "a center of evangelization not only for the city, but for Italy and the whole world!" Pointing out that thousands of miracles had taken place he said that before the statue of Our Lady of Medjugorje had arrived

> *"The Madonna of Civitavecchia will do great things!"*
> Pope Benedict XVI

"Civitavecchia was considered 'the Stalingrad of Latium' – 60% communist, an anti-clerical and anarchic city."

26

Four months later **Pope Benedict XVI** told the Italian Bishops Conference: **"Papa Wojtyla venerated the Madonna of Civitavecchia!"** And as he was greeting Bishop Grillo at the end of the meeting: **"The Madonna of Civitavecchia will do great things!"** (*Il Messagero*, 6/01/05) The statue of Our Lady of Medjugorje in Civitavecchia began weeping again in October, 2006.

President Tudjman of Croatia came on pilgrimage to Medjugorje on March 15, 1997. On that occasion in front of the Bishop of Mostar, the local Franciscans and the media he repeated publicly a state-

> *"I also wish to come to Medjugorje!"*
> Pope John Paul II

ment made to him on two occasions by Pope John Paul II: **"I also wish to come to Medjugorje!"**

After a July, 1987, pilgrimage to Medjugorje, **Archbishop Gaetano Allibrandi, the Papal Nuncio** in Dublin, paid one of his normal visits to Rome and was surprised to find a message from the Pope waiting for him at the Papal Secretariat of State: the Holy Father wanted to speak to him! This kind of message was quite unusual. When he met the Pope, the first thing John Paul II said to him was: "I hear you have been to Medjugorje, tell me all about it!" The Nuncio described how he had found Medjugorje, the graces he had received there, and his visit with the visionaries. As the meeting was ending, the Holy Father took six rosaries and blessed them; then he asked the Nuncio to make sure that these rosaries were given to each of the visionaries on his behalf!

In personal letters written by the Holy Father now made public, Pope John Paul II often expressed gratitude for Medjugorje and his belief in the authenticity of Our Lady's apparitions there (see pp. 151 - 174).[6]

That the Holy Father had said (and not just privately) that he wanted to go to Medjugorje could be taken as an important step towards recognition. It was considered a remarkable gesture of recognition, for example, when in 1979 the Pope visited the apparition site at Knock in Ireland.

Let us note the declarations of **Blessed Mother Teresa** to pilgrims visiting Medjugorje: "Say to all those going to Medjugorje: Pray to the Virgin of Medjugorje to give us the medicine to cure AIDS." "I give thanks to Our Lady of Medjugorje. I know that

> *"I, too, go there [to Medjugorje] every day as a pilgrim in my prayers: I unite in my prayers with all those who pray there or receive a calling for prayer from there. Today we have understood this call better."*
> Pope John Paul II

many people go there and are converted. I thank God for guiding us in this way at this period." On her 85th birthday she told the Croatian Ambassador to India of her desire to go to Medjugorje (Vjesnik, 8/31/95, p. 4).

On April 8, 1992, Mother Teresa wrote *in her own hand* to the author (see p. 16): "We are all praying one Hail Mary before Holy Mass to Our Lady of Medjugorje..." (On August 12, 1991, she gave him written permission to publish her letters referring to Medjugorje specifically

> *"We are all praying one Hail Mary before Holy Mass to Our Lady of Medjugorje."*
> Blessed Mother Teresa

in order to refute attacks against its authenticity: "I give you permission to use my words for the glory of God and the good of souls").

Archbishop Angelo Kim, President of the Korean Episcopal Conference, reported in the *Korean Catholic* weekly, 11th of November, 1990, the following dialogue with John Paul II: "Thanks to

> *"When it is a question of prophetic revelations, the Pope is the sole judge!"*
> Pope Leo X
> 5th Lateran Council

you, Poland has now been freed from Communism." The Pope replied, "No, not me, but by the works of the Blessed Virgin, according to her affirmations at Fatima and Medjugorje." [7]

Since some critics of Medjugorje have said that it comes from a diabolic source, we are fortunate that Medjugorje has been the subject of sustained analysis by the world's leading expert on the Devil, Fr. Amorth, chief exorcist of the Diocese of Rome and also the founder of the Church's Association of Exorcists. An example will show the relevance of this: if a new substance is discovered, any lay person can speculate on its chemical com-

> *Poland has been freed from Communism "by the works of the Blessed Virgin, according to her affirmations at Fatima and Medjugorje."* Pope John Paul II

position. But, in the final analysis, it is the assessment of a trained chemist equipped with the appropriate apparatus that is likely to yield the most accurate account of the compound's composition. In the present situation, the best evaluation of the presence of the Devil will come from someone who, so to speak, identifies and expels the Devil on a daily basis. Hence Fr. Amorth's testimony about Medjugorje is of special importance. Here is what he has to say:

In an interview given in Medjugorje in July, 2002, to Fr. Dario Dodig, Fr. Amorth said, "Medjugorje is a fortress against Satan. Satan hates Medjugorje because it is a place of conversion, of prayer, of transformation of life." He notes further, "I always understood Medjugorje as a continuation of Fatima. According to Our Lady's words in Fatima, if we had prayed and fasted, there would not have been World War II. We have not listened to her and therefore there was a war. Also here in Medjugorje, Our Lady often calls to prayer for peace. In her apparitions, Our Lady always presents herself under another name to show the goal of her apparitions. At Lourdes, she presented herself as the Immaculate Conception, in Fatima as the

> *"Medjugorje is a fortress against Satan. Satan hates Medjugorje!"* Fr. Gabriel Amorth (Official Exorsist, Diocese of Rome)

Queen of the Holy Rosary. Here in Medjugorje, Our Lady presented herself as the Queen of Peace. We all remember the words "Mir, Mir, Mir" (peace, peace, peace) that were written in the sky at the very beginning of the apparitions. We see clearly that humanity is running the risk of war, and Our Lady insists on prayer and on Christian life to attain peace."

Since 1984, Fr. Amorth has been leading a prayer group inspired by the messages of Our Lady in Medjugorje and has authored a regular column in the periodical *Echo di Medjugorje*.

On February 25, 1994, Pope John Paul II wrote to his lifelong friends, Marek and Sophia Skwarnicki: "I guess Medjugorje is better understood these days. This kind of 'insisting' of our Mother is better understood today when we see with our very eyes the enormousness of the danger. At the same time, the response in the way of a special prayer – and that coming from people all around the world – fills us with hope that here, too, the good will prevail. Peace is possible... It can be that there is only one such sanctuary in the world" (see the Pope's letter on page 157).

> "I guess Medjugorje is better understood these days. This kind of 'insisting' of our Mother is better understood today when we see with our very eyes the enormousness of the danger. At the same time, the response in the way of a special prayer - and that coming from people all around the world - fills us with hope that here, too, the good will prevail. Peace is possible... It can be that there is only one such sanctuary in the world."
>
> Pope John Paul II

Chapter 7 End Notes

1. *(text on p. 23)* Ivan Dragicevic was the only Medjugorje visionary not to have met the Holy Father. On April 2, 2005, during her apparition which took place two hours after the Pope's death, Our Lady brought him with her when she appeared to Ivan. He shared the experience on April 25, 2005, during a talk in Lancaster, PA.

2. *(text on p. 23)* The author has pictures of the Holy Father conversing with Vicka during this meeting, and one taken in 1987 of Mirjana with the Pope.

3. *(text on p. 24)* For years the Bishop of Mostar, E. Michael Jones and others were charging that reports of the Pope's belief in the authenticity of these events were pure fabrications. His own letters now dispel any question (See Appendix 1, p. 151). Note also a letter from the pope's secretary (p. v), now the Cardinal Archbishop of Krakow, lending credence to the trustworthiness of what is presented in this book.

4. *(text on p. 24)* Regarding the treatment in 2002 of Fr. Jozo Zovko, OFM, by Bishop Peric (concerning the bishop's personal attacks on Fr. Jozo in the media) the Franciscan Provincial in Mostar, Fr. Slavko Soldo, OFM, Fr. Jozo's superior, told the author: "It's not true that Fr. Jozo was suspended by his Franciscan General. He is not suspended! He is a priest in good standing with his community!" (Note that the November 14th letter from the Provincial and a November 21st letter of clarification from the Franciscan Vicar General in Rome are posted at www.marytv. tv.) "And regarding the charges against him, it's interesting that not one of those women has ever sent any of those letters to me. And I'm the first person who should know. Fr. Jozo is responsible to me as far as discipline goes. I find it interesting that neither has the bishop ever sent me a copy of any of those supposed letters. Let me repeat: never have such charges – or anything like them – ever been brought to my attention – and there are none in my office files preceding my time as Provincial! Of course now they can be invented and sent to me afterwards." The Franciscan Provincial had good reason to be frustrated. Charges of sexual misconduct brought against Fr. Tomislav Vlasic, OFM (who was named pastor in Medjugorje after Fr. Jozo Zovko, OFM, was sent to prison) spread publicly by the Bishop of Mostar, had been refuted countless times by the very woman whose name appears at the end of the letters – that the bishop was using as his proof...the lady who was supposed to have written them and sent them to him. She pointed out to him that two letters he had with her name at the end were even written in different handwriting... "I am ready to swear by the Cross in the presence of anybody and everybody that I never disclosed or wrote who the father of the child is." The bishop's response was to ask her to be quiet and not tell anyone, and he continued spreading those letters to journalists as authentic! (Cf. *At the Sources of Medjugorje: Objections,* Daria Klanac, ZIRAL, Hrvatski mladezi bb, Mostar, 1999, p 39).

31

In 1990 Fr. Rupcic published an account of events that give even a clearer explanation for why the Franciscan Provincial in Mostar would be frustrated by the Bishop of Mostar's treatment of Fr. Jozo Zovko in 2002: "On December 21, 1985, the bishop invited Fr. Tomislav Vlasic (appointed Pastor after Fr. Jozo Zovko went to prison) and the 'provincial' Fr. Jozo Pejic for a discussion. After he had seen fit to defame Fr. Vlasic before his former parishioners, he now sought to blackmail him before his 'provincial.' The bishop told Fr. Vlasic that if he would not sign a statement that the Gospa is not appearing in Medjugorje, and that he (Vlasic) had fabricated the whole thing, Zanic would publish his case against the priest far and wide (that he was the father of the child). When Fr. Tomislav refused to yield, the bishop said, 'Well, Fr. Pejic, there is nothing more we can do with him.' After this, the bishop proved true to his word. He slandered Fr. Tomislav before the whole world." (Rupcic, *The Truth About Medjugorje*, p. 77). It is unfortunate that Our Lady's apparitions were caught up in this scandalous war between the local hierarchy and the Franciscans. Well aware of this sad history (from his tenure as Prefect of the CDF) it would be hard to believe Pope Benedict XVI didn't have this in mind when he addressed Bishop Peric and the other two bishops who make up the Episcopal Conference of Bosnia and Hercegovina during their "ad limina" visits in February, 2006. VIS sent out a press release that included the following:

VATICAN CITY, FEB 24, 2006 (VIS) - "Blessed are the peacemakers." With these words, Benedict XVI received in the Vatican this morning prelates from the Bishops Conference of Bosnia and Hercegovina, who have just completed their "ad limina" visit. ...Love "must translate into that higher measure of justice which is mercy." The Pope underlined the fact that, with this spirit, the bishops "will easily be able to carry out the mission entrusted to you, contributing to healing still-open wounds and to resolving contrasts and divisions left over from past years."

"First of all, it is important that every effort be made to increase the unity of the flock of Christ, ... overcoming, if necessary, misunderstandings and difficulties associated with events of the past...Blessed are the peacemakers," the Holy Father repeated... "As well as to the Church's mission in the outside world, these words are also applicable to internal relations among her members..." The Holy Father reminded them that the bishop should be "a 'builder of bridges,' between the various elements of the ecclesial community," (VIS 060224 [560]).

5. *(text on p. 26)* A history of this event can be found at <http://www.visionsofjesuschrist.com/weeping63.htm>. Note there, for instance, the following AP news article:

"*Update January 25, 2005 — Weeping Medjugorje Statue in Italy is Deemed 'Inexplicable' by Church Experts*"

"Report: Document concludes there's no human explanation for Italy's weeping Madonna. ROME (AP) - A review of the probe into a statue of the Madonna said to have shed tears of blood a decade ago concluded that the phenomenon has no human explanation, a newspaper reported Sunday. The Civitavecchia diocese ordered theologians, historians and doctors to review the case and compile their conclusions in a document, according to *Corriere della Sera*, which published what it said was a summary of the findings.

"*Corriere*, Italy's leading newspaper, said the document presented a critical analysis of all the testimonies given at the time, as well as all possible explanations for the phenomenon. 'Everything – they (the experts) say unanimously – indicates that in that corner of the Earth, at the gates of Rome, an event took place that has no human explanation and points at the mystery of the supernatural,' *Corriere* wrote."

"Vittorio Messori, a leading Catholic author who helped Pope John Paul II write the 1994 best-selling book *Crossing the Threshold of Hope* [and Pope Benedict XVI when Prefect for the CDF, *The Ratzinger Report*] wrote the *Corriere* article."

6. *(text on p. 27)* Regarding the Holy Father's concluding words to his March 30, 1991 letter: **"And may everything work out fine on the Medjugorje to Rome journey,"** note Marek's important clarification at the end of the Pope's letter (p. 165). A statue of Our Lady of Medjugorje weeping in Civitavecchia takes on added significance.

7. *(text on p. 28)* Just prior to signing the Peace Accord in 1987, President Reagan (USA) was given (by Alfred Kingon, at the time America's Ambassador to Europe) a letter from Marija Pavolvic, one of the visionaries in Medjugorje. According to Kingon, President Reagan, visibly moved, phoned his thanks to Marija in Medjugorje, and then proceeded to his meeting with Gorbachev after first exclaiming, "Now I'm going to this meeting with a new spirit!" (Marija would later write Gorbachev, "at the request of Ambassador Kingon," informing him, as she had the American President, of Our Lady's message of peace from Medjugorje. Kingon testifies that it was translated into Russian and put into the hands of Gorbachev at the Kremlin. Also some time later, Reagan wrote Fr. Juan Villanova, chaplain of the Sanctuary of Fatima, Portugal, thanking him for having sent the Pilgrim Statue of Our Lady of Fatima. It was "upstairs in Nancy's and my bedroom" at the White House when he and Gorbachev "were meeting downstairs." A non-Catholic, Ambassador Kingon, Secretary to President Reagan's cabinet before being named Ambassador to Europe, gave this testimony – and also his own after his pilgrimage to Medjguorje – at the 1992 National Conference on Medjugorje at the University of Notre Dame: "Our Lady is now coming for all her children on earth, in preparation for a major turning point in the affairs of men!"

H. E. Mr. Li Shuyuan, Ambassador of the People's Republic of China in Bosnia and Hercegovina, visited Medjugorje on April 23rd, 2002. Eighteen Ambassadors accredited in Bosnia and Hercegovina visited Medjugorje on May 11, 2002. The Russian Ambassador also came. Because so many Americans were going, the US State Department launched its own investigation. The former US

Ambassador to Yugoslavia, David Anderson, sent two poliltical officers who came back and reported, "Mr. Ambassador, you won't believe this, but there's something there!" (NBC, *Inside Edition*, 9/90)

Capt. Scott O'Grady, the American fighter pilot in NATO forces whose plane was shot down in Bosnia in June 1995, credited his rescue to Our Lady of Medjugorje: "On the third day of my hiding out, thinking about how survival is first of all a spiritual test, I experienced something amazing and unrepeatable. All of a sudden, in the stillness of my hiding place, I remembered the accounts of my mother's friend who, before the war broke out in Bosnia, had visited Medjugorje, a little place south in the country, where there is testimony about Our Lady's apparition. That afternoon I turned to Our Lady in prayer. Immediately I felt her presence. It became more and more clear and palpable right up to the moment that I saw her. It is hard to describe in words. The vision came through the strength of my feelings, and that feeling was indescribably warm, full of bliss and peace. Someone existed that prayed and kept watch over my return home. That vision was the most important thing that happened to me in Bosnia. It gave me the courage to hold out in the most difficult moments." (*Return with Honor*, p. 105).

·

"Through his book the American pilot made public his own declaration given immediately after the very rescue operation: 'Our Lady of Medjugorje saved me!'" (Press Bulletin 31, January 31, 1996) Upon his safe return O'Grady's picture graced the front page of nearly every American newspaper and magazine. He was on national TV with President Clinton. *The media – in particular the Catholic media – chose not to report any of Captian O'Grady's references to Our Lady and Medjugorje!*

And testimonies abound: the original symbol for the EU (depicted, for example, on vehicle license plates) was a circle of 12 stars - representing the 12 stars in the crown of Our Lady as she appears during her apparitions in Medjugorje according to the artist who created the design (as a result of grace experienced – during a pilgrimage to the village). Grace extends also to those who haven't been there. On August 1, 1997, Congressmen Chris Smith (R.,NJ), the leader of the pro - life movement in the US Congress, and Tom Lantos (D.,CA) the founder of the Congressional Human Rights Caucus (not a baptized Christian and the right hand of President Clinton in Congress) invited the author to arrange a congressional briefing on the messages of peace being given to the world by Our Lady from Medjugorje. The briefing took place in the Rayburn House Office Building in Washington DC on October 22, 1997. On May 5, 2005, the Executive Director of the Congressional Human Rights Caucus - a holocaust survivor (and also not a baptized Christian) - wrote a letter thanking him for having sent Fr. Donald Calloway's Medjugorje testimony on DVD: "You have a very important mission to spread this information to the world!"

In January, 2005, the author was invited to address an American Evangelization Conference. Cardinals and bishops were present (coming also from the Vatican), America's former Ambassor to the Vatican, the Executive Director of the Catholic Media Association for the US and Canada and numerous representatives of the Catholic media. I admonished the Catholic media for its treatment of Medjugorje...the secular media having been more honest! (One example: Timothy Tindal-Robertson's *Fatima, Russia & Pope John Paul II* quotes the Holy Father: "No, not me, but by the works of the Blessed Virgin, in line with her affirmations at Fatima." But the Pope had actually said, "... at Fatima and Medjugorje." The Pope's reference to Medjugorje had been deleted, and also in its second edition - Ravengate Press, 1998, p. 56). An editor for OSV had told the author 15 years before, "As a journalist I've never seen anything like it in my life! It's as if the Catholic media in this country wants to hide its head in a hole in the ground and hope that Medjugorje goes away." A Catholic newspaper had commissioned her to write an article on Medjugorje. By the time she sent it in a new editor for the paper had been named, who had instituted a new policy: the word "Medjugorje" could not appear in the paper!

The Catholic media continues this policy. The editor of *Today's Catholic* deleted references to Medjugorje in the paper's December 17, 2006 article, "Blessed Mother Leads Guitarist to Music Ministry" and did the same when featuring a talk given at Notre Dame's Edith Stein Conference, "The healing of the Feminine: A Case in Point" (March 4, 2007). "Medjugorje was pivotal in my brginning to heal," the speaker was quoted in the article as saying, but this sentence, and all references to Medjugorje – central to the speaker's testimony and to the article itself - were deleted by the editor before *Today's Catholic* went to print. For years the *National Catholic Register* wouldn't allow the word "Medjugorje" to appear in the paper, even in paid advertisements! A chapter in Jeff Cavin's book, *Amazing Grace for the Catholic Heart*, presented the testimony of Fr. Donald Calloway, titled, "Grateful Dead to Greatly Alive." but before Fr. Calloway recorded his testimony for MARY TV (which can be streamed or downloaded to Ipod at no cost at <http://www.marytv/>), he told the author, "I wasn't allowed to mention Medjugorie." (The couple who wrote and preformed the theme song for *Life on the Rock*, Cavin's television program onEWTN, credit Medjugorie for their music ministry, yet guests were regularly told Medjugorje couldn't be mentioned on the show!). Before recording his testimony in South bend for the 1992 National Conference on Medjugorje, Mark Bavaro, tight end for the New York Giants, told the author he had recorded his testimony the day before for Keep the Faith in new York - but hadn't been allowed to mention "Medjugorje".

Indeed , the secular media has been much more honest, (see also footnote #3 on p. 20 and endnote #9 on p. 35). *"When something important is going on, silence is a lie."* A.M. Rosenthal, New York Times.

8. Cardinals, Archbishops and Bishops Who Have Visited or Mentioned Medjugorje

Thousands of priests have visited Medjugorje, as have millions of pilgrims. Hundreds of bishops, representing every continent, have gone there in order to make a judgment for themselves. They have expressed their joy! (The following list doesn't include names of some bishops and cardinals who chose to come unofficially.) Below are some names, from many others, of visitors to Medjugorje:

- Cardinal Timothy Manning, Los Angeles, California (USA)
- Cardinal Emmanuel Wamala, Kampala (Uganda)
- Cardinal Jean Margeot, Port Louis (Mauritius)
- Cardinal Ruiz Bernardino Echeverria, Quito (Ecuador)
- Cardinal Giuseppe Uhac, Cong. for Evangelization (Vatican)
- Cardinal Franjo Kuharic, Archbishop of Zagreb (Croatia)
- Cardinal Corrado Ursi, Naples (Italy)
- Archbishop Girolamo Prigione, Apostolic Delegate (Mexico)
- Archbishop Frane Franic, (retired), Split (Croatia)
- Archbishop Gorny Kazimierz, Krakow (Poland)
- Archbishop Patrick Flores, San Antonio, Texas (USA)
- Archbishop Philip Hannan, New Orleans, Louisiana (USA)
- Archbishop Giuseppe Casale, Foggia (Italy)
- Archbishop Donat Chiasson, Moncton (Canada)
- Archbishop Sablan Apuron, Guam, (Oceania)
- Archbishop George H. Pearce, Suva (Fiji Islands)
- Archbishop Pantin Anthony, Trinidad (W. Indies)
- Archbishop Joachim Johannes Degenhardt, Paderborn (Germany)
- Archbishop Edwardo G. Amaral, Maceio (Brazil)
- Archbishop Jose Hipolito De Morais, Lorena (Brazil)
- Archbishop Jean Chabbert, Perpignan (France)
- Archbishop Gabriel Gonsum Ganaka, Jos, Plateau State (Nigeria)
- Archbishop George Eder, Salzburg (Austria)
- Archbishop Emilio Ognenovich, Mercedes-Lujan (Argentina)
- Archbishop John Joseph Myers, Newark, New Jersey (USA)

- Archbishop Francisco Spanedda, Oristano (Italy)
- Archbishop Franc Perko, Belgrade (Yugoslavia)
- Archbishop S. Fumio Hamao, Pres., Bishops Conf. of Japan
- Archbishop Fabio B. Tirado, Manizalesa (Columbia)
- Archbishop Andre Fernand Anguile, (Gabon)
- Archbishop Jan Sokol, Trnava, Bratislava (Slovakia)
- Archbishop Edwin O'Brien, US Armed Forces (USA)
- Archbishop Jose Dimas Cedeo Delgado, Pea Blanca (Panama)
- Archbishop Farhat Edmond, (Apostolic Nuncio) (Slovenia)
- Archbishop Paul Kim Tchang-Ryeol, Seoul (South Korea)
- Archbishop Nicodemus Kirima, Nyeria (Kenya)
- Archbishop George Riachi, Tripoli (Lebanon)
- Archbishop Leonard HSU, (retired) Taipei (Taiwan)
- Archbishop Antoun Hamid Mourani, (Maronite) Damascus (Syria)
- Archbishop Luigi Bommarito, (retired) Catania (Italy)
- Archbishop Hieronymus H. Bumbun, Pontianak (Indonesia)
- Archbishop Gaetano Allibrandi, Papal Nuncio, Dublin (Ireland)
- Archbishop Armondo Bortolasio, Papal Nuncio (Syria)
- Archbishop Enrico Masseroni, Mondovi (Italy)
- Archbishop Rubén Héctor di Monte, Mercedes-Luján (Argentina)
- Archbishop Dr. Franc Kramberger, Maribor (Slovenia)
- Archbishop Tomasz Peta, Maria Santissima, Astana, (Kazakhstan)
- Archbishop Harry Flynn, Saint Paul/Minneapolis, Minnesota (USA)
- Archbishop Estanislao Karlic, past Pres. Episcopal Conf. (Argentina)
- Archbishop Bernardo Cazzoro, Puerto Montt (Chile)
- Bishop Boulos Emile Saade, Batroun (Lebanon)
- Bishop Roger Kaffer, Joliet, Illinois (USA)
- Bishop Brendan Comiskey, Ferns (Ireland)
- Bishop Claude Frikart, Paris (France)
- Bishop Joseph Fernando, President of Episcopal Conf (Sri Lanka)
- Bishop Anton Hofman, (retired) Munich (Germany)
- Bishop Damian Kyaruzi, Bukoba, (Tanzania)
- Bishop Salvatore Boccaccio, Frosinone, Aux. Bishop, Rome (Italy)
- Bishop Domenico Sigalini, Palestrina (Italy)
- Bishop John E. M. Terra, Brasilia (Brazil)
- Bishop Jimenez Lazaro Perez, Halisco, (Mexico)
- Bishop Giulio Calabrese, Papal Nuncio (Argentina)

- Bishop Antonius Hofmann, Passau (Germany
- Bishop Christian Werner, Eca, Vienna (Austria)
- Bishop Tonino Bello, Molfetta (Italy)
- Bishop Nicholas D'Antonio, New Orleans, LA (USA)
- Bishop Carl A. Fisher, Los Angeles, California (USA)
- Bishop Michael Pfeifer, San Angelo, Texas (USA)
- Bishop Francis A. Quinn, Sacramento, California (USA)
- Bishop Sylvester William Treinen, (retired) Boise, Idaho (USA)
- Bishop Stanley Ott, Baton Route, Louisiana (USA)
- Bishop Henry Joseph Kennedy, Armidale, New S.W. (Australia)
- Bishop Thomas O'Connell, Los Angeles, Calif. (USA)
- Bishop J. Carboni, Macerata (Italy)
- Bishop Jose Gabriel Diaz Cueva, Guayaquil (Ecuador)
- Bishop L. Graziano y Antionelli, San Miguel (El Salvador)
- Bishop Seamus Hegarty, Derry (Ireland)
- Bishop Paolo Hnilica S.J., Rome (Italy)
- Bishop Murilo Krieger, Ponta Grossa (Brazil)
- Bishop Myles McKeon, Bunbury (Australia)
- Bishop Thomas McMahon, Brentwood (England)
- Bishop Gratian Mundadan, Bijnor (India)
- Bishop John Baptist Odama, Nebbi (Uganda)
- Bishop M. Quedraogo, Quahigouya (Burkina Faso)
- Bishop Mukombe Timothee Pirigisha, Bukavu (Zaire)
- Bishop Matthias Chimole, Lilongwe (Malawi)
- Bishop Antonio R. Tobias, San Fernando (Philippines)
- Bishop Daniel Tomasella, Marilia (Brazil)
- Bishop Severiano Potani, Solwezi (Zambia)
- Bishop Hilario Chavez Joya, Casas Grande (Mexico)
- Bishop Santana Hermin Negron, San Juan (Puerto Rico)
- Bishop Mazzardo Angelico Melotto, Solola (Guatemala)
- Bishop Mauriche Chequet, Ottawa (Canada)
- Bishop Juan Rodolfo Laise, San Luis (Argentina)
- Bishop Manuel Menendez, San Martin (Argentina)
- Bishop Lahaen Petrus Frans, Sakania (Zaire)
- Bishop Aloysio Jose Leal Penna, Bauru (Brazil)
- Bishop Paolo Afonso, (Brazil)
- Bishop George Henry Speltz, St. Cloud, Minnesota (USA)

- Bishop Janos Penzes, Subotica (Yugoslavia)
- Bishop Vitalis Djebarus, Bali, (Indonesia)
- Bishop Patrick Quenon, Manila (Philippines)
- Bishop Ricardo Ramirez, Las Cruces, New Mexico (USA)
- Bishop Armando Ochoa, El Paso, Texas (USA)
- Bishop Raymond Mpezele, Livingston, (Zambia)
- Bishop Jean-Louis Jobidon, (retired), Mzuzu (Malawi)
- Bishop Bonaventura da Gangi (Italy)
- Bishop Francis Paul McHugh, Ontario (Canada)
- Bishop Thomas Connolly, Baker, Oregon (USA)
- Bishop Homero Leite Meira, Irece (Brazil)
- Bishop Paetau Luis Maria Estrada, Izabal (Guatemala)
- Bishop Serafino Faustino Spreafico, Grajau (Brazil)
- Bishop Andre Richard, Bathurst (Canada)
- Bishop John Mone, Glasgow (Scotland)
- Bishop Donald William Montrose, Stockton, California (USA)
- Bishop Domingos Gasbriel Wisniewski, Apucarana (Brazil)
- Bishop Daniel Nunez, Chiriqui (Panama)
- Bishop John Jobst, Broome (W. Australia)
- Bishop Joseph Devine, Motherwell (Scotland)
- Bishop Nicola De Angelis,Toronto, Ontario (Canada)
- Bishop Michael Pearse Lacey, Toronto, Ontario (Canada)
- Bishop Gilbert Aubry, St. Denis, Le Reunion (France)
- Bishop Roman Danylak, Toronto, Ontario (Canada)
- Bishop Basil Filevich, Saskatoon, Saskatchewan (Canada)
- Bishop Sebastian, Olinda (Brazil)
- Bishop P. Arokiaswamy, (India)
- Bishop Agostinho Kist, Diamantino (Brazil)
- Bishop Lorenzo Castellani, Rome (Italy)
- Bishop Barraza Isidoro Quinones, Mazatlan (Mexico)
- Bishop André-Mutien Léonard, Namur (Belgium)
- Bishop Paul Bakyeng, (Uganda)
- Bishop Carrero Raul Horacio Scarrone, Florida (Uruguay)
- Bishop Patrick Power, Canberra (Australia)
- Bishop John Dew, Wellington, (New Zealand)
- Bishop Girard Dionn, Edmonson, New Brunswick (Canada)
- Bishop Adelio Giuseppe Tomasin, Quixada (Brazil)

- Bishop Silverio J. Paulo de Albuquerque, Feira de Santana (Brazil)
- Bishop Albin Malysiak, (Poland)
- Bishop Kenneth D. Steiner, (auxiliary) Portland, Oregon (USA)
- Bishop Louis Kebreau, Hinche (Haiti)
- Bishop Joseph Lafontant, Port-au-Prince (Haiti)
- Bishop Victor Maldonado, (Ecuador)
- Bishop German Pavon Puente, Tulcano (Ecuador)
- Bishop Carlos Altamirano, (auxiliay) Quito (Ecuador)
- Bishop Tadeusz Werno, Koszalina (Poland)
- Bishop Michael Marshall, (Anglican) (England)
- Bishop Joseph Mugeny Sabiti, (Uganda)
- Bishop Christopher Kakooza, (Uganda)
- Bishop Stanislas Lukumwena Lumbala, Kole (Congo)
- Bishop Jose de Jesus Nunez Viloria, (retired) Guyana (Venezuela)
- Bishop L. Bataclan, (Philippines)
- Bishop Robert Rivas, Kingstown (Caribbean)
- Bishop Franziskus Eisenbach, (auxiliary) Mainz (Germany)
- Bishop Waldemar Chavez de Aranjo, Sao Joao del Rei (Brazil)
- Bishop Kauneckas Jonas, (auxiliary) Telsiai (Lithuania)
- Bishop Janez Moretti, (Apostolic Nuncio) Brussels (Belgium)
- Bishop Joseph Das, Berhampur (India)
- Bishop Florencio Olvera Ochaoa, Tabasco (Mexico)
- Bishop Leo Drona, San Jose (Philippines)
- Bishop Nestor Carino, Secretary of Bishops' Conf., (Philippines)
- Bishop Cirilo Almario, (retired) Malolos (Philippines)
- Bishop José Antûnez de Mayolo, Ayacucho (Peru)
- Bishop Jean-Claude Rembaga, Bambari (Central Africa)
- Bishop Mario Cecchini, Fano-Fossombrone - Cagli Pergola (Italy)
- Bishop Irynei Bilyk, (Byzantine rite) Buchach (Ukraine)
- Bishop Hermann Raich, Wabag (Papua New Guinea)
- Bishop Matthias Ssekamanya, Lugazi (Uganda)
- Bishop Denis Croteau, Mc Kenzie, Northwest Territories (Canada)
- Bishop Jérôme Gapangwa Nteziryayo, Uvria (Congo)
- Bishop Nguyen Quang Tuyen, Bac Ninh (Vietnam)
- Bishop Silas S. Njiru, Meru (Kenya)
- Bishop Julio Ojeda Pascual, San Ramon (Peru)
- Bishop Gerard Anton Zerdin, San Ramon (Peru)

- Bishop Jean-Vincent Ondo, Oyen (Gabon)
- Bishop Ricardo Guerra (vicar) Valencia (Venezuela)
- Bishop Salvador Pineiro Garcia-Calderon, Lima (Peru)
- Bishop Gerard Ndlovu, (retired) Umzimkulu (South Africa)
- Bishop Dr. Ludwig Schwarz, (auxiliary) Vienna (Austria)
- Bishop Donal Mc Keown, (auxiliary) Down and Connor (Ireland)
- Bishop Abilio Ribas, Sao Tome and Principe (Africa)
- Bishop Jesus a Cabrera, Alaminos (Philippines)
- Bishop Thomas L. Dupre, Springfield, Massachusetts (USA)
- Bishop Tarcisio Ziyaye, Malawi (Africa)
- Bishop Bernardo Witte, Conception (Argentina)
- Bishop Bruno Tommasi, (retired) Lucca (Italy)
- Bishop Francisco VIII, (retired) Huambo (Angola)
- Bishop Mauro Parmeggiani, Rome (Italy)
- Bishop Joseph Oyanga, Lira (Uganda)
- Bishop Adalbert Ndzana, Mbalmayo (Cameroon)
- Bishop William Ellis, Curacao, Neth. Antilles (Caribbean)
- Bishop Stanislaus Szyrokoradiuk, Kiev (Ukraine)
- Bishop Johannes Dyba, Fulda (Germany)
- Bishop Dominic Su, Sibu (Borneo)
- Bishop Bernard Joseph Flanagan, Worcester (USA)
- Bishop Timothy Joseph Harrington, Worcester (USA)
- Bishop Franjo Komarica, Banja Luka (Bosnia Hercegovina)
- Bishop Kazimierz Nycz, Krakow (Poland)
- Bishop Deogratias Byabazaire, Hoima (Uganda)
- Bishop J. Faber MacDonald, Saint John, New Brunswick (Canada)
- Bishop M. Wiwchar, Byzantine Eparchy of Chicago (USA)
- Bishop Francesco Mirabella, Palermo (Italy)
- Bishop Georges Lagrange, Gap (France)
- Bishop Pierre R. DuMaine, San Jose, California (USA)
- Bishop Augustine Harris, Emeritus of Middlesborough, (England)
- Bishop Zbigniew J. Kraszewski, Warsaw-Praga (Poland)
- Bishop Carvalheria Marcelo Pinto, Guarabire (Brazil)
- Bishop Mario Zanchin, Fidenza (Italy)
- Bishop Ramirez C. Talavera, Coatzacoalcos -Veracruz (Mexico)
- Bishop Moged Elhachem, Be El ' Ahhahmar (Lebanon)
- Bishop Frederick Dranuba, Arua (Uganda)

- Bishop Guiseppi Varelanga, Salerno (Italy)
- Bishop Domenico Pecile, Vicar, St. John Lateran Basilica, Rome
- Bishop Dominique Rey, Toulon (France)
- Bishop Jose Domingo Ulloa Mendieta, Panama (Panama)
- Bishop Thomas Msusa, Zomba (Malawi)
- Bishop Allan Chamgwera, (retired), Zomba (Malawi)
- Bishop Remi Joseph Gustave Saint-Marie, Dedza (Malawi)
- Bishop I. J. Darwish, Eparch, Melchite Rite (Aust. & New Zealand)
- Bishop Jose Luis Azcona Hermoso, Mrajo ((Brazil)
- Bishop G. Mar Divannasios Ottathengil, Bathery, Kerala (India)
- Bishop Lazaro Perez, De Autlan Jalisco (Mexico)
- Bishop Daniel E. Thomas (auxiliary) Philadelphia, PA (USA)
- Bishop Antal Majnek, Mukachevo (Ukraine)
- Bishop Robert W. Finn, Kansas City-St. Joseph (USA)

Without having gone there, many cardinals and bishops have noticed the good fruits of Medjugorje and many have openly expressed their belief in the presence of Our Lady there. Some names:

- Cardinal Agnelo Rossi, Dean of the College of Cardinals (Vatican)
- Cardinal Alfonse Maria Stickler, (Vatican)
- Cardinal Franjo Seper, past Prefect for the CDF (Vatican)
- Cardinal L. Antonetti, Pro-Pres. Admin, Pat. Apos. See (Vatican)
- Cardinal Augustine Mayer, Pres.,Pont. Com. Ecclesia Dei (Vatican)
- Cardinal Joseph Glemp (Primate of Poland)
- Cardinal Ernesto Ahumada Corripio, (Primate of Mexico)
- Cardinal Frantisek Tomasek (Primate of Czechoslovakia)
- Cardinal Joseph Bernardin, Chicago, Illinois (USA)
- Cardinal John Joseph Carberry, St. Louis, Missouri (USA)
- Cardinal Hans Urs von Balthasar (Switzerland)
- Cardinal William Joseph Levada, Prefect for the CDF (Vatican)
- Cardinal Silvano Piovanelli, Florence (Italy)
- Cardinal Jaime L. Sin, Manila (Philippines)
- Cardinal Edward Bede Clancy, Sydney (Australia)
- Cardinal Giuseppe Siri, Genoa (Italy)
- Cardinal Hans Hermann Groer, Vienna (Austria)

- Cardinal Joseph Gordon Gray, Edinburgh (Scotland)
- Cardinal Francis George, Archbishop of Chicago (USA)
- Cardinal Christoph Schoenborn, Archbishop of Vienna (Austria)
- Cardinal Ersilio Tonini, Archbishop of Ravenna (Italy)
- Cardinal Francesco Colasuonno, Apostolic Nuncio (Italy)
- Cardinal Moratinos Jose Ali Lebrun, Caracas (Venezuela)
- Cardinal Juan Jesus Posadas, B, Gudalajara (Mexico)
- Cardinal Nesellah Boutros Sfeir, (Lebanon)
- Cardinal Nicolas Lopez Rodriguez, Primate of America (Dom Rep)
- Cardinal Stanislaw Dziwisz, Krakow (Poland)
- Cardinal John O'Connor, New York (USA)
- Cardinal Eugenio di Arujo Sales,Archbishop Rio di Janero (Brazil)
- Cardinal Jorge Bergoglio, Archbishop of Buenos Aires (Argentina)
- Archbishop Angelo Kim (President, Episcopal Conf. of Korea)
- Archbishop Navas (President, Episcopal Conf. (Ecuador)
- Archbishop Wilfrid Napier, Durban (South Africa)
- Archbishop Hernandez H. Enrique Santos, Tegucigalpa (Honduras)
- Archbishop Marcos McGrath, Panama (Panama)
- Archbishop Carlos Quintero, Hermosillo (Mexico)
- Archbishop Rafael Ruiz Bellow, Acapulco (Mexico)
- Archbishop Gregory Sooi Ngean Yong (Singapore)
- Archbishop Barry James Hickey, Perth (Australia)
- Archbishop Avalos Felipe Santiage Benitez, Asuncion (Paraguay)
- Archbishop Daniel Eugene Sheehan, Omaha, Nebraska (USA)
- Archbishop Alois Sustar, Ljubljana (Slovenia)
- Archbishop Hinojosa Luis Sainz, La Paz (Bolivia)
- Archbishop Leonard Anthony Faulkner, Adelaide (Australia)
- Archbishop Zumarraga Gonzalez, Quito (Ecuador)
- Archbishop Varela T. Manuel Chirivella, Barquisimeto (Venezuela)
- Archbishop G. Bonicelli, Ciena-Colle de Var'dElsa-Mont. (Italy)
- Archbishop Antonio Maria Mucciolo, Botucatu (Brazil)
- Archbishop Domingo Perez Roa, Maracaibo (Venezuela)
- Archbishop Geraldo Maria de Morais Penido, Aparecida (Brazil)
- Archbishop Franc Rodeo, Ljubljana (Slovenia)
- Archbishop Peter Chung, Archbishop of Kushing (Borneo)
- Archbishop Mario Rizzi, Apostolic Nuncio Emeritus to Bulgaria
- Archbishop Maradiaga Oscar Rodriguez, Tegucigalpa (Honduras)

- Bishop Leon Roberto Luckert , Coro (Venezuela)
- Bishop Robert Healy, Perth (Australia)
- Bishop Antonio Pagano, Ischia (Italy)
- Bishop Eugenio Binini, Massa Carrara-Pontremoli (Italy)
- Bishop Gomiero, Rovigo (Italy)
- Bishop Cormac Murphy-O'Connor, Brighton (England)
- Bishop Luciano Giovannetti, Fiesole (Italy)
- Bishop Girolamo Grillo, Civitavecchia-Tarquinia (Italy)
- Bishop Martino Gomerio, Adria-Rovigo (Italy)
- Bishop Kirby, Klonfert (Ireland)
- Bishop Rogers, Auckland (New Zealand)
- Bishop John Jerome Cunneen, Christchurch (New Zealand)
- Bishop Carlo Aliprandi, Cuneo (Italy)
- Bishop Lino Esterino Garavaglia, Cesena-Sarsina (Italy)
- Bishop Silvio Bonicelli, San Severo (Italy)
- Bishop Joseph Mercieca, Valletta (Malta)
- Bishop William Zephyrine Gomes, (retired) Poona (India)
- Bishop Teky Joesph Niangoran, Man (Malta)
- Bishop Nikol Chuchi, Goao (Malta)
- Bishop Enrique Hernandez, Caguas (Puerto Rico)
- Bishop German Morales, Zipaguira (Columbia)
- Bishop Alfonso Maria Toriz, Queretaro (Mexico)
- Bishop Franciso Aguilera, Mexico City (Mexico)
- Bishop Calderon Antonio Troyo, San Jose (Costa Rica)
- Bishop Javier Navarro, Guadalajara (Mexico)
- Bishop Brendan Oliver Comiskey, Wexford (Ireland)
- Bishop Chi-nan Bosco Lin, Kaohsiung (Taiwan)
- Bishop Andrea Gemma, Isernia - Venafro (Italy)
- Bishop Paul Edward Waldschmidt, Portland, Oregon (USA)
- Bishop Kuo-hsi Paul Shan, Koahsiung (Taiwan)
- Bishop Joseph Yu-jung Wang, Taichung (Taiwan)
- Bishop Luke Lin Hsien-Tang (Taiwan)
- Bishop Ka Tseung Domingos Lam, Macau (Macao)
- Bishop Oscar Rodriguez, (auxiliary) Tegucigallpa (Honduras)
- Bishop John R. Sheets, Fort Wayne/South Bend, Indiana (USA)
- Bishop Maurice Couve de Murville, Birmingham (England)
- Bishop Michael Ambrose Griffiths, Newcastle (England)

- Bishop Vincent Logan, Dunkeld (Scotland)
- Bishop Roderick Wright, Argyll (Scotland)
- Bishop Mario Joseph Conti, Aberdeen (Scotland)
- Bishop Edward Kojnok, Rosnava (Republic of Slovakia)
- Bishop Kevin L. Rafferty, St. Andrews & Edinburgh (Scotland)
- Bishop Charles Grahmann, Dallas, Texas (USA)
- Bishop Lazaro Perez, Autlan (Mexico)
- Bishop Luis Robles Diaza, Papal Nuncio (Uganda)
- Bishop Innocent H. Lotocky, Byzantine Eparchy, Chicago, (USA)
- Bishop Reginald Michael Cawcutt, Cape Town (South Africa)
- Bishop Alojz Tkac, Kosice (Slovakia)
- Bishop Jan Hirka, Presov (Slovakia)
- Bishop Wladyslaw Miziolek, Warsaw (Poland)
- Bishop John M. D'Arcy, Ft. Wayne/South Bend, Indiana (USA)
- Bishop Joseph F. Maguire, Springfield, Missouri (USA)
- Bishop J. Magee, (past sec. to Pope John Paul II), Cloyne (Ireland)
- Bishop Luigi Bettazzi, Ivrea (Italy)
- Bishop Pier Giorgio Micchiardi, (auxiliary) Acqui (Italy)
- Bishop Maurice Piat, (Mauritius)
- Bishop Pakul Emile Saad, (Lebanon)
- Bishop Armondo Bortolasio, (Lebanon)
- Bishop Antonio Troy Calderon (Costa Rica)
- Bishop Gastone Simoni, Prato (Italy)
- Bishop Carter (Australia)
- Bishop Edward Albert Bahragat (Uganda)
- Bishop Paul Emile Saadeo, Batrun (Lebanon)
- Bishop Tod Brown, Orange County, California (USA)
- Bishop Ludwig Schick, (auxiliary), Fulda (Germany)
- Bishop Robert Cavellero, Chiavaria (Italy)

9. Cardinals, Archbishops, and Bishops Comment on Medjugorje

"Medjugorje is better understood these days... I, myself, am very much attached to that place. It can be said there is only one such sanctuary in the world!"

POPE JOHN PAUL II*

• **Cardinal Siri** of Genoa gave his assessment to Bishop Hnilica in 1989: "I have noticed that the people who come from Medjugorje become apostles. They renew the parishes. They form groups in which they get together, prayer groups. They pray before the Blessed Sacrament. They hold lectures, lead discussions and bring

> *"I have noticed that the people who come from Medjugorje become apostles... They renew the Church!"*
> Cardinal Siri

others to Medjugorje. And these circles – these prayer groups – spread out more and more. They renew the Church!" (*Gebetsaktion*, #4, 1990).

• When presenting the coveted Sapienza Award in 1985, **Cardinal Agnelo Rossi**, at the time Dean of the College of Cardinals, said: "As President of the jury of the 'Letter to the Believers' book award, I award the prize to the book, *A Thousand Encounters with the Gospa in Medjugorje*, in which Fr. Janko Bubalo, OFM, relates his dialogue with the

> "I award the prize to the book, *A Thousand Encounters with the Gospa in Medjugorje.*"
> Cardinal Angelo Rossi, Dean of the College of Cardinals

visionary Vicka Ivankovic from Medjugorje."

---

* See p.157. The Holy Father also held in the highest the first-hand testimony of pilgrims. he wrote: "*Concerning [Sophia's] pilgrimage to Medjugorje...These are then the impressions of a first-hand witness, that is to say, they are reliable in every respect. may God reward you! ...We every day return to Medjugorje in prayer.*" (See pp. 155, 160.)

• During his homily while celebrating Mass at Fatima on October 13, 1995, **Cardinal Glemp**, the Primate of Poland, said, "Through the Mother of God, the Mother of the Church, people draw close to one another. People who meet one another in prayer, at Lourdes in France, Fatima in Portugal... Einsideln in Switzerland, Medjugorje in the Balkans... not only do they encounter divine peace, but they strengthen the life of faith." That same month, **Cardinal Echeverria Ruiz** at Ecuador's Marian Conference in Quito stated in his homily: "My presence here wishes to confirm my certainty that the impetus for a renewal in the Church comes from the Medjugorje groups, in Ecuador and the world over!" (Press Bulletin 124).

> *"Through the Mother of God ... people who meet one another in prayer at...Medjugorje in the Balkans...not only do they encounter divine peace, but they strengthen the life of faith!"*
>
> Cardinal Glemp
> Primate of Poland

> *"My presence here wishes to confirm my certainty that the impetus for a renewal in the Church comes from the Medjugorje groups, in Ecuador and the world over!"*
>
> Cardinal Echeverria

• After finally getting to visit Medjugorje June, 26 - 28, 1999, **Cardinal Bernardino Eccheverria Ruiz** made public his testimony: "I heard about Medjguorje a long time ago. It was my great desire to immediately come here, but until now it had not been possible. I'm so pleased that I came... God speaks through Mary here to all peoples and cultures... This is a Godly moment on earth. I personally feel here the beginning of Europe's conversion."[1]

• **Cardinal Frantisek Tomasek** stated for publication on November 21, 1987, "I would say to priests who want to go to Medjugorje: Most important is your own personal experience; this experience will require then no further words. The experience of nearness to God is decisive. Then the consequence of this experience is to carry that which was experienced, the message, further and to spread it," (Interview, *Gebetsaktion*, 1988, #1). In December, 1989,

Cardinal Tomasek invited the author to come to Prague to videotape his testimony in support of the authenticity of Our Lady's apparitions in Medjugorje for the 1990 National Conference on Medjugorje at the University of Notre Dame.

•The former Apostolic Nuncio in Paris, **Cardinal Lorenzo Antonetti,** is glad to express his faith in the Medjugorje events in private: "Our Lady has been speaking in Medjugorje for 10 years, and nobody is listening!"

• **Cardinal Francesco Colasuono**, the former Apostolic Nuncio in Yugoslavia, stated on July 31, 1985, (at the time he was also the representative of the Holy See in Russia), "Medjugorje represents the event of the century. And we need to study it very well from the theological and the scientific points of view."

> *"Medjugorje represents the event of the century!"*
> Cardinal Colasuono
> Apostolic Nuncio, Italy

• On September 12, 1996, the Feast of the Holy Name of Mary, **Cardinal Christoph Schönborn,** principal author of *The Catachesim of the Catholic Church*, told 10,000 people in Vienna's major stadium: "Medjugorje bears marvelous and immense fruits... Mary is

> *"Almost all the candidates [in Vienna's Seminary] have received their call to the priesthood through Medjugorje!"*
> Cardinal Schönborn

calling us, consoling us, strengthening us and exhorting us today. She takes her mantle and gives it to us as a protection." The Cardinal, Archbishop of Vienna, declares: "If I was an opponent of Medjugorje I'd have to close down my seminary since almost all the candidates have received their call to the priesthood through Medjugorje!"

• Testimonies from 40 bishops (10 Cardinals among them) have been collected and published in the author's book *Medjugorje: A Time For Truth And A Time For Action.* Let us note, for example, from

Cardinal Frantisek Tomasek: "Personally, I am convinced that Medjugorje is the continuation of Lourdes and Fatima. Step by step the Immaculate Heart of Mary will triumph. And I am also deeply convinced that Medjugorje is a sign for this," (*Gebetsaktion*, #17, 1990).

> *"Personally, I am convinced that Medjugorje is the continuation of Lourdes and Fatima. Step by step the Immaculate Heart of Mary will triumph. And I am also deeply convinced that Medjugorje is a sign for this."*
>
> Cardinal Tomasek
> Primate of Czechoslovakia

• **Cardinal Gordon Joseph Gray** (Scotland) has testified: "I know that the Pope wanted the Marian Year because of the message of the Mother of God in Medjugorje. I know that the Pope himself accepts the apparitions of Medjugorje... for there are many results that prove the authenticity of these ap-

> *"I know that the Pope wanted the Marian Year because of the message of the Mother of God in Medjugorje."*
>
> Cardinal Gordon Gray
> Primate of Scotland

paritions," (*The Apparitions of Medjugorje: A Critical Consideration*, Ivan Kordic, Zagreb: K. Fresimeir, 1994, p.70). On June 15, 1987, the Cardinal invited visionary Ivanka Elez to his episcopal office for a joyful meeting that lasted several hours. (A picture of Ivanka with the Cardinal graces page 56 of the book cited above.)

• An entire continent has welcomed Medjugorje – indeed, **Cardinal Edward Bede Clancy**, of Australia, encouraged all the bishops of the continent to permit Ivan the visionary and Father Slavko of Medjugorje to come and speak in their dioceses. They were thus able to meet 150,000 persons in January, 1993.

• Numerous other bishops have welcomed the visionaries in their dioceses, some of them receiving them in their residences. Bishop Hnilica visited Russia with the visionary Marija Pavlovic in 1991. **Cardinal Godfried Danneels** (Belgium) invited Ivan the visionary to a private meeting when he was in Belgium in August, 1994.

49

• The Archbishop of Sarajevo, **Cardinal Vinko Pulic**, just after being installed as a cardinal by the Holy Father in Rome, visited Medjugorje on his return to Sarajevo in early December, 1994.

• From among the greatest theologians of our century[2], let us note further testimony from **Cardinal Hans Urs von Baltasar**: "The theology of Medjugorje rings true. I am convinced of its truth. Everything concerning Medjugorje is authentic from the Catholic point of view. All that happens there is so evident, so convincing!" (Interview with Fr. Richard Foley, S.J., November, 1985.) Von Balthasar met with visionary Marija Pavlovic in Germany. Before being named a cardinal he stated for publication: "There is only one danger alone for Medjugorje – that people will pass it by!"

> *"The theology of Medjugorje rings true. I'm convinced of its truth."*
> Cardinal Hans Urs von Balthasar

> *"Medjugorje is authentic from the Catholic point of view. All that happens there is so evident, so convincing!"*
> Cardinal Hans Urs von Balthasar

• On May 14, 1989, **Bishop Sylvester Treinen** (USA) testified before 7,000 people at the University of Notre Dame that during his "ad limina" visit earlier that year he had spoken privately with the Holy Father, Pope John Paul II. He told him, "I've just come from Medjugorje, there are wonderful things going on there!" The Pope replied: "Yes, it is good for pilgrims to go to Medjugorje and do penance. It is good!"

> *"Yes, it is good for pilgrims to go to Medjugorje and do penance. It is good!"*
> Pope John Paul II

• In an interview with Msgr. Kurt Knotzinger, President of the Ecclesiastical Institute, Marian Lourdes Committee, **Bishop Paolo Hnilica, S.J.**, stated: "An ecclesiastical recognition of Medjugorje would not be possible so long as the apparitions continue. However, the Church's reserve also implies that until now Rome finds everything legitimate. The Church would have had to say something against it long ago if there were millions of pilgrims coming and something were not in order in a theological, biblical or moral sense."

• On March 25, 1994, Bishop Hnilica, advisor to Pope John Paul II for the countries of the East, chose Medjugorje to celebrate the 10th anniversary of the Consecration of Russia and the World to the Immaculate Heart of Mary by John Paul II. On this occasion, he invited Marian faithful throughout the world to come to Medjugorje in order to renew the consecration there in union with the Holy Father. **Archbishop Frane Franic** came, as did **Bishop Nicholas D'Antonio** from New Orleans (USA), and many priests. Numerous bishops from around the world wrote letters expressing their solidarity with the consecration taking place in Medjugorje.

• On August 5, 1988, **Bishop Michael Pfeifer**, ordinary of the Diocese of San Angelo, Texas (USA) published a Pastoral Letter to his diocese, *The Gospel, Mary and Medjugorje:*"During my 'ad limina' visit to Rome with the Bishops of Texas this past April,

> *"The Pope spoke very favorably about the happenings at Medjugorje...To say nothing is happening there is to deny the living, prayerful witness of hundreds of thousands who have gone there."*
>
> Bishop Michael D. Pfeifer

in a private conversation I had with our Holy Father, I asked his opinion about Medjugorje. The Pope spoke very favorably about the happenings at Medjugorje...To say nothing is happening there is to deny the living, prayerful witness of hundreds of thousands who have gone there."

• The bishop of the Diocese of Bolzano-Bressanone, **Bishop Wilhelm Egger**, on the Feast of the Most Holy Rosary, October 7, 1990, released for his diocese *Pastoral Directions for Marian Devotion* and guidelines for pilgrimages to Medjugorje: "The message aims at the renewal of the individual, the Church and the world. It is a call to prayer and penance.... Medjugorje has become for many people a place of prayer and conversion."

• The invitation of three Slovakian bishops to the visionaries from Medjugorje via an official letter to the local parish office is further testimony of a positive outlook from bishops on Medjugorje. The Slovakian **Metropolitan Archbishop Jan Sokol** of Trnava, who had himself visited Medjugorje several times, **Bishop Alojz Tkac** of Kosice, and the Greek-Catholic **Bishop Jan Hirka** of Presov signed the invitation which achieved the result of Ivan Dragicevic visiting their country and giving his testimony before thousands of people, mainly young adults, in March, 1990.

• **Archbishop Johannes Joachim Degenhardt** titled his report to his diocese (Paderborn) in March, 1991, *Medjugorje: Impulse to Renewal of the Christian Life.* Starting with the confusing press reports, and then citing an opinion by Cardinal Ratzinger, and the fact that in Medjugorje "deep springs of religious life are bursting open," Archbishop Degenhardt gave his personal judgment: "Just as in the great classical pilgrim shrines there is going on in Medjugorje the call to renewal of life after cleansing and conversion ... It appears that this invitation applies to the entire Church."

> *"Deep springs of religious life are bursting open... This invitation applies to the entire Church "*
> Archbishop Degenhardt

• **Archbishop Gregory Yong** of Singapore and **Archbishop Phillip Hannan** of New Orleans both publicly credited the renewal of their dioceses to Medjugorje. "Never have we seen the church packed with so many daily Masses as now. We are seeing the fruits of what is happening in Medjugorje," (from Archbishop Yong's homily at the June 25, 1988, Queen of Peace Mass in Singapore's Cathedral of the Good Shepherd, celebrating the seventh anniversary of Our Lady's apparitions in Medjugorje; quoted in *The Tablet*, July 30, 1988).

• On his third trip to Medjugorje, **Archbishop Gabriel Gonsum Ganaka** of Nigeria said: "Even though it is not always easy or possible, I would like my diocesan priests

> *"I would like my diocesan priests to come to Medjugorje ...As an Archbishop, I would like to invite all those who have not yet done so, to come to Medjugorje!"*
> Archbishop Gabriel Ganaka

to come to Medjugorje because it is important for them to come, see and experience. I permit no one, myself included, to be prejudiced, because that means to judge without seeing. As an Archbishop, I would like to invite all those who have not yet done so, to come to Medjugorje!" (Press Bulletin 8, March 15, 1995).

• **Bishop Robert Cavellero**, from the shrine to Our Lady of Orta in Chiavaria (Italy), testifies that following Mass in the Pope's private chapel at the beginning of October, 1997, the following conversation took place: "Holy Father, I have just come from Medjugorje!" The Pope responded, "Do you believe?" He replied, "Yes, Holy Father!" And then he asked the Pope, "And you, Holy Father, do you believe?" After a moment of silence **Pope John Paul II replied, "I believe! I believe! I believe!"** [3]

> *"I believe! I believe! I believe!"*
> Pope John Paul II

• Commenting on the fact that pilgrims from around the world were returning from Medjugorje and beginning programs of Adoration of the Blessed Sacrament in their parishes, **Archbishop Franz Kramberger** testifies, "That is one of the secrets, grace! Just like at Lourdes and Fatima, today the same thing is happening in Medjugorje. Medjugorje has become a place of God's grace. In fact that is what serves as proof that God is present and something Divine is occuring there. People who come to Medjugorje not only realize this but experience it in a special way. To experience God in this way is something unique...and this is where we see that Medjugorje is something special...it has great meaning for the general and local Church." [4]

• **Bishop Denis Croteau** of Makenzie-Fort Smith (Canada) went to Medjugorje in 2003 and again with groups from his diocesan 2004 and 2005. He testifies: "I've tried all kinds of things in my diocese to transform the people because we live in a dysfunctional society. I've spent thousands and thousands and thousands of dollars with sessions and workshops, and I haven't accomplished, spending all that kind of money, 10% of what has been accomplished here with one pilgrimage!" [5]

• **Archbishop Frane Franic** (Split, Croatia): "If Jesus has sent his Mother to preach about conversion, then her call is definitely coupled with a great grace of conversion which can only be received at Medjugorje. Jesus wanted exactly those graces, which he is distributing through his Mother, the Queen of Peace, to give peace to our people. That's why I feel that those who have hindered a greater response to Our Lady Queen of Peace in Medjugorje carry a great responsibility. However, it is not too late yet...." (Nasa Ognjista, xxv, 1995, pp. 4, 9).

> *"I feel that those who have hindered a greater response to Our Lady Queen of Peace in Medjugorje carry a great responsibility. However, it is not too late yet..."*
> Archbishop Frane Franic

• "I feel that Medjugorje is the continuation of Fatima....Our Lady is constantly telling us, free yourselves from sin and open your hearts to God's love. When I go back I will proclaim again what I have heard and experienced here. That is what re-evangelization means. I invite everyone to take advantage of this time of grace that God is giving us here through Mary!" **Bishop Albert Ndzana,** Mbalmayo, Cameroon (Press Bulletin, 68, July 2, 1997).

• "People come from all over the world and they pray together. The world today is in need of Medjugorje!" **Bishop Stanislaus Szyrokoradiuk,** Ukraine (Glas Mira, VI, 1997 no. 6, p. 13).

> *"The world today is in need of Medjugorje!"*
> Bishop S. Szyrokoradiuk

• "The fact that pilgrims are constantly coming here and in ever greater numbers is a proof that miraculous gifts are being distributed here...What saddens me most is the negative position of the local bishop, both the current bishop as well as his predecessor. Let us pray that this negative position changes. The Pope privately proposes pilgrimages to Medjugorje. Privately he approves them. That is enough for us now." **Bishop P. Arokiaswamy,** India (Press Bulletin 72, August, 27 1997).

• "I see Medjugorje as a gift and a responsibility. Medjugorje is a gift of grace. Our Lady gives to everyone who comes here the possibility to find the same love and tenderness that she revealed at Cana at

> "*I see Medjugorje as a gift and a responsibility...You cannot even imagine how important is the role of this parish for the Church and the world!*"
> Archbishop Murillo Krieger

Galilee. Medjugorje is a great responsiblity. I understood that immediately, from the first time I set foot on the soil of Medjugorje. That was in May, 1985, immediately after my Episcopal Consecration. Observing and listening to the visionaries I came to the conclusion that they need our prayers so they may be able to be faithful to their mission. From that moment I decided to dedicate to them the first five mysteries of my daily Rosary. That is my small gift. I thereby offer my support and help because they have an important mission.....You cannot even imagine how important is the role of this parish for the Church and the world!" **Archbishop Murillo Krieger,** Brazil (Press Bulletin 86, March 11, 1998).

• "I see that a great number of the faithful who have visited Medjugorje return with a renewed faith, a renewed experience of prayer, fasting, confession, Holy Mass, and adoration. People who are faithful to Our Lady are also faithful to the Church!...I especially want to pray for the Franciscans, because what is happening here is great and the Franciscans have a great responsibility. I know about all your troubles and difficulties, but persevere in doing good!" **Bishop Donald Montrose**, Stockton, California, USA (Press Bulletin 89, April 22, 1998).

• "In Medjugorje I experienced a new spiritual motivation. I have discovered God again and for me that is the proof that Our Lady is here!" **Bishop Kenneth Steiner,** Portland, USA (Press Bulletin 105, December 2, 1998).

• "One cannot talk lightly about Medjugorje. It is a profound experience, intimate and personal! For me this is a time of renewal!"

Bishop Louis Kebreau, Port au Prince, Haiti (Press Bulletin 105, December 2, 1998).

> *"I believe that Our Lady is appearing here!"*
> Bishop Emilio Bataclan

• "I believe that Our Lady is appearing here!" **Bishop Emilio Bataclan**, Philippines (Press Bulletin 131, 1999). "Medjugorje is a huge chance for the Church!" **Bishop Hermann Raich**, Papua New Guinea (Rupcic, "A Door to Heaven...," Mostar, 1999, p. 181).

> *"Medjugorje is a huge chance for the Church!"*
> Bishop Hermann Raich

• "I can personally say that it is clear to me that all that is happening in Medjugorje, especially the great number of people, cannot be interpreted in any other way than a special intervention from God...I personally am praying that the moment of recognition comes as soon as possible. I would recommend to all communities that do not have vocations to come here and pray in this spirit that is alive in Medjugorje and they will certainly have vocations!" **Bishop Stanislas Lukumwena**, Kile, Congo (Press Bulletin 131, December 1, 1999).

• "It is clear to me that in Medjugorje is something very strong and supernatural. Without this supernaturality these events could never hold out to such an extent and spread like this throughout the whole world...What is being announced here is the essence of the Gospel, therefore we have to accept it!" **Bishop Jose Viloria**, Guayana, Venezuela (Press Bulletin 131, December 1, 1999).

> *"I would recommend to everyone to come to Medjugorje."*
> Bishop Robert Rivas

• "I would recommend to everyone to come to Medjugorje, because here they will deepen their faith!" **Bishop Robert Rivas**, Kingstown, St. Vincent (Press Bulletin 139, March 22, 2000).

• "Medjugorje is a special place of prayer so its.. a prayer that also brings forth the fruits in service of man, especially of man in afflic-tion. It was especially important for me to

> *"I wish that this message and this experience be carried also to Germany!"*
>
> Bishop Franziskus Eisenbach

get to know the "Mother's Village" where mothers with children, abandoned children and orphans of war find a refuge...the community of Sr. Elvira in which those addicted to drugs and other evils find a place of refuge...the God-Parent program for children...I saw that many families from Germany cooperate helping every month with a financial contribution for the families torn apart by the war. These works of active love for the needy especially showed me that Medjugorje is not just a matter of the correct spirit of prayer. Love for God that is shown in prayer has brought fruits that are recognized in the care of man. The message of Medjugorje for the world is clear: it has to overcome wars and conflicts by the power of love. No one needs to be afraid of Medjugorje even if it has not yet been officially approved by the Church. I wish that this message and this experience be carried also to Germany because we Germans are inclined to rationalism rather then to feeling. And here it is a matter of a message for man in his entirety." **Bishop Franziskus Eisenbach**, Mainz, Germany (Press Bulletin 139, March, 2000).

• "I believe that Our Lady is appearing here. Medjugorje is a message of hope!...With Mary our path is sure. Accept what she says, she knows the Way, she knows her Son and will help us on our path to the final homeland in heaven!" **Bishop Waldemar Chaves de Araujo**, Brazil

> *"I believe that Our Lady is appearing here. Medjugorje is a message of hope!"*
>
> Bishop Chaves de Araujo

(Press Bulletin 145, June, 2000).

• "I met Medjugorje through my seminarians. Some of my students in theology came to me seeking permission to go to Medjugorje [in 1983]... I told them 'Go and see!' In 1984 I decided myself to go and see. ...Some people say where there is prayer, there is grace and miracles. But this logic does not seem to me completely correct. There are many other places in the world where there is prayer, where there is confession, where Eucharist is celebrated, but there are not the same kind of evident fruits! ...I think that on the spiritual plane we are living in a period that demands urgency!" **Bishop Andre Leonard**, Namour, Belgium (Press Bulletin 150, August 22, 2000).

• "I think we owe a lot to Medjugorje for this great spring - time of faith we are experiencing. It was given to us by God through Mary....I am deeply grateful to God for Medjugorje. And it fits in well for me in this 70th anniversary of Fatima...I hear a lot, but I would always like to hear more about Medjugorje. Oh, how I would love to go on pilgrimage to Medjugorje and there fill myself with new hope! That's what many of the faithful of my diocese would like to do too." **Cardinal Frantisek Tomasek**, Archbishop of Prague (*Medjugorje in the Church*, Marija Dugandzic, p. 32).

> *"I am deeply grateful to God for Medjugorje...Oh, how I would love to go on pilgrimage to Medjugorje and there fill myself with new hope!"*
> Cardinal Frantisek Tomasek

• "I will tell Bishops not to be afraid to come here.[6] The apparitions are a gift from God! It would be good if every bishop could come and experience what Mary is doing here!" **Bishop John Baptist Odama**, Uganda (Press Bulletin 52, November 20, 1996).

> *"The apparitions are a gift from God! ...It would be good if every bishop could come and experience what Mary is doing here!"*
> Bishop Johnn Baptist Odama

• "Medjugorje is being talked about much in Poland... In church here one feels the prayer of the people. Praying the Our Father together was a unique experience for me; to hear all the different languages as they pray as in one voice and one could make out the Polish language particularly clear... We all must try to accept and live the messages of Our Lady. Peace in the world is at stake... I hope that this message will spread througout the world and that more and more people will come here and accept the messages, while we all wait together for the Vatican to recognize Medjugorje!" **Bishop Albin Malysia**, of Krakow, Poland worked closely with Pope John Paul II for more than 20 years: ten years as a parish priest and professor in theology and ten more years as an assistant bishop. (*Medjugorje in the Church,* Information Center Mir, 2002, p. 153; Press Bulletin 103, November 4, 1998).

> *"I hope that this message will spread througout the world and that more and more people will come here and accept the messages."*
> Bishop Albin Malysia

> *"We all wait together for the Vatican to recognize Medjugorje!"*
> Bishop Albin Malysia

• "I had a strong experience in this place in 1989 when I prayed in Medjugorje for the breakdown of communism in my country. Because of communist repression, I was ordained a bishop secretly, because public ordinations were not possible." Fr. Bilyk had prayed in Medjugorje on his way to Rome for his secret Episcopal ordination, to ask for the intercession of the Queen of Peace. He returned in 2003 to give thanks.

"For my personal life, as a bishop and as a believer, Medjugorje is a power and a grace! Our Lady is present in a very special way here. I will surely come again to this place of prayer, because here, we are all closer to Jesus through Our Lady!" **Bishop Irynei Bilyk** (Byzantine rite) Buchach, Ukraine, (Press Bulletin 189).

> *"Medjugorje is a power and a grace!"*
> Bishop Irynei Bilyk

• "I heard about Medjugorje for the first time from my parishioners. Those who went to Medjugorje came back with good fruits: the spirit of prayer, fasting, returning to the life of the sacraments and becoming active members of the parish

> *"These events in Medjugorje made a profound impression on me!"*
> Bishop John Dew

community. Numerous prayer groups were established. These events in Medjugorje made a profound impression on me! I do not see any kind of oddities. People talk about the apparitions in a simple way and a large number of the faithful try to live Our Lady's messages. The experience of prayer and fasting are to me especially useful. I will try in a special way to find time for prayer before Holy Mass. I will try also to propose all that to the parishes of my diocese!" **Bishop John Dew**, auxiliary bishop, Wellington, New Zealand (Press Bulletin 89, April 22, 1998).

• "Everything I have seen here during my stay has impressed me deeply. Something like this is hard to find anyplace else. The faith of the people here, the attendance at Holy Mass and the spirit of self-denial cut deeply into my heart. I watched how crowds of countless people go up mountains that are not easy to climb, go to confession and pray. They were from every part of the world. It is difficult therefore to conclude that all this is accidental, that this is an ordinary place and that nothing has happened here. In my opinion, only faith could lead these people to come here, faith that is convinced of something concrete...According to the fruits that I see, I can say there is something really special taking place here. It is not the Franciscans who are drawing the people here. I also have Franciscans in my parish, but there is nothing special going on. God is the one who is drawing the people to come."

"I believe Our Lady is appearing here. I don't know how I would in any other way explain the phenomenon that is alive here. It

> *"I believe Our Lady is appearing here!"*
> Bishop Gerard Dionn

is not possible that the devil is at work, since

people are praying. Likewise, all this cannot be an ordinary deception. People can be deceived for a while, but not a full seventeen years and then not millions of people. I believe that something special is happening here because of the fruits. There cannot be so much good fruit on a bad tree.

"Observing the liturgical life in the parish of Medjugorje I didn't notice anything particular. It is the everyday customary life of the Church. Mass is celebrated just like in other places. There is nothing here out of the ordinary. Last night we had adoration before the Most Blessed Sacrament of the Altar. Everything was so simple: a few words, a few songs, just like the Church wants it to be. People are so strongly attracted to it that they are prepared to spend hours on their knees. We do the same thing in our churches, but people do not come in such great numbers. Why? I cannot answer differently than to say that God is present here in a special way.

"Many pilgrims who come here carry in their hearts a remembrance of the faith and the hospitality that they encountered in the parish of Medjugorje. It is a great honor for this parish that Our Lady has visited it in a special way and that she has spoken in the Croatian language. I hope that the parish of Medjugorje and the entire Croatian people will never lose sight of that!" **Bishop Gerard Dionn**, Edmonson, New Brunswick (Press Bulletin 91, May 20, 1998).

• "I have experienced something special here. In May, 1993, I was in Rome. After that I came to Dubrovnik with Bishop Zelimir Puljic, the bishop of Dubrovnik, since I had three days free. I took advantage of the opportunity and came to Medjugorje incognito. There was still war. There were not many pilgrims.

> *"This is the second time that I come to Medjugorje and it really is a time of great grace. Our Lady has prepared many graces also for me. This all helps me again to decide for my vocation as a priest and for my ministry as a bishop!"*
> Bishop Patrick Power

However, many things impressed me. I was already a bishop then, but I did not come here as a bishop. I remained a private person. I celebrated Mass. This is the second time that I come to Medjugorje and it really is a time of great grace. Our Lady has prepared many graces also for me. I have found a profound peace, especially after I heard Vicka's testimony. I felt the same peace that I felt in 1993 when I heard about the messages the first time. This all helps me again to decide for my vocation as a priest and for my ministry as a bishop. Medjugorje is PEACE.

"I have felt internal peace and I have witnessed about it to everyone… Not only I, but also Bishop Kennedy who has been here several times, recommend to the faithful to come to Medjugorje!" **Bishop Patrick Power**, Canberra, Australia (Press Bulletin 87, March 25, 1998).

• "I am **Edwin O'Brien, the archbishop responsible for the entire armed forces of the United States of America**. That is, the responsibility for every American in all branches of the military, for military hospitals and for all members of the diplomatic corps. I began this ministry in September, 1997. Recently I became an archbishop. My assignment is to visit

> *"I am Edwin O'Brien, the archbishop responsible for the entire armed forces of the United States of America…The fact that I celebrated Holy Mass in the parish church of St. James is for me a great privilege. I have heard many good things about Medjugorje!"*
> Archbishop Edwin O'Brien

American military personnel where they are serving. I have been in the Pacific and now I'm in Europe (Italy, Germany, England, Belgium and Bosnia-Hercegovina). For Christmas I visited Sarajevo and I was very disappointed that I did not succeed then in coming to Medjugorje. I had to answer: No! I did not have the opportunity. I was living in Rome from 1985 to 1990, but I did not come. When I was in Sarajevo I asked my superiors if I could visit Medjugorje. Today I am here. The fact that I celebrated Holy Mass in the parish church of St. James is for me a great privilege.

"I have heard many good things about Medjugorje. I was in Medjugorje very briefly. Now I am already planning my second visit to Medjugorje. I would like to go on Podbrdo, the place of the apparitions, but I don't have time and that bothers me. I am happy that I have celebrated Holy Mass here today. I prayed before Our Lady's statue. I have decided to come another time to have more time to be here. I will do everything that the other pilgrims also do. I will try my best for my next visit to be this summer. Till then let us remain united in prayer for peace in the world." **Archbishop Edwin O'Brien** (Press Bulletin 86, March 11, 1998. Several months earlier another military bishop had visited Medjugorje. **Bishop Johannes Dyba** had come to visit the German SFOR units stationed in Bosnia-Hercegovina).

"The strongest impression made on me was the simplicity of prayer and the strong faith of those that I met. There is no kind of fanaticism here!" **Bishop Silverio J. Paulo de Albuquerque**, Feira de Santana, Brazil (Press Bulletin 93, June 17, 1998).

"I often went on pilgrimage to Fatima, Lourdes and other places. Here I discover a big difference. There is nothing stereotyped. Everything is different from the other places. Everyone has his own personal experience. Here people find peace and are reconciled!" **Bishop Joseph Lafontant,** Port-au-Prince, Haiti (Press Bulletin 105, December 2, 1998).

> *"Here people find peace and are reconciled!"*
> Bishop Joseph Lafontant

• "I have met many priests who have come to Medjugorje. They have a better idea of their own priesthood. That is what I personally will take with me. I will tell people that Medjugorje is a place where people can go and be renewed in their faith." **Bishop Kenneth Steiner**, Portland, Oregon (Press Bulletin 105, December 2, 1998).

• "Medjugorje indeed opens the way for us to be able to plunge into the life of the Most Holy Trinity. Mary is doing that here. I am so grateful to her!" **Bishop Louis Kebreau** of Hinche, Haiti (Press Bulletin 105, December 2, 1998).

• "I have to be honest and say that when we bishops hear news about apparitions and similar phenomena we are cautious in our statements. Usually it happens that in the first instance we say that it is impossible, we want to immediately oppose it. We are always afraid...

"This morning we talked with a visionary, Vicka. She presented to us Our Lady's messages on conversion, fasting, prayer, forgiveness and holy confession, about all these values that are gradually being lost today. I personally believe the following: If Our Lady through Christ is endeavoring to quicken these values then that ought to be the fundamental duty of a priest, especially of us bishops...

"On one occasion I was conversing with a friend who was a theologian. He counseled me not to go to Medjugorje and said that he would not risk his theological honor. Fr. Laurentin told me that this type of theologian talks a lot about Mary, but does not genuinely love her. They use Mariology for teaching, but they do not have a felt relationship with Mary. All of this helped awaken in me a great interest in Our Lady...

"I think that above all one has to pay great attention to the fruits of Medjugorje. I will invite my faithful to come to Medjugorje!" **Bishop Lazaro Perez**, De Autlan Jalisco, Mexico (Press Bulletin 82, January 14, 1998).

> *"A theologian counseled me not to go to Medjugorje ... 'this type of theologian talks a lot about Mary, but does not genuinely love her!'"*
> Bishop Lazaro Perez

• "We are living in a special time. God is giving us special graces through this place. Many people who have problems with their faith should come here to Medjugorje. Medjugorje is a chance,

> *"I believe that the persons who lead the Church should come here and experience the graces and gifts of this place!"*
> Bishop Joseph Mugeny

a privilege, special gifts given by God through the Blessed Virgin Mary to help us. There is no doubt about what is happening here!

"I believe that the persons who lead the Church should come here and experience the graces and gifts of this place!" **Bishop Joseph Mugeny**, Uganda (Press Bulletin 129, November 3, 1999).

•"I greatly trust in Our Lady of Medjugorje... When, at some time in the future, the credibility of the events here will be accepted, what will happen to those who did not believe? There is no doubt about it: what happens here is good. What happens here is what should happen in the Church: prayer, Mass, confession, adoration, conversion, the formation of prayer groups, vocations. These

> *"I greatly trust in Our Lady of Medjugorje!"*
> Archbishop Georg Eder

are all in light of the events which are being guided by Mary, with which She is preparing us for the new millennium. Much is happening here that we in the Church have forgotten. Mary calls and teaches us. For the Church in Austria, I can say: 'We have forgotten much and we must begin anew with what Mary tells us in Medjugorje!'" **Archbishop Georg Eder,** Salzburg, Austria (Press Bulletin 128, October 20, 1999).

• "Medjugorje is a meeting place of God and man. Here there is found an authentic source of salvation... I have to admit that this visit here has opened my eyes to many things and that I will do a

> *"Medjugorje is a meeting place of God and man!"*
> Bishop Victor Maldonado

lot of things differently in all the tasks of my life. Here I have better understood the role of Mary in the life of a Christian!" **Bishop Victor Maldonado**, Ecuador (Press Bulletin 122, July 28, 1999).

• "When I first heard of Medjugorje I had a great desire to come immediately…I understood that, besides the message that Our Lady gives, her presence here is so important. God is speaking here through Mary not only to you, but to all nations and to all cultures. One does not come here because of tourism. One comes here for confession, for encounter with God. This is a divine moment for the world!" **Cardinal Bernardino Echeverria Ruiz**, Ecuador (Press Bulletin 122, July 28, 1999).

> *"God is speaking here through Mary. This is a divine moment for the world!"*
> Cardinal Bernardino Echeverria Ruiz

• "I am an Archbishop in Panama, Central America, and President of the Bishops Conference. This is my first time to Medjugorje, but there are already many fruits of Medjugorje in Panama. For example, we have a parish community led by Fr. Francesco Verar. He often comes to Medjugorje and their church is identical to St. James Church in Medjugorje! Francesco has also founded a community that is called: 'The Sisters of Mary Queen of Peace.' Every evening they have the same prayer program as here in Medjugorje! They are very active.'"

> *"There are already many fruits of Medjugorje in Panama!"*
> Archbishop Jose Dimas Cedeo, President of the Bishops' Conference

"The community has been given recognition by the Church. I recognized the community on the diocesan level when I sensed their spirituality, saw what they are doing and how they are living, and that their main work is to pray for peace.

"The community has already been in existence for several years. They are having good experiences. I recognized the community precisely on June 25, 1998. And that is exactly also the anniversary of the apparitions. I am fully conscious that this is a fruit of Medjugorje!"[7] **Archbishop Jose Dimas Cedeo, President of the Bishops Conference**, Panama (Press Bulletin 117, May 19, 1999).

• "Here in Medjugorje one senses a special devotion to Our Lady... I am in Medjugorje for the first time and unexpectedly. For me it is like a small miracle to find myself here. You know, I am a professor of the Bible and I should now be in Brazil for lectures, but some unexplainable circumstances have led me here. For me and for the whole group this has been in some way a miraculous pilgrimage...

"Yesterday I was at dinner with the Medjugorje Friars and their simplicity amazed me as also afterwards at prayer and at the time for confessions. I had a feeling like I was among the first churches in Jerusalem. I lived and worked in Jerusalem for two years as an archeologist and professor of Scripture. I worked in the Syrian desert as a chaplain to a Levitic tribe. I think all that work prepared me to be able now to feel great grace and Our Lady's blessing...

"It does not bother me that your local bishop is not favorable to these events because there are also other bishops who think otherwise.[8] One time the archbishop of Pescara who is my great friend, told me that he asked the Holy Father about these events. 'Holy Father, what should I do when the faithful from my diocese of Pescara want often to go on pilgrimage to Medjugorje?' 'What are they doing?' asked the Holy Father. 'They pray and go to holy confession.' 'Well, isn't that good?' answered the Holy Father. I worked for ten years with the Holy Father and with Cardinal Ratzinger. Cardinal Ratzinger is a wonderful man, full of spirituality and very pleasant. Sometimes I hear it said about him that he is very strict and serious, but I think he is a man with a big heart. Once I asked him what he thinks about Medjugorje. He answered that the tree is recognized by the fruits, because good fruits are a sign of God's presence.

> *"Once I asked Cardinal Ratzinger what he thinks about Medjugorje. He answered me that the tree is recognized by the fruits, because good fruits are a sign of God's presence! ...I have come now to thank Our Lady for this beautiful gift."*
>
> Bishop John Evangelist Martins Terra

67

"In Brazil we have organized pilgrimages to Medjugorje and moreover we have pilgrimages to other shrines. The most numerous are the pilgrimages to Medjugorje which was for me very interesting and therefore I have come now to thank Our Lady for this beautiful gift." **Bishop John Evangelist Martins Terra**, Brasilia, Brazil (Press Bulletin 79, December 3, 1997).

• "People from my diocese have often come to me after having been in Medjugorje. I wanted to see for myself what is happening here. I know of the many good fruits of Medjugorje. Those who had been here, after returning home become testimonies of faith on all levels. And that's what is most needed at this moment.

"The first thing that deeply impresses me is the spirit of prayer here in Medjugorje. I see pilgrims from the whole world here. The evening program alone is enough to show how much and how deeply people pray here. Those inside the church and those who cannot enter

> *"You can feel the spirit and presence of Our Lady."*
> Archbishop Andre Fernand Anguile

(because there is no more space) still pray ardently and devotedly. I see all the priests here confessing for hours and who pray more devotedly than they would normally. But the thing that really delighted me was the sight of so many young people praying and confessing. Here it's not difficult to feel the presence of God and the workings of grace in action…You can feel the spirit and presence of Our Lady.

"Our Lady's apparitions are a good sign for our times. She wants to prepare us for the third millennium through Medjugorje and we must do as she says. If we're obedient, all will be well and the world will have hope. It's good that Our Lady

> *"Our Lady's apparitions are a good sign for our times. She wants to prepare us!"*
> Archbishop Andre Fernand Anguile

has appeared here and that the priests, the visionaries and the parish community have managed to remain faithful to her. You have become an example to many. Here great good is being done. Please remember me in your prayers and I promise to remember all of you also. When I return home I will tell people that I have been to Medjugorje and I will call all the laity to pray and fast more, and to allow Mary to lead us all into this new time." **Archbishop Andre Fernand Anguile,** Libervill, Gabon (Press Bulletin 75, October 8, 1997).

• "This is the first time that I am coming to this place. Here I feel the presence of God. I feel the grace that God is granting to his faithful through the intercession of His Holy Mother." **Archbishop Fabio Betancourt Tirado**, Archbishop of Manizales, Columbia (Press Bulletin 71, August 13, 1997).

• "I am in Medjugorje for the first time. I came here to pray before my episcopal consecration. Here I found a place and people who pray a lot in Church, on Podbrdo and Cross Mountain. I saw deep devotion on the mountains. I welcomed this experience because for me it means that people are ready to pray, when they are given the opportunity and when they are led well. But this is not only a place of prayer, but a place where one can learn a lot. It is particularly important to me that I understood that we are all pilgrims. Pilgrims who come here discover the gift of life. God heals them here. They come back to God, they grasp the law of life and become messengers of peace. I want in my own ministry to tell people not to be afraid to accept life, even though I know it isn't easy. When we climb the Medjugorje mountains, we can understand those difficulties. That can be experienced especially on Cross Mountain. The lesson one gets on Cross Mountain says: One has to accept everything one encounters in life and complete one's assignment!" **Bishop Damian Kyaruzi,** Tanzania (Press Bulletin 68, July 2, 1997).

• "This is really an important experience for me, especially at the level of prayer. I cannot say that Our Lady is not appearing. Fifteen years have gone by and the visionaries are always repeating the same message. They don't change at all. The message is simple: to pray, to fast, to believe, to confess and to adore. That's precisely why we must be dealing with a supernatural event, because they are steadfast in their one message. People come and change their lives. Many confess. In these last ten years as a bishop I hardly ever heard confessions. Here people were constantly asking me to hear their confessions, and I did. In these days I must have heard over 100 confessions. I'm certain that the Lord is using this place for the conversion of nations!" **Bishop Frederick Dranuba**, Arua, Uganda (Press Bulletin 66, July 4, 1997).

> *"In these last ten years as a bishop I hardly ever heard confessions. Here people were constantly asking me to hear their confessions. I'm certain that the Lord is using this place for the conversion of nations!"*
>
> Bishop Frederick Dranuba

• "I've spent a week in Medjugorje and I felt that it emanates much prayer, peace and friendliness. I met so many people who really pray and who seek prayer. I visited Krizevac and Podbrdo. I saw many, many people praying…

"The evening Mass made a deep impression on me. The church was full every evening, and there were even more people hearing the Mass from outside. And even though they didn't understand the language they were deeply united in devotion and prayer. But even so, the most beautiful part of the prayer program was the Adoration of the Blessed Sacrament. I saw a great number of priests confessing and a multitude of pilgrims and local people confessing.

"My impression is that we are dealing with something profoundly real here… On my return home I will emphasize the simplicity of the Gospa's messages, and how it is this simplicity which breaks through to the hearts of her children." **Bishop Deogratias Byabazaire**, Hoime, Uganda (Press Bulletin 66, July 4, 1997).

> *"My impression is that we are dealing with something profoundly real here… On my return home I will emphasize the simplicity of the Gospa's messages!"*
>
> Bishop Deogratias Byabazaire

70

• "This is a place of contemplation and prayer . Everyone who comes here takes part in an interpersonal togetherness. I saw people from Europe, America, Japan, Australia. They all feel as one. This made a strong impression on me. Here one really prays. I couldn't go up the hill but it really touched me when a pilgrim brought me back a stone from the Apparition site. Adoration is a special experience. It is something unique. I saw people fasting. In the house where I was staying the pilgrims ate nothing for dinner other than bread and a little salad. This spirit of penance, sacrifice and mortification is something which I haven't seen in such a long time. This experience will give me the strength to preach about the 'Gospa.' I feel now that I haven't given her enough attention. She is very close to us. That is the main message of this place." **Bishop Joseph Oxyanga**, Lir, Uganda (Press Bulletin 66, July 4, 1997).

> *"This experience will give me the strength to preach about the Gospa. I feel now that I haven't given her enough attention."*
> Bishop Joseph Oxyanga

> *"Thousands of pilgrims are coming to Medjugorje, they pray, they discover faith. It is a great gift!"*
> Cardinal Ersilio Tonini

• "Thousands of pilgrims are coming to Medjugorje, they pray, they discover faith. It is a great gift!" **Cardinal Ersilio Tonini**, Archbishop of Ravenna, Italy (Luciano Moia: Parola di Maria, Edizione Segno, Udine, 1996, p. 13).

• "Every priest should pray three hours a day, and every bishop four. Every retired bishop should pray five hours a day. I personally learned how to pray at Medjugorje, with the Queen of Peace...I thank God that I was personally able to observe the development of this mystical theology and mystical phenomenon so closely. I recognize and accept the truth of Mary's message at Medjugorje!" **Archbishop Frane Franic**, Split, retired (Press Bulletin 57, January 29, 1997).

> *"I recognize and accept the truth of Marys message at Medjugorje!"*
> Archbishop Frane Franic

• "In this shrine I have always felt an atmosphere of deep peace and faith. I find that peace in all the people who have visited it. They come home with a deepened faith, they return to sacramental life and prayer. They start prayer groups that are the source of grace

> *"I recommend everyone, but mainly young people, to come on pilgrimage to the Queen of Peace!"*
> Archbishop Philip Hannan

for many. For that reason I recommend everyone, but mainly young people, to come on pilgrimage to the Queen of Peace and to take their powerful experiences to others. In that way may a chain of peace and faith be made in the world!" **Archbishop Philip Hannan**, (retired) New Orleans (Press Bulletin 32, February 14, 1996).

• "This is my first visit to Medjugorje. It is a grace for me to stay here two days. Providence has brought me here. I am satisfied and I did not know that it has this kind of great dimension. The apparitions in Medjugorje are

> *"The apparitions in Medjugorje are known throughout the whole world!"*
> Bishop Carrero Raul Scarrone

known throughout the whole world. Popular devotion must be purified. It is a question, namely, of religious motivation. That holds true for each one of us. So that we might firmly go on the way of holiness we need a purification of motivation. When I think of myself, before my own personal confession, I always ask myself, 'Am I a bishop in order that I might serve the church or only so that I might have authority?'

"You in this parish have a great gift that is called Mary. She can always help us in evangelization for the reason that she always leads us toward Jesus. She opens the doors of hearts and the doors of homes. I have seen that also in my own people which is so secularized and has so many sects. Where Mary is, there the heart is open. Accordingly, that which has to be done is to evangelize with Our Lady's help." **Bishop Carrero Raul Scarrone**, Florida, Uruguay (Press Bulletin 43, July 17, 1996).

• "For me as well as for the soldiers with me it's been really wonderful to be in Medjugorje. I told the soldiers what a great number of conversions had taken

> *"It really is a place of great grace and life!"*
> Bishop Christian Werner

place here...thousands of people go to confession and pray on the mountains. And also there is the fact that so many young people come. It really is a place of great grace and life!" **Bishop Christian Werner**, Vienna, Austria ("Oase des Friedens," Vienna, July 1996; Press Bulletin 44, July 31, 1996)

• "When I was born in 1917 there was a war, and when in 1942 I was ordained to the priesthood there was a war then also. Now I am in Medjugorje and much is being said about the peace after the terrible war in your homeland. It seems to me though, that we are treating the subject of peace far too superficially. If we desire real peace, we need something deeper. That which Our Lady wishes to say is: Don't make the same mistake again, speak about peace, and not go deeper into the soul and the heart, where true peace is made. Here, Mary is teaching us true peace.

"Confession is also important here. People are really ready to meet themselves face to face here. They are ready for repentance and penance and I believe that this is the important experience of Medjugorje: to renew ourselves and to convert.

"Without judging the local bishop I would say when someone comes here and wishes to pray, to confess, to change their lives, you cannot say

> *"Without judging the local bishop I would say when someone comes here and wishes to pray, to confess, to change their lives, you cannot say "No!"*
> Bishop Augustine Harris

'No!' So many people are confused, so many live in fear, they do not know what to do. I would say that it is good to come to Medjugorje. Here you clear your conscience, and conquer confusion. I see this in so many people here... I have no reason not to believe in the apparitions. If people ask me, can I go to Medjugorje, my answer will be: 'If you wish to clear your conscience, and if you are confused, go!'

"On the feast day of the Exaltation of the Cross I saw over 50 Franciscan priests hearing confessions. This was really wonderful. Immediately after the Mass that day which I celebrated in the church of Medjugorje, a pilgrim stopped me and wished to confess. Was I supposed to say no?" **Bishop Augustine Harris**, Middlesborough, England (Press Bulletin 52, November 20, 1996).

• "Since the time my faithful are coming to Medjugorje, I too, as Archbishop, feel the duty to come, to see what happens and to have a personal experience of this place of intense prayer. I still remember the strong impressions I had after my previous visits. Our Lady's messages are simple, practical and life changing...

"I have preached in 12 dioceses and I always mention Medjugorje. The messages changed a lot of people in my diocese. Even life in convents changed after they had become known. But we must still spread them more and more. That's why I wish to have as much information as possible about these events...

> *"Our Lady's messages are simple, practical and life changing...I have preached in 12 dioceses and I always mention Medjugorje!"*
>
> Archbishop Gabriel Gonsum Ganaka

It is important for everyone to respond and then peace will dwell within us." **Archbishop Gabriel Gonsum Ganaka**, Nigeria (Press Bulletin 8, March 15, 1995).

• "The Church has still not expressed its official position regarding the Medjugorje apparitions. With confidence and prayer we are yet waiting for it. I have visited Medjugorje. I came and I am convinced of the authenticity of what is taking place there.

"The perseverance with which Mary is speaking to us in these times of ours made a very strong impression on me. Sometimes someone will say to me, 'How are such long – lasting apparitions possible?' or 'Mary talks so much!' I personally do not have any preconceived plans either about how or how much Mary should talk. I tell myself that perhaps Mary is knocking on our doors with such unusual persistence just because there are such great and urgent needs in our times. I interpret Mary's persistence as a stimulus to our conversion. The Medjugorje fruits are blessed fruits. Frequently people confide in me relating their experiences for which I can testify that they are rich with fruits of conversion, discovery of prayer, love, peace, penance, fasting and returning to sacramental life and the Eucharist.

"In order to achieve peace in the world, peace in families and in our hearts, I want to invite both you and myself to accept all those unceasing invitations into our life and in a special way to accept the call to prayer and fasting."

> *"We need to accept the messages. Because all who are accepting them are renewing the Church!"*
> Bishop André-Mutien Léonard

Bishop André-Mutien Léonard, Namur, Belgium (Bulletin 26, Nov. 22, 1995). Referring to Our Lady's messages from Medjugorje during his homily at Mass with 3,000 of the faithful at the National Shrine of Beauraing, **Bishop Léonard** said, "We need to accept the messages. Because all who are accepting them are renewing the Church, and the Church needs renewal!" (Press Bulletin 23, October 11, 1995).

• "The memory of my pilgrimage to Medjugorje is still alive in me. My experience of that holy place could be summarized in three points: prayer, penance and communion in faith. It seems to me those are also the main features of Medjugorje. Truly we have reasons to be grateful to God!" **Cardinal Emmanuel Wamala,** Uganda (Press Bulletin 24, October 25, 1995).

> *"My pilgrimage to Medjugorje is still alive in me."*
> Cardinal Emmanuel Wamala

• "It is clear to me that in this place there is something very strong and supernatural. Without this supernaturality these events could never hold out to such an extent and spread like this throughout the whole world. I know that all the more people are coming from the whole world and that many pray here and are converted. This is a great supernatural reality of which the facts themselves speak....

"Mary is helping us in a special way to come to Christ, and He is the only Mediator and Savior. To her Jesus said from the cross: 'Behold your son,' but to the disciple He said: 'Behold your Mother!' I am convinced that is the reason for the apparitions, that is giving Mary the right and from which comes the duty that she appear and help us... What is being announced here is the essence of the Gospel, therefore we have to accept it!" **Bishop Jose de Jesus Nunez Viloria**, Guyana, Venezuela (Press Bulletin 131, December 1, 1999).

• "I believe that Our Lady is appearing here. She is the Mother and she cares for us. I believe that she is always with her children, especially when they have to suffer, when they have so many problems. I have no difficulties believing that Our Lady is here because, above all, the 'sensus fidelium' [sense of the faithful] says that Mary is here, and also my priestly and pastoral experience through a full 25 years, and now also that of being a bishop helps recognize the special signs that Mary is present here and that she is caring for her children. I would like to say to everyone: 'Mary is the Mother who loves and truly has to come to this world. She comes and says what we have to do, because she cares for us.' I hope that the world will open its heart and soul to this good Mother." **Bishop Emilio L. Bataclan**, Philippines [9] (Press Bulletin 131, December 1, 1999).

• "In Medjugorje, people plunge into an atmosphere of prayer and silence. This is very positive. They pray a lot, go to confession; the Eucharistic celebration is beautiful and alive, which is not the case everywhere. I would say: Look at the fruits! The fruits show the quality of the tree. The fruits that I see and

> *"Our Lady is at work here!"*
> Bishop Hermann Raich

experience, that I hear about, are so positive and so convincing that I am personally convinced that Our Lady is at work here, that she appears!" **Bishop Hermann Raich**, Wabag, Papua New Guinea (Press Bulletin 190, September 26, 2003).

• "The Blessed Mother is actively concerned for our well-being. She wants all of us to be really happy and to have peace. All we have to do is to listen to the messages, to read them, to put them into practice. I remember what is written in the Psalm of today: 'If today you hear his voice, harden not your hearts!' Make sure that your heart is receptive of the messages and put them into practice! I feel very much at home here in Medjugorje. It is as if Our Lady was telling me, 'This is your home!' " **Bishop Jesus a Cabrera,** Alaminos, Philippines (Press Bulletin 192, November 26, 2003).

> *"Listen to the messages!"*
> Bishop Jesus a Cabrera

> *"The apparitions are a sign!"*
> Bishop Abilio Ribas

• "The apparitions are a sign that people went astray from God's path. This is why the Mother comes with love and warns us, she tells us that we really have to turn to God!" **Bishop Abilio Ribas**, Islands of Sao Tome and Principe, Africa (Press Bulletin 191, 2003).

• "I find the challenge in Medjugorje absolutely in accordance with the teaching of the Church and with the theological training we have gone through as priests. I find it rather a challenge to put into practice what we have already learned. I want to call Medjugorje 'a rumination station'. Here, I am challenged to bring up all that I was taught in my heart and in my mind, and question myself concerning my life. I am deeply impressed by what is going on here in Medjugorje...My advice will be short: 'Go there and experience it yourself.' That's all!" **Bishop Gerard Ndlovu**, Umzimkulu/South African Republic (Press Bulletin 188, May 26, 2003).

• "Faith is alive here in Medjugorje. I can feel here how much every person needs God. While climbing Cross Mountain, I saw many young and old, healthy and sick people, praying sincerely. It is evident that God is being praised here, and I thank God for this!" **Bishop Salvador Pineiro Garcia-Calderon**, military

> **"Faith is alive here in Medjugorje!"**
>
> Bishop Salvador Garcia-Calderon

bishop in Lima,Peru (Press Bulletin 187, 2003).

• "My position towards the events of Medjugorje is identical to the position of Croatian bishops. Medjugorje exists and as such is a fact. People go there, and I see that Medjugorje is a place of grace. Many faithful from Slovenia who went there said that they

> **"Medjuguorje is a place of grace.... I think that soon [the Church's official pronouncement] will happen."**
>
> Cardinal Franc Rode, Prefect, Vatican Congregation

received great graces! They made their confession, came back to the life of the Church and started to live a Christian life. This is the grace that they received in Medjugorje. Why not allow this? I have nothing against the fact that people go there. However, I wait until the competent and legitimate authorities of the Church pronounce themselves on the question of Medjugorje and I think that, soon, this will happen." **Cardinal Franc Rode**, Perfect of the Congregation for Institutes of Consecrated Life and Societies of Apostolic Life, (Press Bulletin 187, June 26, 2003).

• "Medjugorje is a place where an intensive mission-station of heaven obviously exists, where thousands upon thousands of people find prayer, confession,

> **"Medjugorje is a place where an intensive mission-station of heaven obviously exists!"**
>
> Cardinal Schönborn

conversion, reconciliation, healing and deeper faith."[10] **Cardinal Schönborn**, Archbishop of Vienna, during a catechesis given in St. Stephen's Cathedral in Vienna on December 1, 2002 (Press Bulletin 182, January 26, 2003).

- "I came to Medjugorje in 1987. Things were much more primitive then than they are today,

but the Spirit is still here and the presence of Our Lady is all around. You can't move anywhere without sensing the marvelous grace of God affecting the lives of people. I have met people who are here because they are on drugs, on alcohol. I have met people with tragic situations in their lives and the miraculous way in which God is reflecting, manifesting Himself. One of the priests told me that he was hearing Confessions, he eventually stopped and left, and they drew him back! The magnitude of the Confessions is enough if you want to be satisfied that God is present here. For me, that's Medjugorje.

"Our Lady's apparitions are no problem for me. Fundamentally, it is a question of belief. We can't inflict faith and devotion on people. Mostly you can show it by your own example. This is the freedom that God has given to all of us. He wants us to respond out of faith and love.

"The basic message of Medjugorje is absolutely solid. We are living in 2002, but men and women are still made of a body and a soul. We all have traces of the Original Sin. Our needs are the same as in the times of the Apostles and in any generation. Basically, we are the children of God and our cries are as huge as of any generation. Therefore, the message has to be the same! We cannot do without God. This is the marvelous thing about Medjugorje. This is an

"Medjugorje is the shining light today in our society!"
Bishop Pearse Lacey

oasis of God, this is the life of the Church as it should be. Tradition is not a dirty word, although it seems to be to some people! The life of a priest consists in bringing people back to God, people who have wandered away because they thought religion was irrelevant. Thank God that He is God and provides places like this. I have been to other places, but Medjugorje is the shining light today in our society." **Bishop Pearse Lacey**, Toronto, Canada (Press Bulletin 180, November 26, 2002). During his fifth pilgrimage to Medjugorje (October 11 to 16, 2006) Bishop Lacey stated during an interview with Radio "Mir" Medjugorje that he believes Our Lady is indeed appearing in Medjugorje!

• Commenting on the fact that there are thousands of prayer groups in the USA inspired by Medjugojre, **Archbishop George Pearce** testified: "We have a little group in the Cathedral in Providence, where I am. They call it 'Little St. James.' They meet every evening; they have Exposition and Adoration of the Blessed Sacrament, Benediction and Holy Mass....

"I think that we have not got the message yet. There was a great turn to the Lord right after September 11, but I think we need more than that before my country

> *"Come to Medjugorje!"*
> Archbishop George Pearce

really turns to the Lord. So we just pray for that day. We hope we will turn to the Lord before we have to learn too many lessons, but this is also an act of the mercy of God. Everything is an act of the mercy of God. We know very well that God in His merciful love, in His permissive Providence, will take all the means possible so none of the least of His children will be totally lost. That's all that really matters. I would say: Come to Medjugorje in the spirit of an open mind, in prayer, and entrust your journey to Our Lady. Just come and the Lord will do the rest!

"I have no doubt about the authenticity of Medjugorje. I have been here three times already and I say to any priest who asks about it: 'Just go and sit in the confessional, and you will

> *"I have no doubt about the authenticity of Medjugorje!"*
> Archbishop George Pearce

see miracle after miracle, after miracle...'I have no doubts whatsoever. This is the work of God!" **Archbishop George Pearce**, retired Archbishop of the Fiji Islands (Press Bulletin 180, Nov. 26, 2002).

• "I fell in love with Medjugorje! The motherly voice full of tenderness that resounds through Our Lady's messages leads the faithful to prayer and to Christ. Our Lady calls us 'little children,' and this word deeply touches the human heart...the faithful feel that this call is authentic and they respond!" (Bishop Guerra had already been to Medjugorje. That experience led him to found a youth prayer

> *"I fell in love with Medjugorje!"*
> Bishop Ricardo Guerra

group, which lives according to the spirituality of the messages of the Queen of Peace. When he was asked why he came again to Medjugorje and what attracts the faithful to Medjugorje, the Bishop gave the preceding answer.) **Bishop Ricardo Guerra**, Juridical Vicar of the Archdiocese of Valencia, Venezuela (Press Bulletin 179, October 26, 2002).

• "This is not the first experience of this kind in the world. There were apparitions in Fatima and in Lourdes. Now everyone talks about Medjugorje[11]...Here, Our Lady reveals herself as the Queen of Peace...Young people in their parishes feel too much luke-warmness. In

> *"Christians are coming from all horizons and speaking one and the same language – the language of prayer!"*
> Bishop Jean-Vincent Ondo

Medjugorje they discover a living, warm, awakened Church...I believe that those who come here are not tourists, but they come in the hope of finding rest in Mary... I am enthusiastic to see Christians coming from all horizons and speaking one and the same...language – the language of prayer!" **Bishop Jean-Vincent Ondo**, Oyem, Gabon (Press Bulletin 178, September 26, 2002).

• "We read about the Medjugorje apparitions in newspapers. … We have come to see, but even more to experience...We were especially touched by the desire of people to come closer to God, to use every occasion to come closer to God. They have seen that a door towards God was open!" **Bishop Gerard Anton Zerdin**, Bishop-coadjutor San Ramon/Peru

> *"A door towards God was open!"*
> Bishop Gerard Anton Zerdin

(Press Bulletin 177, August 26, 2002)

• "I heard about the apparitions for the first time from the newspapers… For me, it meant nothing more than other strange names and I was skeptical, but I have noticed conversions and this is what impressed me most of all.... There was an occasion to come to Medjugorje and I did it. I see so

> ## *"I will tell what I have seen and experienced!"*
> ### Bishop Julio Ojeda Pascual

many people coming here; people who want to come closer to Jesus through Mary. Let us thank God for having given us Mary... There are many conversions here, which can lead to spiritual vocations: a priestly vocation, a religious vocation, an active lay vocation... When I go back home, I will tell what I have seen and experienced!" **Bishop Julio Ojeda Pascual**, San Ramon, Peru (Press Bulletin 177, August 26, 2002).

• "Medjugorje is really known throughout the world. Wherever I go, in my country, in the USA or in Europe, people talk about Medjugorje! Last year I was in Orlando, in Florida, and someone took me by car to the Space Center. He told me that he went to Medjugorje several times, and that I should go there too. I answered him that I regret that I cannot, for three reasons: I have no time, it is far and I have no money. He answered me that Our Lady would work a miracle. This year, a missionary from Italy told me that he

> ## *"Whoever has been here cannot remain silent!"*
> ### Bishop Silas S. Njiru

was going to Medjugorje and asked me if I would like to come with him. I answered in the same way: I have no time, it is far and I have no money. When he went back home, he sent me a letter saying: The money is here, everything is ready, just open your heart to Our Lady. This is why I am here, because I venerate the Blessed Virgin Mary. I am profoundly impressed by the faith of people in the Church. It is a strong faith. I especially see many young people. I see that many people go to confession and ask to be reconciled with God. Today, this is a real miracle. People told me that for many years they did not go to Church, and since they have been to Medjugorje, they go regularly to Mass. This is a real miracle for me. Whoever has been here cannot remain silent!" **Bishop Silas S. Njiru,** Meru, Kenya (Press Bulletin 175, June 26, 2002).

• "We wanted to come to this place where Our Lady calls to conversion, and especially to pray the rosary. When we go back to Vietnam, we will speak about Our Lady's call to conversion, especially her call to adore the Most Blessed Sacrament of the Altar, and to pray for peace. We ask you to pray for the Catholics in Vietnam!" **Bishop Nguyen Quang Tuyen**, Bac Ninh, Vietnam (Press Bulletin 173, April 26, 2002).

• "I am grateful to God for having given us Medjugorje, such a place of prayer!" **Bishop Jérôme Gapangwa Nteziryayo**, Uvira, Congo (Press Bulletin 169, December 26, 2001).

> *"I am grateful to God for having given us Medjugorje!"*
> Bishop Jérôme Gapangwa Nteziryayo

• "Medjugorje is not only the name of a place in Bosnia and Herzegovina, but Medjugorje is a place of grace where Our Lady is appearing in a special way. Medjugorje is a place where those who have fallen get up again, and all of those who go on pilgrimage to that place find a star, which leads them and shows them a new direction in life." **Archbishop Franc Kramberger**, Maribor, Slovenia (Press Bulletin 169, December 26, 2001).

> *"Medjugorje is a place of grace where Our Lady is appearing!"*
> Archbishop Franc Kramberger

• "I would like our people to come to Medjugorje, but Africa is far away. [12] I decided to take the initiative to establish a strong contact with Medjugorje." **Fr. Ghislain Ndondji, OFM,** Provincial of the Franciscan Province, Lumumbashi, Congo (Press Bulletin 168, November 26, 2001).

• "The prayers after the evening Mass are long! People pray!... Pilgrims from my group say we have to do something to make Medjugorje known in Taiwan.

> *"'We have to do something to make Medjugorje known in Taiwan!'"*
> Archbishop Leonard Hsu

83

I wonder how we could organize pilgrimages from Taiwan to Medjugorje, how to bring young people... Personally, I would like to stay in Medjugorje longer!" **Archbishop Leonard Hsu**, Taipei, Taiwan (Press Bulletin 165, August 26, 2001).

• "It is really very beautiful here. It is right that Medjugorje is called a place of prayer for the whole world and 'the confessional of the world.' ...Medjugorje is still quite unknown in Peru, but I promise to

> *"I promise to become an apostle of Medjugorje in my country!"*
> Archbishop José Antúnez de Mayolo

become an apostle of Medjugorje in my country!.. I shall come back, I shall surely come back!" **Archbishop José Antúnez de Mayolo**, Ayacucho, Peru (Press Bulletin 162, May 26, 2001).

• "You who live here must be happy people. Certainly, there are obstacles. The devil is strongly attacking a place where Our Lady appears. We have been attacked, because we have decided

> *"I will tell to everyone: come and see! I have seen the real presence of the Most Blessed Virgin!"*
> Abbot Nicolas Hakim

to go to Medjugorje. They asked us why we do not go somewhere else. The devil is always attacking human goodness. If you want to do good, to be near God, many will be against you. I will tell everyone: 'Come and see!' I have seen the real presence of the Most Blessed Virgin. She is everywhere in the world, but here in a special way!" **Abbot Nicolas Hakim,** Superior General of the Melkite Basilian Order of Chueirites (Press Bulletin 163, June 26, 2001).

> *"Medjugorje is a sign!"*
> Archbishop Georges Riachi

• "I would like to tell the people to come to Medjugorje. Medjugorje is a sign!" [13] **Archbishop Georges Riachi**, Tripoli, Lebanon (Press Bulletin 163, June 26, 2001).

• "I have kept an eye on the events of Medjugorje for the past

84

> **"I am convinced the apparitions are true!"**
>
> **Bishop Bernardo Witte**

20 years and have been convinced they are true! They convey a message of faith and a message of hope, which the Church is conveying, while calling to prayer, to fasting and to conversion. "This intensity is rather surprising, but this is how I interpret it: morality and ethics in the world are in great danger. In an extreme danger for the world, for the Church and for souls, extreme measures are needed. I marvel and I rejoice! Each apparition is a new hope and a new challenge. Also to this question, I have the same answer: In a great danger of the civilization of death, these apparitions promote a civilization of life.

"I have the impression that everything is happening in a harmonious way: these apparitions, the pontificate of John Paul II who encourages the renewal of the pastoral life in the Church, and many bishops who consciously give a Marian orienta-

> **"These apparitions promote a civilization of life."**
>
> **Bishop Bernardo Witte**

tion to their episcopate… To resume, I would repeat the words of Our Lady in Fatima: "At the end, my Immaculate Heart shall triumph!" I think that both, the apparitions of Fatima and of Medjugorje, signify a call to the renewal of Europe. In Medjugorje, the communist East has begun to collapse. Medjugorje is a carrier of joy, of hope and of trust." **Bishop Bernardo Witte**, Conception, Argentina (Press Bulletin 197, April 26, 2004).

• "As a Christian and as a believer, I came to pray and to adore the Lord. I thank the Lord for the experience of faith that I had here, especially concerning the Sacrament of Reconciliation and the Eucharist. I had a special joy in experiencing the spirit of prayer here. The ecclesial communion that reigns here among the pilgrims is a special grace of the Lord." **Archbishop Francisco Viti**, Huambo, Angola (Press Bulletin 202, September 26, 2004).

• **Archbishop Giovanni Moretti,** Apostolic Nuncio from Meina (Italy), came on a private pilgrimage to Medjugorje in the beginning of October, 2004, and expressed his enthusiasm about the devotion and spirit of prayer that reign at the Shrine (Press Bulletin 204). **Bishop Mauro Parmeggiani,** in preparation for the First European Meeting of Eucharistic Adoration Youth Groups in Rome, came for the Youth Festival in 2004. He encouraged the Franciscans to continue to do all they can so that "Medjugorje may preserve the simplicity, the austerity and the intensity of prayer, so that all may encounter Mary, and through her, her Son Jesus, who are inviting us to conversion and the essential Christian experience today." In the diocese of Rome, Bishop Parmeggiani is especially charged with pastoral work with youth (Press Bulletin 202).

• "I heard about Medjugorje for the first time about 15-20 years ago, but I was doubting. I was not very much interested in coming here, but a friend of mine, a priest from Switzerland, told me about Medjugorje and about his experience. His attitude as a priest had tremendously changed after Medjugorje. He was praying well, and in his relationship with others he became very human. He is a real priest now! That made me think: There must be something in Medjugorje!

"Roman Gruether told me that Medjugorje was different from other places of pilgrimages, that the natural atmosphere is kept, and that people are really praying here. Last year, I made up my mind to come and see. My experience is corresponding to my expectations! These three days are a confirmation. One can feel the family spirit here. People who are involved in the service, even the smallest service, do it with love and with joy. This place gives us also the experience of the universal family. Everyone feels here at home, like in one's mother's house. I met the visionaries; I visited Marija, Ivan and Vicka. I think

> *"Medjugorje will be recognized, there is no doubt! Today or tomorrow, maybe a little later, it will surely be recognized! ... It is for the whole world!"*
>
> Bishop Geevarghese Mar Divannasios Ottathengil

that they are real visionaries. Medjugorje will be recognized, there is no doubt! Today or tomorrow, maybe a little later, it will surely be recognized!

"These messages are really needed. Prayer, Holy Mass, penance, confession, fasting, conversion. At any age, they are the fundamentals of spiritual life. Without Jesus, there is no spiritual life. Self-denial, living for God and for others. Often, we are tempted to think that, at the modern age, we are competing with God. But we have to realize that human beings are limited. Catastrophes help us understand our limits. September 11th, or Tsunami… we understand how small we are.

"Medjugorje is for our time a real call from God. The people who live here are fortunate. You have a special vocation. You have to keep this universal brotherhood. This is not only for this parish, this region, this diocese… It is for the whole world!" **Bishop Geevarghese Mar Divannasios Ottathengil**, (Syro-Malankara Rite) Bathery, Kerala, India (Press Bulletin 213, August 26, 2005).

• "I have come to Medjugorje to seek inner peace. A bishop in Africa is a builder, the one who reconstructs roads, builds bridges and schools. A bishop does everything, so there are times when what he really needs is spiritual peace. That is why I have come here. To retire for a few days, to pray together with the pilgrims. What I found very good here is the fact that I can hear confessions. I spent four hours in the confessional yesterday. It is wonderful to see how many people come here for confession.

"The Church has been increasingly insisting on the sacraments of the Eucharist and Reconciliation lately. Exactly these two important sacraments are present here. In the beginning, there was much talk on the apparitions, and now the stress is more on spirituality. A deep spirituality is developing here. A message of peace and conversion has been given. All these messages are now to be used and lived. People like sensations. When messages and seers were discussed, people were flowing in. Now less talk is spent on them, but everything is moving towards a deeper level. Man needs a firm spiritual support. Man's inner life should rely on solid Gospel values. That is why I say that deepening of the message, that is prayer, communion and confession, is becoming the basis of a deep spiritual life...

"I come here because of my own devotion. One should not worry about approval all the time. The approval will certainly be given. Bish-

> *"One should not worry about approval all the time. The approval will certainly be given. Bishops come, and they come to pray. There is something that we are drawn to, something that has impressed us. Little by little, Medjugorje will be approved!"*
>
> Bishop Stanislas
> Lukumwena Lumbala

ops come, and they come to pray. There is something that we are drawn to, something that has impressed us. Little by little, Medjugorje will be approved. Let each one live one's own devotion.

"We are making way to set up a radio station in my Kole Diocese, which will allow us to let people know more about Medjugorje." **Bishop Stanislas Lukumwena Lumbala**, Kole, Congo (Press Bulletin 215, October 25, 2005).

• "Last Sunday, I was in Castel Gandolfo with my group of pilgrims, and we prayed the Angelus with the Pope. After the Angelus, as it was arranged before, I went to visit the Holy Father. The program of this visit was specified in advance. At the end of our conversation, I asked the Holy Father to give his blessing to the group of pilgrims, which was going to Medjugorje the following day. If you have ever met the Pope, you know that he has a splendid smile. He smiled with great kindness and he said: 'May God watch over you and bless you.'

"The devotion towards the Virgin Mary is very widespread among our parishioners. They came to me and they asked me to accompany them this year to Medjugorje. I have much work, but I accepted immediately. Then, I thought that I should have perhaps said no, but now I am glad to have come. For me and for the whole group, coming here is a blessing...

"The number of pilgrims coming to Medjugorje is a sign of God. The atmosphere of prayer spread by the priests from here is very deep. I believe that Medjugorje is a place of expectation, a place that is questioning our faith: how to deepen our faith? The prayer in front of the cross, adoration, the Eucharist – all this gives the pilgrims a deep spirituality. It is a place of prayer. I think that the role of the priest who accompanies the pilgrims is very important. In order to bring fruits, the pilgrims must be accompanied by a priest.

"The messages of Medjugorje are messages of the Gospel. I do not see anything else. Eucharist, penance, prayer... it is the Gospel. I will write a booklet on my impressions of Medjugorje. I will encourage the faithful to come to make this pilgrim-

> *"I will write a booklet on my impressions of Medjugorje. I will encourage the faithful to come!"*
> Bishop Issam John Darwish

age, to live a few days of prayer and interior conversion. I will encourage them. I also will encourage the priests to come with them. I have a desire: that Medjugorje opens to the environment, to the Orthodox and to the Moslems, that Medjugorje becomes a centre of dialogue with them." **Bishop Issam John Darwish**, Eparch of the Melchite Catholic Church in Australia and New Zealand (Press Bulletin 215, October 25, 2005).

• Archbishop Hieronymus Herculanus Bumbun was in Medjugorje on May 13 and 14, 2005. He came on a pilgrimage with a group from Jakarta. He said on Radio Mir that he was "very impressed by the message of Medjugorje given to the six visionaries. It is good for people to follow the messages, because they lead to peace, hope and faith. They present a basic Catholic education for the families. It would be good for families to pay more attention to these messages. In my diocese of Pontianak in Indonesia, they increase the community spirit. The messages of Medjugorje can be very well applied to the living philosophy in Indonesia. They are closely related to the life of the people and the Church. In the present globalization of the world, which is affecting rela-

> *I praise the Lord for the possibility to be in Medjugorje and to see with my own eyes and to hear with my own ears!"*
> Archbishop Hieronymus Herculanus Bumbun

tionships in the family, these messages can help the family to feel like the basic cell of the Church." The Archbishop "praised the Lord for the possibility to be in Medjugorje and to see with my own eyes and to hear with my own ears!" **Archbishop Hieronymus Herculanus Bumbun**, Pontianak, Indonesia (Press Bulletin 211, June 26, 2005).

• "In my diocese, I have young people who were converted and whose life was changed in Medjugorje. Their witness was for me a sign of a great presence of God in Medjugorje. I also read what Rene Laurentin

> *Conversions of young people in my diocese are "a sign of a great presence of God in Medjugorje!"*
> Bishop Salvatore Boccaccio

wrote about Our Lady's apparitions, and it also had an influence, but most of all, I was inspired by personal witnesses of the pilgrims. I congratulate the Franciscans who are tirelessly serving the pilgrims and patiently

> *"Unfortunately, there is still a great deal of ignorance within the Church about the great supernatural reality that is happening in Medjugorje."*
> Archbishop Emilio Ogñénovich

and humbly enduring all attacks and provocations." **Bishop Salvatore Boccaccio**, Frosinone (near Rome), Itlay. (Press Bulletin 211, June 26, 2005. The Press Bulletin noted the bishop was visibly filled with joy because he was finally able to come to Medjugorje. Bishop Boccaccio had also served as an auxiliary bishop for Rome, working closely with Pope John Paul II).

90

• "Unfortunately, there is still a great deal of ignorance within the Church about the great supernatural reality that is happening in Medjugorje, at the heart of the modern world. What fills me with hope are the words of John Paul II, who told us, both priests and bishops, to accompany pilgrims to Medjugorje, because here they are praying, converting, fasting and changing their lives. The Church needs some more time to state its position in relation to Medjugorje, just as in its wisdom it took time to state its position towards Fatima and Lourdes.

"Concerning Medjugorje, I will share my own personal conviction with my fellow bishops in the Bishops Conference of Argentina, and also with our cardinal, Mons. Bergoglio, who was

> *Cardinal Bergoglio "was very happy when I told him that I was going to Medjugorje."*
> Archbishop Emilio Ogñénovich

very happy when I told him that I was going to Medjugorje. If you ask me for my opinion about Medjugorje, I will tell you that it can be compared to a mother, a pregnant woman in the sixth month of pregnancy, who impatiently awaits the moment to see her child born, but nobody can hasten it, because the right moment will come in its own good time." **Archbishop Emilio Ogñénovich**, Mercedes-Luján, Argentina (Interview with Parish Information Center, May, 2006).

• **Bishop José Domingo Ulloa Mendieta** began an interview on Radio Mir Medjugorje by explaining why he had come to the Shrine: "A priest with whom I was in the seminary, Fr. Francisco Verar, spoke to me about Medjugorje long ago. Now, the time has come for me to see for myself. What I have experienced here goes far beyond my expectations. The encounter with so many pilgrims is an excellent experience. I can see their desire to convert and to change. For me, it is also important to notice the social activity practiced here in Medjugorje. It articulates what Mary is doing, namely, to be always ready to help others. My pilgrims were prepared for this pilgrimage. Medjugorje amazes them, and they will remain under the influence of seeing so many people coming here to pray.

"The spirituality inspired by Medjugorje is very developed in my country. We especially want to involve children. The parish church consecrated to Mary, Queen of Peace, founded by Fr. Francisco Verar, was built according to the model of St. James Church in Medjugorje. In Panama, there are many prayer groups based on Our Lady's messages.

"The simplicity of these messages is enticing. The Medjugorje messages are an evangelical call to conversion and to peace; there is nothing apocalyptic in them. Without prayer, without

> *"What I have experienced here goes far beyond my expectations...One cannot leave Medjugorje without this burning desire to change!"*
> Bishop José Domingo Ulloa Mendieta

fasting and without the Eucharist – and these are the foundations of Christianity – we cannot answer the call to holiness addressed to us by Mary. Those who come to Medjugorje want to answer the evangelical call that is coming from the Lord, especially by means of the Eucharist and the Sacrament of Confession. I have heard from many people that they experience the need to change, and to change within the Church and through the sacraments. One cannot leave Medjugorje without this burning desire to change and to start anew. Many groups are coming accompanied by their priests who help them, and this generates the beginning of a new life for them.

"The greatest miracle happening in Medjugorje is the spiritual healing that people experience here. The specificity of Medjugorje is the gift of peace pilgrims receive. This is what humanity is longing for today, and this gift is received in Medjugorje through our Mother Mary. It is not only about inner peace, but also about discovering that we are all brothers, and that conflicts and violence are not a solution. This peace should be shared with others.

"All of the visionaries of Medjugorje are married, they have families, and I am very glad about this because this means that the call to holiness is for all. The family path is a way of holiness; holiness is not only for priests and for religious. God is calling all men. Christians are invited to give witness, to live in the world without belonging to the world. We are called to be witnesses of joy.

"We cannot keep silent about what we have seen [in Medjugorje] and we cannot ignore what Our Lady is asking. In Medjugorje, pilgrims find peace, they encounter

> *"We cannot keep silent about what we have seen [in Medjugorje] and we cannot ignore what Our Lady is asking"*
> Bishop José Domingo Ulloa Mendieta

Jesus, and their lives change. Towards all those who are like the lost sheep, we have to be like Jesus, so that people can come back to Him and receive from Him all the good that He is giving. Let us be like Mary, let us see what people need, what their sufferings are, and let us help them. Let us be witnesses of the great gift of living our faith within our Holy Mother Church." **Bishop José Domingo Ulloa Mendieta**, O.S.A., auxiliary of the Archdiocese of Panama, was interviewed on *Radio "Mir" Medjugorje* in September, 2005.

• In September, 2005, three bishops from Malawi visited Medjugorje: **Bishop Thomas Msusa** (Zomba), **Bishop Allan Chamgwera**, his retired predecessor, and **Bishop Remi Joseph Gustave Saint-Marie** (Dedza). Bishop Msusa (who gives the following testimony) is the youngest bishop in Malawi. He is the son of a Muslim mullah. "Because of our poverty," he says, "I was educated by the missionaries. My father was a Muslim minister, and I became a priest in the Church of Jesus Christ.

"The central problem in our country is famine. The population engages mainly in agriculture. During recent years, we had terrible drought, and the food shortages increased. About four and a half million are facing the problem of famine, and if the administration does not act, who knows if those people will survive? Another problem is the great number of HIV-positives. Many are dying, and leaving orphans behind. The third problem is the Muslims, who have the support of other Muslim countries and have great financial resources also.

They are buying food and giving it to the people, but on condition that they become Muslims. Islamic countries are giving money and scholarships to young people, but under the same conditions – that they embrace Islam.[14] Unfortunately the young people, desiring a better life, are accepting these conditions.

"I heard about Medjugorje a long time ago, and I read about Medjugorje when I was a seminarian. My rector intended to send me to Medjugorje, but it was not possible then. Recently, I met a woman who is in charge of the Medjugorje Peace Centre in Malawi. She asked me if I wanted to go to Medjugorje, and I accepted. My desire was to pray here, because

> *"I am so amazed... I have no words to describe what I feel. I ask myself why Medjugorje is so distant from Malawi. We also need such a place, but my people have no funds to come to Medjugorje. I have received an answer: I am the one who has to spread news of the events of Medjugorje!"*
> Bishop Thomas Msusa

in Malawi I am very busy, and have very little time for prayer. I am very enthusiastic about my visit here. I saw pilgrims from all over the world, all united in prayer. I am delighted to see the piety here. People take very seriously the Sacrament of Confession, and the Blessed Eucharist also. I am so amazed... I have no words to describe what I feel. I ask myself why Medjugorje is so distant from Malawi. We also need such a place, but my people have no funds to come to Medjugorje.[15] I have received an answer: I am the one who has to spread the news about Medjugorje. Furthermore, there are the experiences of people who come here. Previously I read about this in books, but now I have

> *"Previously I read about this in books, but now I have experienced it personally!"*
> Bishop Thomas Msusa

experienced it personally. I observed this also in my own group, with the other bishops. We became united, and this tells me that this is a gift from God. God is telling us... you have to be apostles.

"Everything started under the direction of the Peace Centre in Malawi, when they began to speak about the spirituality of Medjugorje. The idea was to give to the Malawians something similar…We understood that Our Lady wanted us to have such a place in our own country. We then went to ask for permission from our archbishop, which he granted, because he had a positive attitude towards Medjugorje.

"The Stations of the Cross, and the cross on our mountain – the same as that on Krizevac – are already finished. The foundations of the church, identical to the church in Medjugorje, are laid (see pp. 132 - 135). The donor came with us on this pilgrimage, and he wants to continue to finance the construction.

> *"I have seen how strong the spirituality is here. I believe that we can transmit this experience to Malawi."*
> Bishop Thomas Msusa

"The building of this center will deepen our spirituality. I have seen how strong the spirituality is here. I believe that we can transmit this experience to Malawi. The difficulty for the believers is how to live the word of God in their own lives. The building of the center will help them to deepen their faith and to come back to God. The Catholics in my country are scattered and exposed to attacks, and the center may help them to be more united.

"The Church will be the last to pronounce a judgment about Medjugorje. In the meantime, the experience of the faithful is essential. However, I see that the attitude of the Church is positive, because it doesn't prevent anyone from coming. On the contrary, the Church allows people to go to Medjugorje. Unofficially, we can say that the Church has already accepted Medjugorje. As for the official judgment, we will have to wait some more time…

> *"The Church allows people to go to Medjugorje. Unofficially, we can say that the Church has already accepted Medjugorje."*
> Bishop Thomas Msusa

I always think of the words the angel spoke to the Virgin Mary, when he told her not to be afraid. People should have hope and faith. Roused by Our Lady's words, we need to pray primarily for conversion, because what is happening in Medjugorje also helps the Church to advance. I do not believe that the Church will ever refuse conversions. This is why I believe that, one day, the Church will recognize Medjugorje." **Bishop Thomas Msusa**, Zomba, Malawi, (Press Bulletin 216, November 26, 2005).

• "I know people from the north of Brazil, professors and industrialists, who were atheists, and who were converted in Medjugorje some 15 years ago. Now, they go to Mass every day and are very active in the Church. There is a big difference between pilgrims who come here and those who go somewhere else. The experience of Medjugorje is an experience of conversion. Pilgrims speak in a different way about other places. Here, lives are changed. I see the authenticity of the conversions of Medjugorje. The reason for my coming, my hope and the grace that I desire to receive here, is my personal conversion, the deepening of my personal conversion." **Bishop José Luís Azcona Hermoso**, Marajó, Brazil (Press Bulletin 214, September 26, 2005).

> *"I know people from the north of Brazil, professors and industrialists, who were atheists, and who were converted in Medjugorje...Here, lives are changed!"*
> Bishop José Luís Azcona Hermoso

> *"There is a big difference between pilgrims who come here and those who go somewhere else."*
> Bishop José Luís Azcona Hermoso

• "Modern culture is pulling people away from God, pulling people away from religion. We see that everywhere. That is why we need strong faith, to renew our commitment to God and to His Church. Ultimately, God is not going to force us against our will.

"I have heard from people who have come here over the years. This is the first time I have come to Medjugorje. I am coming here to see with my own eyes and hear with my own ears....I believe that many wonderful spiritual fruits have been produced here. I see much good fruit…you meet people from all over the world. Many people from Europe, but also people from America, people of different races, white and brown and black… and everyone is a brother and sister here. It is an expression of the universal Church, of the faith that we all share together. That is marvelous!" **Bishop Thomas L. Dupre**, Bishop of Springfield (Massachusetts, USA) came to Medjugorje at the end of October, 2003.

• "I was deeply moved by my visit to Medjugorje!" **Cardinal Timothy Manning**, USA. [16]

• "I have been coming to Medjugorje for many years. I have realized during this stay more than ever that this is a school of prayer for the world. We are taught by our Mother Mary in this beautiful mountain reality and in the church to be in the central part of the world, in the central part of our hearts, real honest Catholics of great prayer.

"Just this week I was reading a paper by a very well known cardinal in Europe who wrote, regarding Medjugorje, that there was nothing to worry

> *"In Medjugorje you learn how to pray!"*
> Bishop George Tracy

about in a critical way – he had only praise. In Medjugorje you learn how to pray! Medjugorje began to have a great influence when I came here for the first time and it has continued…I want to be Mother Mary's child.

"I have learned a lot from Mother Teresa[17]…Together with Mother Teresa I went to see the Holy Father. Mother Teresa and the Holy Father together was the most beautiful thing anybody could be part of and it will never be repeated in history. It is difficult to speak about this. Observing two children together. The way they relate to each other, the way their hearts connect. They both understood the Little Way of St Therese of Lisieux.

"Mother Teresa was the person who said to me: 'Jesus has told me that this is the work that you will be doing.' I had never thought of it before. The Cor Christi missionary community gives retreats and conferences to people in leadership and in business. Mother Teresa told me: 'These are your poor.' Our charism is to lead them to the Eucharistic Heart of Jesus and the Immaculate Heart of Mary. The point of the conferences that we give is to bring them back to that way, which they have lost." **Bishop George Tracy**, USA, founder of Cor Christi, has been coming to Medjugorje every year since 1984 (Information Centre "Mir" Medjugorje, May 22, 2004).

• "I came here to pray and not to discuss. I desire my entire personal conversion. What a joy and what an immense grace to be present here!" **Cardinal Corrado Ursi**, retired Archbishop of Naples (Press Bulletin 169, December 26, 2001). During his December, 2001, pilgrimage Cardinal Ursi met with the visionaries and was present during an apparition of Our Lady. He did not hide his enthusiasm. In his booklet "Rosary," already in its sixth edition, he had written that Our Lady is appearing in Medjugorje!

> *"What a joy and what an immense grace to be present here!" In Medjugorje "Our Lady is appearing!"*
>
> Cardinal Corrado Ursi

• "Our Lady of Medjugorje, you who inspire and are the only owner of Redevida, obtain for the Family Channel – TV Good News to be an instrument of communication according to moral, ethical, social, civil and Christian principles, at the service of the Brazilian people. May Your Son, our Lord Jesus Christ, bless and forever protect Redevida and the effort to create TV Maria in Brazil." **Archbishop**

Antonio Mucciolo, Archbishop of Botucatu, Brazil, President of the General Council of the Brazilian Institute for Christian Communication in Brazil, when consecrating TV Maria. (Press Bulletin 167 October 26, 2001).

• "I came to know Medjugorje while reading the messages of Our Lady and my impression was that this is her usual way of speaking. The conversion of my two cousins during their pilgrimage to Medjugorje is what urged me to come to Medjugorje. One of them had been a communist and the other a fascist. This fruit and my desire to see what is happening in this place motivated my coming to Medjugorje.

"Our Lady's theology in Medjugorje seems to be healthy and I understand it to be a continuation of the theology of her apparitions in Fatima. In the past century a Our Lady had already begun her work: Rue du Bac, Lourdes, Fatima and, in my opinion, Medjugorje is the nucleus of her

> *"The messages of Medjugorje are messages of hope."*
>
> Archbishop Rubén Héctor di Monte

work. Through this nucleus she is continuing what she began in Rue du Bac. She invites us to conversion of heart. Here, where there is so much suffering today, people pray a lot and are being reconciled through the Sacrament of Penance to arrive at that conversion. The messages of Medjugorje are messages of hope." **Archbishop Rubén Héctor di Monte**, Mercedes-Luján, Argentina (Press Bulletin 6, February 15, 1995).

• "I had heard about the events in Medjugorje not long after their beginning. In recent times there is a lot of talk about apparitions and, as a bishop, almost every week I was receiving something about apparitions, visions and revelations. I have to admit that during the Communist period in Yugoslavia I often came on vacation to Istria, but I did not go farther south even though I could have. I just did not have sufficient motivation. Then I began to ask myself more and more often: Why these completely simple messages that are still even being repeated? It is always a call to prayer, fasting, penance, prayer for peace. I said: That must have some meaning!

"What does a mother do when she raises her child? I experienced that at home: she always repeats the same thing: I have already often told you that! But I cannot stop saying: Pray, or do so and so. Mary acts the same way in Medjugorje. She always says the same thing to her children who are already now adult persons. And what else would a priest have to do in his parish? He is always calling to prayer. John Paul II once said that priests have to be the first to pray and have to be the teachers of prayer. That is what Mary, a good Mother, does. She teaches us to pray, really in a very simple way. Now I have to say truly that Christ's word has the value for me of being the recognizable sign: By their fruits you will know them!

"My impressions here are not surprising. I know that groups from Salzburg very often go to Medjugorje, that new prayer groups are constantly being started, that there are more and more people who say: 'In Medjugorje I received my vocation!'

> "New prayer groups are constantly being started, that there are more and more people who say: In Medjugorje I received my vocation!"
> Archbishop Georg Eder

I am reflecting: We are losing three things that we are getting back again in Medjugorje: penance, conversion and vocations. In Austria we look in vain for these things: Conversion is not even mentioned anymore because people do not need it; Confession is dying out with us except in shrines and in the churches of religious orders where this sacrament is sought and lived; spiritual vocations are less

> "We are losing three things that we are getting back again in Medjugorje: penance, conversion and vocations."
> Archbishop Georg Eder

and less. In Medjugorje this is happening constantly: Confessions, conversions and spiritual vocations!

"That is what I ask myself: What must we do for conversion to happen to someone? I have repeated to the members of Peoples' Initiative that, for me, conversion in their program has disappeared. Are we the ones who do not need conversion, the way Jesus says it in the Gospel? Conversion is being excluded, and Confession is being lost, spiritual vocations are less and less, and we are asking ourselves how can we at all keep up a seminary? But all that is found in Medjugorje. We are finding exactly that which for us has disappeared.

"I still have one more wish: That peace come here between the Franciscans and the bishop, and that Medjugorje can truly develop in the way that Our Lady wishes. I am now convinced of the authenticity of Medjugorje. I have believed it for quite a while. I still wanted to come and take a look. When pilgrims called me to go with them to Medjugorje, I answered: 'I am spiritually closer to Medjugorje than some others are!' My impression was confirmed because of the simplicity of the visionaries and the evening program. Everything is in the Church's spirit and that very, very simply. At the same time also very devoutly, with strong faith and above all with a strong will for conversion and real renewal." **Archbishop Georg Eder,** Salzburg, Austria (Press Bulletin 108, January 13, 1999).

> *"I am now convinced of the authenticity of Medjugorje!"*
> Archbishop Georg Eder

• "The experience of the people coming to Medjugorje affirms that this place is a place of special grace. You Franciscans must persevere. This is magnificent!" **Bishop Tadeusz Werno**, Koszalina, Poland (Press Bulletin 126, September 22, 1999).

• "Because of my responsibility as a bishop of the Catholic Church, I have come personally to see if this event is real, if it is acceptable. From the very first time that I came to Medjugorje, my conviction is that these events are authentic. In Medjugorje, Our Lady is coming in a very powerful way, an outstanding way, different than her other comings. It is impossible not to see here the Lord our God. Impossible! I come here to pray to Our Lady, to feel her presence, not only because I feel the need for it, but because this is giving me a consolation on the road, a strength to continue, to walk with one additional reason, with the conviction that God truly loves us all.

"At other places of pilgrimage where Our Lady was appearing, some miracles have happened, and this is beautiful. But here, for such a long time, Our Lady is giving messages, is continuing to speak.

> *"It is impossible not to see here the Lord our God. Impossible!"*
>
> Bishop Domenico Pecile, *Vicar of St. John Lateran Basilica in Rome*

I would say that, here, Our Lady continues to speak to humanity. She is not doing it from a pulpit, but as a mother. Those who want to hear and to obey: they listen. Those who do not want: they don't listen. Our Lady is continuing to speak here. I think that this is because the time in which we live is powerful and important as no time before. In our time, Our Lady is observing as a mother,

> *"Here, for such a long time, Our Lady is giving messages, is continuing to speak!"*
>
> Bishop Domenico Pecile, *Vicar of St. John Lateran Basilica in Rome*

seeing our reality and coming to help us to think again about our way of life and about the world in which we live...

"In Eucharistic celebrations, I saw something extraordinary: pilgrims were attentive, concentrated, although we had Holy Mass in a conference hall. Nothing could distract them; they experienced something deep within them. The presence of the mystery can almost be felt in the air here. The faithful come to the churches elsewhere also, but you see them talking. But not here! Here, they are attentive! In all our churches throughout the world, it should be as it is here in Medjugorje." **Bishop Domenico Pecile,** Vicar of St. John Lateran Basilica in Rome, talk given in Medjugorje on October 4, 2005.[18]

• Archbishop Bruno Tommasi came for his second pilgrimage to Medjugorje in September, 2005. He gave his testimony for the Parish Bulletin published on September 24, 2005: "Several years ago, I met a priest and some laymen who had gone to Medjugorje and who were internally transformed, converted. I was impressed. If a place is able to transform, to convert people, that means that this is a place of grace! Last year, I had the occasion to come here with two priests who accompanied me this year also. Then I had the occasion to know Marija, and this year I met Vicka. Although for the moment there is no official position by the authorities on the authenticity of these apparitions, thanks to

> *"In all our churches throughout the world, it should be as it is here in Medjugorje."*
>
> Bishop Domenico Pecile, *Vicar of St. John Lateran Basilica in Rome*

my encounter with these persons, I am convinced that they do not lie, that they are sincere and that they have a true experience of grace. [19]

"The apparitions have already lasted for 24 years. I believe that this is an extraordinary event. I remember that once Our Lady was asked a question about this matter. She replied: 'Are you already bored?...'

"To those who ask me questions about Medjugorje, I say that this is a place of prayer, a place where people are converted... I think that for the moment Medjugorje has become a shrine. The choice of the Holy Virgin to appear here, in the context and in the time of Communism, is a special event. It is really appropriate that she appears here and not in a place where liberty reigns.

"I think that one can consider Medjugorje as an impulse for the renewal of the Church. This is a renewal that comes from below, through changes in persons.

> *"Medjugorje is an impulse for the renewal of the Church!"*
>
> Archbishop Bruno Tommasi

"The fact that so many go for confession here is very positive. In the western countries, many go for communion, but very few go for confession. One could say that the sense of sin got lost, and

> *"We should receive with faith Our Lady's messages."*
>
> Archbishop Bruno Tommasi

103

therefore also the need to go for confession. We should receive with faith Our Lady's messages." **Archbishop Bruno Tommasi**, Lucca, Italy, (Press Bulletin 214, September 26, 2005).

• "The spiritual renewal that is coming from Medjugorje has done more in three years than what we have been able to accomplish within the last 40 years in our pastoral service!" **Archbishop Frane Franic**, Archbishop of Split (statement given in 1984).[20]

• "In 1984 when I first came to Medjugorje I was impressed by the fact that even before the evening prayer the poorly lit church was full of faithful, so many of whom were young. I was also struck by the profound devotion – which was not fanaticism – and by the confessions, and the prayer on the hills. I went to the church and remained there in prayer nearly the entire day. That's how I spent my days in Medjugorje; I did not speak to any of the Franciscans or the visionaries.

"Back home I felt profoundly renewed. I understood Mary better; also that thanks to Her the Church is renewed. I came again ... deeply convinced that many things happen here that theology or psychology cannot explain. I discovered the true meaning of faith and its fruits. No one can doubt the fruits of Medjugorje, for God's presence and His mercy are obvious; the Church can see that God's grace is handed out by the Mother of Mercy, the Mother of Sinners, who was close to the Cross. This is a truth which cannot be denied." **Bishop Adelio Tomasin**, Quixada, Brazil (*Echo di Medjugorje*, 140, 1998). Back home in Brazil, Bishop Tomasin was inspired to build a Shrine to Our Lady "Virgin of Serteo," where conferences run by Medjugorje apostolates could be held. It is staffed by a new religious order, "Oassi della Pace," recognized by the Church and given birth through Our Lady's apparitions in Medjugorje (see p. 118).

> *"No one can doubt the fruits of Medjugorje!"*
> Bishop Adelio Tomasin

• "I have desired to visit Medjugorje ever since the apparitions began. In 1983, two years after the apparitions began, I became a bishop. I heard consistent reports from those visiting Medjugorje, who spoke in glowing terms of their truly tremendous spiritual experiences. 'You have to go there, you have to see..,' they would say to me.

"I believe Medjugorje is a place that has been touched by the divine. Otherwise, you cannot understand the kind of immediate spiritual atmosphere that the senses experience... One of the things that I was told was that I would be hearing confessions. How wonderful! This is Our Lady's work. Secularism is spreading very quickly. Values are changing. Our Lady always comes to give the message of conversion... of sacrifice. I think it is badly needed. Just observe what is happening in the world: Israel, Palestine, Lebanon, India, Kashmir, Sri Lanka, East Timor... God must be deeply concerned about this situation. At the Cross, Jesus gave us Mary as Our Mother!" **Bishop Joseph Vianney Fernando**, President of the Bishops Conference of Sri Lanka (July, 2006 interview in Medjugorje).

> *"Medjugorje is a place that has been touched by the divine."*
>
> Bishop J. Fernando, Pres.
> Bishops Conf., Sri Lanka

• At the beginning of August, 2006, **Bishop Domenico Sigalini**, Ordinary of Palestrina near Rome, spent three days on pilgrimage in Medjugorje. Bishop Sigalini had been consecrated a bishop only fifteen months before. He was the last bishop to be appointed by Pope John Paul II. Before his episcopal ordination, for ten years he was the delegate for pastoral work with youth. In summer, 2005 in Cologne, during the World Youth Days, he was one of the bishops who gave catechesis in this context. On August 1, Bishop Sigalini assisted in the opening of the 17th International Youth Festival in Medjugorje. On the morning of August 2, he gave catechesis to thousands of young people in attendance from all over the world. (Parish News, August 2, 2006).

Having announced in his diocesan newspaper that he would be going on pilgrimage to Medjugorje, **Bishop Robert Finn**, Ordinary of the diocese of Kansas City-Saint Joseph, came to the Shrine in the beginning of September 2006, along with a group from his diocese. Each day he celebrated Mass, heard confessions and visited the prayer places in Medjugorje together with other pilgrims. "In the celebration of the Holy Sacraments I see the

> *"I see that the Spirit of God is at work here!"*
>
> Bishop Robert Finn, Kansas City (USA)

proof and the confirmation of the faith of God's people, and I also see that the Spirit of God is at work here," Bishop Finn said. "I came to pray for Christian laws to prevail in our country. I also pray for priestly and religious vocations and for the spreading of devotion to, and adoration of, the Most Blessed Sacrament of the altar in my own diocese" (Parish News, September 9, 2006).

Two archbishops visited Medjugorje in early October, 2006, and were present for the feast of the Rosary. **Archbishop Luigi Bommarito**, emeritus of Catania (Italy), came with a group of pilgrims from Italy. This was his second visit to Medjugorje. **Archbishop Harry Flynn**, Ordinary of Saint Paul and Minneapolis, Minnesota (USA), came with a group of pilgrims from Minnesota. It was his first visit to Medjugorje. Archbishop Flynn met the Franciscans serving the Medjugorje parish and spoke with them about the pastoral aspects of the work with the pilgrims, and especially with those who come from his own archdiocese, where numerous prayer groups have been established, groups that have reintroduced Adoration of the Blessed Sacrament into their parishes. He said that he came to Medjugorje to pray. Having celebrated the morning Masses in St. James Church for Italian and English speaking pilgrims, both archbishops visited the places of prayer and also spent many hours hearing confessions (Parish News, October 8, 2006).

After his pilgrimage Archbishop Flynn wrote an article

strongly endorsing the authenticity of the apparitions in the October 19, 2006, issue of his archdiocesan newspaper, *The Catholic Spirit*. In his article, titled "In Medjugorje, 'people are turning to God,'" he remembered the answer given by Pope John Paul II during his first ad limina visit in 1988 when he had been asked, "Holy Father, what do you think of Medjugorje?" The Holy Father kept eating his soup and responded: "Medjugorje? Medjugorje? Medjugorje? Only good things

> *"Only good things are happening at Medjugorje!"*
> Pope John Paul II

are happening at Medjugorje. People are praying there. People are going to Confession. People are adoring the Eucharist, and people are turning to God!"

• We conclude this chapter with the testimony of a great apostle of Mary, **Bishop Paolo Hnilica**, a friend of Sister Lucia of Fatima and Blessed Mother Teresa of Calcutta. A trusted confidant of Pope John Paul II (see p. viii), Bishop Hnilica died on October 8, 2006.

After escaping from a Soviet concentration camp he was ordained a bishop on January 2, 1951. In 1978, **Bishop Hnilica** had traveled by train with Cardinal Karol Wojtya to Rome for the conclave that elected him – and was sought out afterwards by Italian television to find out something that could be reported about the new Polish Pope.

The Parish Bulletin begins by quoting the editors of the German magazine, *PUR*, who first published Marie Czernin's interview with Bishop Hnilica: "This article follows two other articles about Medjugorje published in October, in the magazine of the Italian Bishops Conference, *Avvenire*, which speak in a positive way about Medjugorje. One of them reports that the Italian UN forces based in Sarajevo went on pilgrimage to Medjugorje in order to thank the Queen of Peace for her protection during their peace mission in Bosnia. The other article, published on October 10, 2004, by Allessandro

Fo, professor of Latin Literature at the University of Sienna, speaks about his conversion as a fruit of his pilgrimage to Medjugorje. The fact that the magazine of the Italian Bishops Conference gives much space to the events of Medjugorje is interesting to us." (Editors of *PUR*).

Bishop Hnilica began the following interview (republished in the Medjugorje Parish Press Bulletin) by sharing the encouragement given him on March 25, 1984, by the Holy Father to go to Medjugorje, making reference to its connection with Fatima (see page viii) .... " 'Our Lady is appearing in a Communist country primarily because of problems that originate in Russia,' the Pope said, who had already taken this as a mission of his pontificate. This is why I immediately understood the connection. After the conversation with the Pope, I visited Medjugorje incognito three or four times. But, the former Bishop of Mostar-Duvno, Pavao Zanic, wrote a letter to me asking me not to visit Medjugorje anymore; if I refuse, he will write to the Pope himself, he said. It seems that somebody informed him about my visit. However, there was no reason for me to be afraid of the Holy Father.

> *"Our Lady is appearing in a Communist country."*
> Pope John Paul II

"The next time we spoke about Medjugorje was on August 1, 1988. A group of doctors from Milan, who were testing the children, came to visit the Pope in Castel Gandolfo. One of the doctors mentioned that the Bishop of Mostar was giving them hard times. The Pope said: 'As he is the Bishop of that place, you have to respect him. Then he continued in a cordial tone: 'But he will have to answer before God if he has not acted in a right way.' After this, the Pope was pondering a few moments, and then he said: 'Today's world has lost the sense of supernatural, in

> *"As he is the Bishop of that place, you have to respect him...But he will have to answer before God if he has not acted in a right way."*
> Pope John Paul II

other words, the sense of God. But many people rediscover this feeling in Medjugorje through prayer, fasting and the sacraments.' For me personally, this is the strongest explicit witness about Medjugorje. What has especially and profoundly impressed me is the fact that the doctors, who were present, declared, 'Non constat de supernaturalitate.' The Pope, for his part, recognized a long time before that supernatural events are really at work in Medjugorje![21] Through many sources, the Pope came to the conviction that God can be experienced in this place.

"In response to those who might say things like Medjugorje can be invented, some years ago, there was a youth meeting in Marienfried, and I was invited. During the encounter, a journalist asked me: 'Bishop, don't you believe that

> "The Pope, for his part, recognized a long time before that supernatural events are really at work in Medjugorje!"
> Bishop Paolo Hnilica

all that is happening in Medjugorje comes from the devil (Satan)?' I answered: 'I am a Jesuit. Saint Ignatius taught us how to discern spirits, but he also taught us that each event can have three different sources: human, divine or diabolic.' At the end, he agreed with me that what is happening in Medjugorje cannot be explained from a human point of view – the fact that every year normal young people, thousands of them – are attracted, they stream in order to reconcile with God. Medjugorje has already been named 'confessional of the world,' because, as a phenomenon, neither Lourdes nor Fatima managed to spur that many crowds of people to go for confession.[22] What is happening during confession? The priest is delivering the sinner from the devil. Then I replied to the journalist: 'Of course, Satan is capable of many things, but he

> "Medjugorje has already been named 'confessional of the world.'"
> Bishop Paolo Hnilica

is not capable of one thing: Is it possible that Satan spurs people to go for confession in order to be delivered precisely from him?' The journalist laughed, understanding what I wanted to say. Therefore, the only cause remains in God. Later on, I told the Holy Father about this conversation.

"In Lourdes, Fatima and Medjugorje – all three places – Our Lady is inviting us to repentance, forgiveness and prayer. In this aspect of the message, these three apparitions are similar. However, the difference in Medjugorje is that the apparitions are lasting for 23 years now. The intensity of the continuation of the supernatural is neither declining nor diminishing during all these years, and the result is an even greater number of intellectuals that are converted here.

"In 1991 (10 years after the first message: 'Peace, peace and only peace'), when the war broke out in Croatia, I met the Pope once again, and he asked me: 'How can the apparitions of Medjugorje be explained in the midst of the war in Bosnia?' Really, the war was terrible, so I answered: 'It seems that we are in the same situation as in Fatima. If Russia had immedi-ately been consecrated

> "*Maybe if the bishops of former Yugoslavia had accepted these messages more seriously...*"
> Bishop Paolo Hnilica

to the Immaculate Heart of Mary, the Second World War and the spread of Communism and atheism would have been avoided. Holy Father, as soon as, in 1984, you consecrated Russia to the Immaculate Heart of Mary, countless changes took place in Russia, and the fall of Communism began.

"In Medjugorje, Gospa started with the warning that there would be a war if we were not converted. Nobody took these messages seriously. Maybe if the bishops of former Yugoslavia had accepted these messages more seriously it would not have gone that far – but in any case, this would not have been a guarantee of the definitive recognition of the official Church, because the apparitions are still going on today. Then the Pope told me: 'Then, Bishop Hnilica is convinced that my action of consecration to the Immaculate Heart of Mary was valid?' I answered: 'Certainly it was valid; the only question is how many bishops really did the same consecration in union with the Holy Father.'

"Such would have expressed the collegiality of the Church; in other words, the unity of the bishops with the Pope gives to it a far deeper meaning. When Karol Wojtyla was elected Pope in 1978, I congratulated him, but I immediately told him that something would be missing from his pontificate if he did not consecrate Russia, together with all the bishops. He told me then: 'If you manage to convince the bishops about this, I will do it tomorrow.' This is why, after the consecration (on March 25, 1984), he asked me, 'How many bishops do you think concelebrated with me?' As I could not answer this question, the Pope said: 'Every bishop must prepare his diocese, every priest his community, every father his family, because Gospa said that lay people also must consecrate themselves to her Heart.'"

As previously noted, Bishop Hnilica first went to Medjugorje at the encouragement of Pope John Paul II. He would later give his own testimony: "Thousands of priests and hundreds of bishops have celebrated Holy Mass, and dedicate a lot of time listening to the confessions of penitents who've been transformed by Mary's motherly grace. Many of these have returned to their dioceses with the conviction that 'at Medjugorje people convert,' and these conversions are being noticed by the pastors because they are longlasting conversions. So many are the people who have experienced the presence of Mary at Medjugorje that they cannot be counted, just as the stories of spiritual and even physical healings can no longer be counted. Countless, as well, are the vocations to the priesthood and consecrated life born of the grace of Medjugorje. These are just some of the main spiritual fruits which have brought many to the conclusion that the Queen of Peace is truly present in Medjugorje.

"It is our conversion that decides the fate of mankind of the future. It is not the programs, or meetings, or words that will change the world. The Queen of Peace has shown us the highway that leads one to conversion of heart. This way leads to the Cenacle, or Upper Room, and it is here that by means of prayer in communion with Mary, Bride of the Holy Spirit, we are able to acknowledge our sins, do penance and convert. We must not be surprised if Satan tries many ways to destroy the supernatural fruits which have matured within the spiritual movement of Medjugorje. As our defense we must sincerely love, serve and imitate our Queen and Mother of Peace by living her messages.

"Let us unite our hearts to the Immaculate Heart of Mary. Many of us have clearly understood that these are her times; the times announced at Fatima and confirmed by the message of Medjugorje! These are the times of the universal 'Totus tuus.' The Queen of Peace wants us united in prayer as we trustfully await the New Pentecost which will renew the face of the earth. Together with her, let us journey towards the Lord!" (*Echo of Mary Queen of Peace*, 190, p. 4).

Chapter 9 End Notes

1. *(text on p. 47)* *Medjugorje in the Church*, Marija Dugandzic, Information Center Mir, 2002, pp. 36, 37.

2. *(text on p. 50)* Hans Urs von Balthasar, the late Swiss theologian, is widely regarded as one of the leading Catholic theologians of the 20th century. His work *The Glory of the Lord* is viewed by many as the "Summa Christiana" of modern times. He was the director of Pope Benedict XVI's doctoral thesis, his mentor and guide. Moreover, Cardinal von Balthasar was widely regarded as Pope John Paul II's favorite theologian. Fr. Henri de Lubac, S.J., wrote "he is the greatest Christian thinker of our era" *(30 Days*, July, 1988). He was awarded the Paul VI Prize for theology, conferred in Rome by the Holy Father, for his many achievements over a long lifetime. After writing the following December 12, 1984, public letter to Bishop Zanic, at the time ordinary of Mostar, the diocese in which Medjugorje resides, he was named Cardinal by Pope John Paul II (although he died on the eve of the consistory): *"My Lord, what a sorry document you have sent throughout the world! I have been deeply pained to see the episcopal office degraded in this manner. Instead of biding your time, as you were recommended to do by higher authority, you fulminate and hurl thunderbolts like Jupiter. While you denigrate renowned people who are innocent, deserving of your respect and protection, you bring out accusations that have been refuted a hundred times over."* To Laurentin, von Balthasar expressed his horror at the slanders thrown at the pastor of Medjugorje: *"Fr. Tomislav,"* he wrote, *"seems to me a model of humility, of deep wisdom, of discretion, a man whose obedience is nothing less than heroic. He is a true Christian man of God"* (Craig, *Spark From Heaven*, pp. 149, 150).

3. *(text on p. 53)* Press Bulletin 85, February 25, 1998.

4. *(text on p. 53)* *Glas Mira — Medjugorje,* March, 2002.

5. *(text on p. 53)* Bishop Croteau has spread this testimony throughout his diocese and shares it with Medjugorje groups. Many in his diocese who are coming with him to Medjugorje are Native Americans... Note the following testimony regarding Native Americans from another part of Canada: "The over-all Chief of the Mic-Maq Nation, Ben Syllboy, came to Medjugorje in March, 2001, for the second time. The tribe of 40,000, scattered in the US and in the northeast of Canada, had received the sacrament of Baptism in 1610. Today, the Christian faith and religious practice are decreasing, and many are searching for their identity in old pagan traditions. The pilgrims of Medjugorje represent a real spiritual renewal, because they have started prayer groups and are giving a new breath to the religious practices of their people.

"Today the tribe of Mic-Maq face the same difficulties as other nations: drug addiction and the loss for the sense of life, seen mostly among young people.

Their overall Chief, Ben Syllboy (chosen for life) and whose role is mostly spiritual, visits all the reservations, one after the other. He accompanies the priest on his pastoral journeys and invokes the Queen of Peace for the well - being of his tribe. He is deeply attached to Medjugorje because of the many signs he has received from God while here and also after returning from his pilgrimage to Canada. He is convinced that God is near, that God sees and knows each one of those He has created, and that He watches lovingly over everyone" (Press Bulletin 161, April 26, 2001).

6. *(text on p. 58)* Towards the end of the Balkan War the late Cardinal John O'Connor, Archbishop of New York, accompanied a planeload of goods for refugees sent by his archdiocese to Mostar. In response to his request to go to Medjugorje, the Bishop of Mostar told him it wouldn't be possible because the village wasn't safe. The cardinal returned to New York without realizing his desire. But in fact it was Mostar that wasn't safe. Pilgrims continued going to Medjugorje throughout the war. It is worth noting that only one bishop of the region stood by the authenticity of Our Lady's apparitions in Medjugorje, the late Archbishop Frane Franic of Split, and his was the only diocese untouched by the war. The Serb Navy sailed to the Port of Split with the intention of destroying the city - but at the last minute turned around without firing a shot. The Serb Army came down to the border of his diocese from the North, to the border of his diocese from the East and up to the border of his diocese from the South - but left his diocese completely untouched. And all during the Balkan conflict a slim corridor remained open between Split and Medjugorje. Pilrimages never ceased! (See footnote #9, p. 14.)

7. *(text on p. 66)* Also see p. 137 in Chapter 10.

8. *(text on p. 67)* All bishops have been encouraged by the Church to come to Medjugorje...see top of p. 5.

9. *(text on p. 76)* See p. 127 in Chapter 10.

10. *(text on p. 78)* See also p. 21.

11. *(text on p. 81)* "Medjugorje is the Fatima of our day. The hours of the apparitions follow a progression. At Lourdes, they took place in the morning. At Fatima, at noon. At Medjugorje, in the evening. Is it the end of a long day?" Fr. Rene Laurentin (*Queen of Peace*, Pittsburgh Center for Peace, Winter, 1993, p.11).

12. *(text on p. 83)* Providence has established a Medjugorje Shrine in Africa. See Chapter 10, page 132.

13. *(text on p. 84)* The Blessed Mother said in her messages: **"Medjugorje is a sign to all of you and a call to pray and live the days of grace that God is giving you. Therefore, dear children, accept the call to prayer with seriousness. I am**

with you and your suffering is also mine. Thank you for having responded to my call" (Parish office, April 25, 1992).

14. *(text on p. 94)* What Our Lady said in Medjugorje about other religions fits perfectly with what Pope John Paul II taught about interreligious dialogue during his April/May, 2000, Wednesday General Audiences. To Vicka the Gospa had said that respect must be given to all religions. Fr. Rene Laurentin clarifies: "When the visionary commented that Our Lady had said: 'All religions are the same before God,' she meant (and later explained) that all races are the same before God. In fact, for the cultural conception of those lands, 'religion' is identified with 'race.' For them, Catholic means Croatian, Orthodox means Serb, and Muslim means Bosnian."

15. *(text on p. 94)* On August 5, 2006, three bishops along with 21 priests from the region consecrated Malawi's own Medjugorje Shrine to Our Lady, the Queen of Peace. See Chapter 10, p. 132.

16. *(text on p. 97)* March 3, 1989 letter to the author.

17. *(text on p. 97)* Note Blessed Mother Teresa's testimony, p. 16 & p. 28.

18. *(text on p. 102)* For the bishop's complete testimony: <http://www.medjugorje.hr>; and in English also at <http://www.medjugorje.ws/en/articles/testimonies/testimony-domenico-pecile/>

19. *(text on p. 103)* This attitude is to be contrasted with the attitude of the Bishop of Mostar. (See endnote #1 p. 183.)

20. *(text on p. 104)* *Is Medjugorje a Spiritual Movement in the Church?* Fr. D. Grothues, 1998.

21. *(text on p. 109)* One commentator observes: What cannot be disputed, as it is on record, is how close the parallels are between the messages of Medjugorje and the teachings of Pope John Paul on such subjects as peace, forgiveness and reconciliation, prayer, repentance and confession, the rosary, the call to inactive Christians to return to God, fasting, adoration of the Blessed Sacrament, and the importance of the family. The list is endless. The following message from Our Lady in the early days of the apparitions throws a light on this aspect of Pope John Paul's pontificate:

"In my messages I recommend to everyone, and to the Holy Father in particular, to spread the message which I have received from my Son here at Medjugorje. I wish to entrust to the Pope the word with which I came here: Mir (peace), which he must spread everywhere. And here is a message which is especially for him: that he bring together the Christian people through his

words and his preaching; that he spread particularly among the young people the messages which he has received from the Father in his prayers, when God inspires him" (Parish office, September 16, 1983).

Who can seriously doubt that the Pope read those words and that they guided his life and his great work of peace, reconciliation and all his missionary journeys, the Interreligous Prayer Meetings for Peace he began in Assisi and his outreach to the young through World Youth Days!

22. *(text on p. 109)* This, in spite of the fact that until October, 2000, Bishop Peric, the Bishop of Mostar, granted faculties to only three priests in Medjugorje so that they could administer the Sacrament of Reconciliation. In October, 2000, he was forced by the Vatican to grant faculties to all the Franciscans of the parish. He continues, however, forbidding his diocesan priests from going to Medjugorje in order to help administer the Sacrament of Reconciliation to pilgrims.

10. Examples of Good Fruit, Including New Religious Orders and Bishops and Cardinals Consecrating Medjugorje Shrines Throughout the World...

Several points remain clear for priests and the faithful:
– Everyone can come to Medjugorje on private pilgrimages.
– Everyone can read or publish the messages because no caution has been given by Rome.
– Rome has not yet officially recognized the apparitions, as it has recognized, for instance, Lourdes. The question remains open.
– Medjugorje has been accepted as a place of prayer and as a Marian shrine by the bishops of former Yugoslavia: "All bishops should visit Medjugorje and personally witness what is happening there," so their decisions would be based "on our own experence."
– The local bishop's view regarding the authenticity of the apparitions is the same as anyone else's – it "is and remains his personal opinion."
– On July 15, 2006, it was announced there will be a new international commission, with the list of members supplied by the Vatican.

In conclusion: **"One must follow the authority of the Church, of course. However, before she expresses an opinion it is necessary to advance spiritually because she will not be able to pronounce herself in a vacuum, but in a confirmation which presupposes growth of the child. The Church will come to confirm what is born of God"** (answer given by Our Lady to a question asked by the visionaries in 1986 regarding the Church's recognition of the apparitions).

Six children, from unsophisticated backgrounds – are they capable of keeping up such a pretense for a quarter of a century? Could the so called fabrication of a small team of priests give rise to millions of conversions across the entire world, to the transformation of millions of lives by Christ? Could it lead to the renewing of whole dioceses, the creation of thousands of small prayer groups, the reconciliation of thousands of families, the blossoming of an incalculable number of priestly or religious vocations and the recognition of new religious orders and the consecration of Medjugorje shrines by bishops and cardinals throughout the world? *Does one not know a tree by its fruit?*

THE FRATERNITY OF THE DISCIPLES OF JESUS
TO THE GLORY OF GOD THE FATHER

www.mosteiroreginapacis.org.br

During a May, 1988, apparition in Medjugorje Our Lady gave Vicka a message for a visiting priest from Brazil: he was to leave his parish and begin a new congregation in the Church that would take care of children living on the streets of Sao Paolo. (Our Lady's initiative was in response to petitions she had been receiving from the faithful.) Fr. Eugenio Pirovano didn't believe in the authenticity of the apparitions, he had only gone to Medjugorje at the insistance of his confessor.

Back in Brazil he was surprised to receive encouragement from his bishop, who would later officially recognize the new congregation. Cardinal Minguzzi would arrange for Fr. Eugenio to have a private meeting with Pope John Paul II, who encouraged him to continue responding to this call. On February 22, 1999, The Fraternity of the Disciples of Jesus to the Glory of God the Father was given official recognition as a Public Association of the Faithful. On March 19, 2005, their monastery, Regina Pacis, was officially recognized as "Priorato sui juris."

In a message to Vicka in January, 2004, Our Lady said Fr. Eugenio's new congregation was called "to live the messages and bear fruits of perseverance and humility. You are like a town built on top of a mountain that cannot remain hidden."

The congregation's brochure states: *"We are a community of priests and laymen consecrated as disciples of Jesus, through the mediation of the Queen of Peace, for the Glory of God the Father. Guided by 'Gospa's' messages, we strive to live a monastic life helping homeless children. Father Eugenio Maria, after a deep experience of God in Medjugorje, founded the Fraternity in response to Our Lady's call: 'Dear Children, I invite you today to surrender yourselves totally to God,' (July 25, 1988)."* A picture of Our Lady of Medjugorje in the center of a cross worn around the neck is part of their religious habit.

OASI DELLA PACE (Oasis of Peace)
http://www.oasispacis.org

Fr. Gianni Sgreva was encouraged by Our Lady, through an apparition to the visionary Marija in Medjugorje, to begin a new community in the Church. Concerned that it would be based on an apparition not yet approved by the Church, he quotes Cardinal Ratzinger's encouraging words to him on September 9, 1986: *"Why are you worried about it? Medjugorje – I'll take care of it... go ahead."* The following day, September 10, he unexpectedly obtained an audience with the Holy Father. He quotes John Paul II's words to him: *"But, Father, what are you concerned about? This problem with Medjugorje, my services are concerned with it. The Madonna will open all the ways. Pray also for me."* With emotion he spoke to Father Sgreva, embraced him and then gave him his rosary. (Fr. Giannii shared the preceding testimony at the 1991 National Conference at the University of Notre Dame. It is also documented in *Seven Years of Apparitions*, Fr. Rene Laurentin, the Riehle Foundation, pp. 60, 61).

The first ecclesial recognition for Oasi della Pace was given on December 25, 1990, in the Diocese of Sabina-Poggio Mirteto and on December 25, 1995, juridically, it became a "public association of the faithful." There are presently several hundred internal members including brothers, sisters and priests. There are also married couples living their charism within family life.

As of 2003 members have joined from Italy, Germany, Belgium, France, Austria, Slovenia, Switzerland, Spain, Ireland, U.S.A., Canada, Panama, New Zealand, Mauritius, South Korea, Brazil, Croatia, Bosnia-Hercegovina, Cameroons, the Czechoslovakian Republic, Romania, Poland and Lebanon. The religious garb worn by the members of Oasi della Pace was designed by one of the visionaries based on Our Lady's appearance when she comes during her apparitions in Medjugorje.

NUOVI ORIZZONTI (New Horizons)
http://www.nuoviorizzonti-onlus.com

Founded in Italy, the community Nuovi Orizzonti (New Horizons) is comprised of "survivors," young men and women who have been living on the streets. The foundress, Chiara Amirante, decided to go to Medjugorje and, while there, in prayer, she understood that nothing would happen if she did not take the first step, the step of "folly" found in the Gospel: "Go, sell all you have, give it to the poor, then you will have a treasure in Heaven! Then come, follow me!" (Mt. 19:21). With her Bishop's approval, she left her job and decided, on a feast of Mary, to leave her home and live with the people suffering on the street.

She had gone to Medjugorje during the war, and it was actually there (on January 1, 1993) that Our Lady had placed in Chiara's heart Her own love for Her children "who have not yet known the love of God," and were therefore dying in their souls. Having founded many Nuovi Orizzonti houses in Italy, Chiara continued to answer the urgent call from Our Lady and with her bishop's blessing, in 2004, she gathered twelve elders in the community and opened a center in Medjugorje. On June 6, 2004, the bishop in charge of Nuovi Orizzonti came from Rome to Medjugorje to bless their house and receive the promises from a number of youth coming into the community (poverty, chastity, obedience and JOY!) There are now more than 300 consecrated members. In 2004, they reached out to 650,000 youth through evangelization in the streets.

On March 10, 1997, Cardinal Camillo Ruini, Papal Vicar for the Diocese of Rome, granted New Horizons official recognition as a private association of the faithful. Cardinal Ersilio Tonini testifies: "This new community has taken on the street as its mission field, i.e., young people who populate it during the day and the night living by drugs, prostitution, alcohol, imprisonment, violence. ...What may be impossible for man is possible for God. New Horizons is a work of God!" In July, 2004, Chiara was appointed by Pope John Paul II as a Consultant for the Pontifical Council for the Pastoral Care for Migrants and Itinerant People.

YOUTH 2000

http://youth2000ny.com/info.htm

The following is taken from the Archdiocese of New York Youth 2000 web sit: "It is hard to describe what happens at a Youth 2000 Prayer Festival to someone who has never experienced it; words alone just don't seem to express the reality. When you are able to express something that happens people don't always believe you! But we will give it a try. First of all we call this a Prayer Festival instead of a retreat because there is an atmosphere of joy and celebration, and of enthusiasm that is unique...

"How it all began... The first Youth 2000 Prayer Festival took place in 1990 in Medjugorje and included 7000 young people from 24 countries and it was a resounding success. In 1992, Youth 2000 came to the US through the efforts of some of the participants of the original Prayer Festival. The first retreat was held in Dallas, Texas, in June, 1992, with 700 young people. The Franciscan Friars of the Renewal were among the preachers at the event...

"In May of 1993, Youth 2000 came to New York. The first event in New York was held at Our Lady of the Angels Parish in the Bronx. Since that time, Youth 2000 NY has held monthly prayer festivals and has touched the lives of thousands of young people in the Metropolitan area. Youth 2000 Prayer Festivals occur almost every week somewhere in the US. At present, Youth 2000 is active in the US, in England, Ireland, Germany, Australia, Panama, the West Indies, and hopes to expand into other countries in Europe and in Africa. Youth 2000 Prayer Festivals in the US, in New York in particular, have been led by The Franciscan Friars of the Renewal....

"Youth 2000 was invited by the World Youth day committee to lead Eucharistic Adoration at the World Youth Days in Manila in 1995, Paris in 1997, Rome in 2000, and again in Toronto in 2002. Youth 2000 is for youth and young adults between the ages of 15-30... Every major language, group, and nationality is represented..."

CRAIG LODGE: FAMILY HOUSE OF PRAYER
http://www.craiglodge.org/history.htm)

The following is taken from the Craig Lodge web site "In 1983 a family from the highlands of Scotland visited Medjugorje in Bosnia. They went because they had heard that Mary, the Virgin Mother of God, was appearing to a group of children. Their visit affected their lives in many ways. On their return they decided to turn their guest house into a house of prayer – a retreat center. Craig Lodge Family House of Prayer began to take shape. Very soon a group of young people inspired by the messages of Our Lady Queen of Peace formed a community at Craig Lodge. Over the next 10 years many young people came and devoted a year to living out Our Lady's call to holiness through prayer, fasting and service. Today, Craig Lodge Community is made up of families as well as single people. The same desire unites us; to journey along the road to holiness together by listening to Our Lady and doing our best to put her messages into practice.

"In 1992 when war had engulfed Bosnia, many refugees ended up in the area around Medjugorje. Their suffering could not be ignored. Craig Lodge Community responded by collecting and delivering aid to Medjugorje. This was intended to be a one-off delivery but the scale of the suffering and the level of response to our appeal at home gave rise to further deliveries. Before long an overseas aid charity, Scottish International Relief (SIR), was set up. The work of SIR and Craig Lodge Community are inextricably linked as they share the same root – Medjugorje. The community is continually blessed by the privilege of being able to reach out to the poorest of the poor around the world through helping in the work of SIR. In response to Our Lady's message, 'I invite you to be apostles of love and goodness,' Scottish International Relief (SIR), one of the fruits of the community, reaches out to some of the world's poorest people. Mary's Meals campaign, a work placed under the patronage of Our Lady, feeds more than 100,000 children every day throughout the world.[1]

---

[1] "The Junior Chamber International organizes The Outstanding Young Persons of the World program to award 10 individuals between the ages of 18 and 40 who exemplify the best attributes of the world's young people. Past honorees have included John F. Kennedy, Orson Welles and Henry Kissinger.

"Craig Lodge Community has recently established an outreach community in Medjugorje itself where they will work in a cafe/information point to share the good news about Mary's Meals. There is a sense of homecoming about this move as we return to the place where it all began. Praise God!"

(1 Cont) "There are 10 categories and this year Magnus MacFarlane-Barrow, Director of Scottish International Relief, won the award for Contribution to Children/World Peace, and/or Human Rights. His Acceptance Speech:

"Despite my personal embarrassment, I'm honored and grateful to accept this award on behalf of all of those around the world involved in our work – particularly those participating in our Mary's Meals campaign.

"This award is as much for Esther, a woman I met in Malawi recently, as it is for me. Esther rises at first light every morning to prepare and cook Mary's Meals for the children at her village school. Her own children attend the school. There are over 3,000 people like Esther in Malawi, giving their time freely to help the poorest children in their communities.

"Mary's Meals is not about rich people in affluent countries giving in a patronizing way to people waiting with begging bowls in poor countries; rather, it is a movement of people – rich and poor – walking in solidarity, working together to improve the lot of the world's poorest children, people united by their belief that their efforts can change things. Mary's Meals consists of lots of little acts of love, little sacrifices made by people all over the world. Already thousands of children are attending school for the first time because of Mary's Meals, and the education they are gaining can transform them and their communities.

"I believe passionately that every child has a right to one good meal every day in school...We can feed a child for an entire school year in Malawi for 10 euros. And yet today, 16,000 children died of hunger-related causes. There is no excuse!

"Mary's Meals is named after Mary the Mother of Jesus. She knew the struggle of bringing up a child in poverty. Under her patronage I believe that Mary's Meals can grow to reach every hungry child and that some of the chains binding the poorest communities will be broken. I believe in a good and loving God. I believe everything we have has been given by Him. We have a duty to share with those who have nothing – we have no right to continue to eat our obscenely large slice of the world's cake while children starve. We cannot keep what is not ours to keep.

"I thank God for this opportunity He has given me to serve Him in His poorest little ones. It is a work that fills me with joy.

"Thank you, Lord, for my small part in your team."

During an interview in Medjugorje in October, 2004 Magnus said: *"Our faith, the Gospel and Medjugorje are at the center of our life, of our family life. It is the most important thing in our life. The starting point for everything that we do is to pray and to try living Our Lady's messages. It is not about going out and doing things, but doing what Our Lady asks every day. Then, perhaps, God will call us to do other things."*

RACHEL'S VINEYARD
Founded by Theresa Karminski Burke, MA, PhD, DAPA, NCP, LPC
http://www.rachelsvineyard.org/aboutus/endorse.htm

In 1983, Stan Karminski traveled to Medjugorje with his family to observe firsthand the apparitions of the Blessed Virgin to the 6 children. They brought back to America some of the first film ever taken, and the family (with Theresa's sister, Katie, editing and Theresa writing the narrative) put together, A Message of Peace, the first video on Medjugorje circulated throughout America. Theresa testifies that before she went to Medjugorje she was working as a ski instructor in Switzerland, living "as a pleasure seeking youth very selfish and concerned about my fun and entertainment." As a result of seeds planted in Theresa's heart by Our Lady, her life changed dramatically. Theresa's prayer life deepened and led her into a ministry to post-abortion victims that has grown exponentially over the past 20 years. Theresa witnessed at the 2006 National Conference on Medjugorje at the University of Notre Dame, testifying that her ministry can be seen as a direct fruit of Medjugorje.

In 1986 Theresa began one of the first therapeutic support groups for post-aborted women after founding The Center for Post Abortion Healing. In 1994 Theresa began Rachel's Vineyard. A Psychological and Spiritual Journey for Post Abortion Healing. Without a budget, office or advertising, Rachel's Vineyard became a grassroots national outreach. By word of mouth only, the retreats began to spread across the country because of the retreat's dramatic effectiveness, from 18 retreats in 1999 and growing to 35 retreats in 2000. Currently, Rachel's Vineyard has grown to 250 retreats annually, held in 47 states and 11 countries, with many new sites in development. The international outreach of Rachel's Vineyard is now growing in Australia, New Zealand, Canada, Africa, South America, Ireland, England, France, Portugal, Scotland, Spain, Taiwan and Russia, with new translations in progress for Korea, Japan and China. Retreatants are lead to Jesus in the Blessed Sacrament – the source for healing from the horrors of abortion.

Twice in 2006 Theresa addressed the US Bishops Conference.

THE HOLY SOULS APOSTOLATE
Susan Tassone

In 1983, Susan Tassone spent 4 months convalescing after being struck by a taxi while crossing a street in Chicago. Doctors said her left leg had been permanently damaged. For 10 years she was in constant pain. She wanted to go to Medjugorje "because the Blessed Mother has always been my best friend, and when your best friend is in town you go visit her! I expected to pray, to experience closeness with Our Lady, and to return home. But the Blessed Mother had other plans." Not only did she experience incredible grace through Our Lady's presence, "my permanently damaged leg was healed on the mountain!" (Upon her return to Chicago her doctor was shocked: "This is a miracle. You're blessed! If any doctor saw your leg now he'd never believe what happened to you!" On purpose he waited three years and then wrote a letter formally attesting to the miracle).

After returning home Susan discovered Our Lady had other surprises. She found herself absorbed with the plight of the souls in Purgatory. Having often called attention through her messages to their need for prayer, Our Lady placed a mission upon her heart: *to become their ambassador!* Susan testifies: "Medjugorje changed my life...a miraculous healing of my injured leg and the founding of the Holy Souls Mass Apostolate!" Since 1993 she has raised over $1,000,000 for Mass stipends (200,000 Masses said), and has written five books encouraging prayer for the souls in Purgatory - best sellers among those published by Our Sunday Visitor: *The Way of the Cross for the Holy Souls in Purgatory; Praying in the Presence of Our Lord for the Holy Souls; The Rosary for the Holy Souls in Purgatory; 30 Day Devotions for the Holy Souls;* and *Prayers for Eternal Life.*

Cardinal Francis George of Chicago arranged for Susan to present her books to Pope John Paul II. Both strongly endorsed her apostolate. The Cardinal invited her to deliver the opening address preceding his Mass marking the 1,000th Anniversary of All Souls Day, 1998.

WINTERSHALL ESTATE RELIGIOUS PLAYS
(SURREY) UK (Bramley, Nr Guildford, Surrey GU5 0LR)
wintershall-estate.com

The extensive grounds of Wintershall Estate provide the location for the Wintershall Plays which continue drawing more and more people each year.

Open-air dramas depict the life, death and resurrection of Christ on the 1,500 acre Wintershall estate in Surrey. The audience follows the cast of over two hundred actors around from scene to scene as the remarkable events surrounding the life of Jesus Christ are brought to life...

"The Life of Christ" is the initiative of the Hutley family, owners of Wintershall. They decided to perform a play after a spiritual conversion in Medjugorje, a shrine in the former Yugoslavia where the Virgin Mary continues to appear... After a pilgrimage to Medjugorje the Hutley family converted and became Roman Catholics.

As a 'thank you' to Christ for their conversion, the Hutleys began to perform the Nativity at Christmas more than 12 years ago in a barn on the estate, mainly for their close friends and family. Later, it became a Passion play, performed at Easter. Now there are plays and retreats throughout the year. For the past 6 years at least 3,000 people each day visited Wintershall to watch "The Life of Christ."

Mr. Hutley wrote this play after seeing a letter written by Pope John Paul II urging Christians to do something for the Millennium. Originally it was going to just be for two years....but it has continued every year. The plays attract people from every religious background (and no religious background).

The Wintershall grounds now also have an extensive Rosary Garden and Way of the Cross.

INTERCESSORS OF THE LAMB
bellwetheromaha.org

Nadine Brown converted to Catholicism at the age of 25 and at 30 became a cloistered nun. After 16 years she felt the Lord calling her out of the cloister to bring the charisms of contemplative prayer and intercession to the broader church. The preliminary discerment process took a full year, culminating with a 30-day retreat directed by a discernment board (which included a bishop). Seven months later her superiors gave their permission and blessing for her to begin.

In the early 1980's, during a pilgrimage to Medjugorje, the formation of this new community, the Intercessors of the Lamb, began to take shape in Mother Nadine's heart and mind. She testifies: "Our Lady's ongoing messages calling people to open their hearts to Jesus, prayer of the heart (contemplative prayer), the call to conversion and reconciliation are very much part of what our Formation – for all of God's people – is about."

The Intercessors of the Lamb are a mixed community of laity, consecrated brothers, sisters and priests who have been called to discipleship by the Holy Spirit and formed in the Heart of Mary to continue the redemptive mission of the Lamb of God through His powerful "burden-bearing" ministry of intercession.[1] Companion Prayer Groups have formed in over 46 states in the US and have spread throughout the globe. For example, there are 25 in Lithuania and 20 in the Philippines, and prayer groups are active in Singapore, Canada, Australia, Poland, Russia, France, England, Ireland, Scotland, Tinidad, the West Indies, Jamaica, Grand Cayman, Puerto Rico, Uganda and Ghana, to name a few. Mother Nadine's teaching series (see web site) are being used for formation by Mother Teresa's Missionaries of Charity all over the world and by numerous communities, congregations and religious orders.

---

1. Mons. Elden Francis Curtiss, Archbishop of Omaha, states:"The Intercessors of the Lamb are a Public Association of the Christian Faithful under my authority in the Archdiocese of Omaha. Mother Nadine, as well as the community of the Intercessors of the Lamb, have my approval and I continue to assume the responsibility of protecting and supporting their charism. I consider the community, and Mother Nadine, a gift to our Archdiocese and to the Church!"

SHRINE OF THE QUEEN OF PEACE IN THE PHILIPPINES

Regarding the testimony of **Bishop Emilio L. Bataclan** from the Philippines (p. 76) the Press Bulletin (131) went on to report:

"A reason behind this visit is the fact that the Philippines feel a special debt of gratitude towards the Queen of Peace because of her intervention in 1986, which they experienced during their peaceful revolution that precipitated the fall of the dictatorship in the Philippines.

"According to the testimony of two of priests [on pilgrimage with Bishop Bataclan], who were laymen at that particular time, they took part in the peaceful and silent demonstrations against the dictatorship in the streets of Manila, with nothing but roses and rosaries in their hands, when inexplicably, the soldiers from the helicopters began waving white scarves, just when the tanks and the helicopters were about to shoot on hundreds of thousands of demonstrating citizens. They landed their helicopters among the crowd, called on the soldiers to leave their tanks and witnessed that they could not shoot because they had seen Our Lady, and recognized her as the Queen of Peace.

"According to the Filipino priests [accompanying Bishop Bataclan], Medjugorje was not known in the Philippines at that time, but Cardinal Jaime Sin had declared the year 1985 as a Marian Year for the Philippines, and invoked the help of the Queen of Peace. (Editor's note: Medjugorje was well known to Cardinal Sin. Fr. Rene Laurentin states it was at Cardinal Sin's insistence that he write his first book on Medjugorje in 1984 [coauthored with Fr. Ljudevit Rupcic, OFM]. It was from this book that Pope John Paul II read sections to Bishop Hnilica. see p. viii), When, in 1986, the dictatorship of Marcos was overthrown without shedding a drop of blood, Pope John Paul II called Cardinal Sin and asked him what he had done to cause the peaceful downfall of the dictatorship. The answer was: 'I declared a Marian Year for the Philippines!' After this, the Pope declared the year 1988 as a Marian Year for the whole Church. In 1989, the USSR fell...

"After these events, Cardinal Sin opened a large Marian

Shrine on the street in which those decisive events took place, a shrine in which Our Lady is venerated under the name of the Queen of Peace. The statue made for this shrine resembles the statue of Our Lady of Medjugorje."

Cardinal Sin gave this same testimony at the 1992 Baltimore International Marian Conference (USA). In an interview with *Medjugorje Magazine* during the conference Cardinal Sin said that the people of the Philippines believed in Our Lady and believed in Medjugorje: "I have a Jesuit friend, Father Antonio Olaguer, who was an activist during the time of President Marcos. He was a problem because he lacked a faith dimension. He was somewhat leftist. Then someone invited him to go to Medjugorje, paying his fare, so he went. People there were telling him about the wonders they were seeing but he didn't believe them. Then one day he entered the church there, just to reflect and to meditate. He heard a voice and it was the voice of Our Lady. 'Father, you are my son, as Christ is my son. Follow His footsteps.' And now Father Olaguer is a different man. He is working for Our Lady all the time. He is now superior of the Jesuits in Manila. He said this is a great surprise because before he was a problem and now he is the superior!"

Cardinal Sin was the only cardinal of voting age who did not travel to Rome for the conclave that elected Pope Benedict XVI. His declining health did not allow him to make the trip. For more than 20 years Cardinal Sin believed in the urgency of spreading Our Lady's messages from Medjugorje – giving his support to Medjugorje apostolates. Just before he died he wrote to the author expressing his support for Mary TV's Medjugorje television project (see page 213): *"I want you to know that I gladly support your project. You are a true friend, so priceless and valuable in life. God is so good for sending friends like you. Let us together praise and give thanks to the Lord. I will offer my prayers and sacrifices for your intentions."* Cardinal Sin died on June 21, 2005, the day before the author received his letter in the mail. He is no doubt continuing his intercession from Heaven....

MEDJUGORJE SHRINE SERU DE ORASHON (HILL OF PRAYER) Curacao, Netherlands Antilles (Caribbean)

Piet Campman couldn't understand what had happened to his daughter. After returning from Medjugorje, Hilde, who used to run his business 7 days a week, was devoting all of her time to religion!

During a business trip to Frankfurt in 1997, he decided, without his family knowing, to take a side trip to Medjugorje to find out! After five days of prayer there he found himself transformed, and returned with a burning desire to bring all of his island to Medjugorje. This being impossible, he hit upon the solution: *bring Medjugorje to Curacao!*

He redirected his business enterprise from the object of making money to making a replica of the Medjugorje Shrine in the middle of Curacao. He first build a little Mt. Krizevac (Curacao is flat) upon which he placed a replica of the Cross,...and then constructed a beautiful Rosary garden and a Way of the Cross; an outdoor facility for Mass with seating for several thousand (and a large parking lot); a guest & retreat house and an adoration chapel; a conference center and a retreat center.

Bishop William Ellis designated the Medjugorje Shrine, Seru di Orashon, as the official gift of the Diocese of the Netherlands Antilles and Aruba to God the Father for the Great Jubilee. When consecrating the cross on August 15, 1999, the Bishop declared: "As our Lady of Medjugorje teaches, we must pray with the heart! I hope that this place, Seru di Orashon, will become like Medjugorje, a place of prayer, of penance, of conversion – lots of conversion! We need it in Curacao because many people are far away from God. Let us pray here continuously!" Twice each year the Bishop and local priests (from the islands of Aruba, Bonaire, Saba, St. Eustatius and St. Maarten) hold their meetings and retreats at the shrine. The Bishops Conference of the Netherlands Antilles (AEC) held its 2004 meeting at Curacao's Medjugorje Shrine, April 25 - 30. (AEC is the section of the Catholic Church in the English, French and Dutch territories of the Antilles made up of five archdioceses, fourteen dioceses and two "missiones sui iuris." The region included is composed of thirteen independent nations, three Departments of France, two parts of the Kingdom of the Netherlands having complete internal autonomy, six British colonies and one US dependency with observer status.)

Religious of the Antilles held their 2006 meeting at the shrine with Bishop Francis Alleyne (Ordinary of Georgetown, Guyana), Bishop Secco and the Apostolic Nuncio, Archbishop Thomas Gullickson. The Council of Bishops for Latin America & the Caribbean designated the Medjugorje Shrine to host its international youth conference in preparation for the 5th General Conference (called for by Pope John Paul II in 2001, and inaugurated personally by Pope Benedict XVI in Brazil on May 13, 2007). CELAM's Youth Conference took place at the shrine in July, 2006. Several workshops organized by CELAM were held there in June, 2005. Bishops from surrounding dioceses regularly hold meetings/retreats/conferences there.

Students from the University of Trinidad and Tobago and from Jamaica are often sent to the shrine in Curacao to learn more about the Papiamento language. (Hilda adds, "They also learn about Medjugorje!" *While her father was beginning construction of the shrine, Hilde began producing a local Medjugorje television program that continues airing every week in Curacao and Aruba. Two weeks after finally finishing the translation of the Bible into Papiemento, the Bible Society of Curacao translated the first seven television programs of the series "Medjugorje: Our Mother's Last Call" into Papiemento, for distribution to schools and parishes)!* Bishop Rivas wrote about being "overwhelmed by the awesomeness of the place" in an article he published, titled *Awesome Presence on the Hill*: "Piet is prepared to walk by faith while interpreting the signs along the way. 'I am sure,' he says 'that in the next millennium things will change not only here but in many other parts of the world. The next millennium will become God's time!' ...One thing is clear, Curacao has a center of Peace, a Hill of Prayer..." The Bishop's experience there "was the meeting of the human and the divine!" (Diocesan Newspaper of Kingstown, Vol. 8 No .3, December, 1999. See also p. 206).

Bishops process to Curacao's replica of the original Medjugorje cross on Mt. Krizevac.

Bishops Conferences regularly hold meetings at this Medjugorje Shrine in the Netherlands Antilles.

A REPLICA OF THE SHRINE OF MEDJUGORJE ON THE CONTINENT OF AFRICA, IN MALAWI!

Gay Russell of Malawi writes: "In September, 2000, I was given a ticket to make a pilgrimage to Rome and Medjugorje...I was agonizing with Jesus for three days preparing for the trip before the Blessed Sacrament, 'Why me, Lord? Why am I blessed to go again? What about all the Malawians who can never go?'...On the third day the phone rang, and a voice, obviously long distance, said to me 'Is that Gay Russell...You don't know me. My name is Tony Smith. I love Medjugorje and I want to talk to you about this idea I have...I was hoping to build a replica of Krizevac for all the people in England who could not go, but...last night I heard clearly in my heart: "Build it in Malawi for all the Malawians who can never go"...Now I am asking if you could find a mountain near Blantyre on the summit of which we could build the Krizevac Cross and then place the Stations of the Cross up the mountain just like in Medjugorje. I hope you don't think I am crazy, but it could become a Medjugorje for the Malawians.'"

The Forestry Department gave permission for a replica of the Cross on Krizevac to be built on Mount Michiru and the Archbishop gave permission for the shrine. The bronze plaques depicting the Stations of the Cross were done by Carmello Puzzolo in Italy, identical to the ones he did that are on Krizevac in Medjugorje. (His Rosary plaques, identical to the ones he did for Medjugojre, will soon be placed on an adjoining hill.)

On August 5, 2006, Archbishop Tarcisio Ziyaye of the Blantyre Archdiocese, assisted by Bishop Remi St. Marie of Dedza Diocese and Bishop Peter Musikuwa of Chikwawa Diocese, together with 21 priests from various parishes in the southern region, formally consecrated the new Church, "as an incredible gift from God for all those who cannot go to Medjugorje." More than 5,000 of the faithful attended the first Mass in St. James Church in Blantyre. "Now that the church is complete the keys can be handed over," proclaimed Fr. Kanjira, the Diocesan Administrator who was Master of Ceremonies for the celebration. Mr. Armenio Da Costa (the builder) presented them to Gay Russell (the Medjugorje pilgrim who had overseen the project to its completion), who presented them to Tony Smith (the benefactor), who in turn presented them to the Archbishop, who joyfully handed them over to Fr. Mwapuwa, the parish priest. "At this point great jubilation and ululating broke out in the church; the choir began singing the Gloria, and the church bells rang out loud and clear for the first time. It was wonderful to experience the overwhelming joy!"

The new St. James Church is identical to St. James Church in Medjugore in every way (see p. 135). St. James Church in Malawi lies at the foot of Mt. Michiru (about the same height as Mt. Krizevac in Medjugorje) with a cross on the summit identical to the one on Mt. Krizevac, and about the same distance from the church.

Gay states: "I believe that this has been given to Africa since it is now almost impossible for any group from here to get to Medjugorje. To aquire the proper visa African passport holders have to travel to Johannesburg or Cairo for a personal interview beforehand. It is believed one day this will become a very special place of pilgrimage for all peoples of Africa, *our tie with the grace of Medjugorje!"*

When in Medjugorje with several other bishops and pilgrims from Malawi in September, 2005, Bishop Thomas Msusa said: "I am so amazed... I have no words to describe what I feel. I ask myself why Medjugorje is so distant from Malawi. We also need such a place, but my people have no funds to come to Medjugorje. God is telling us 'you have to become apostles!' ...We understood that Our Lady wanted us to have such a place in our own country... I believe that we can transmit this experience to Malawi... Unofficially, we can say that the Church has already accepted Medjugorje!" (see pp. 93 - 96).

Note: Pope Benedict XVI warmly received the Bishops of Malawi during their *ad limina* visit in September, 2006, (the month after they consecrated their Medjugorje shrine) and later declared his November, 2006, Missionary Intention for the Church: "That through the efforts of believers, together with the living forces of society, the new and old chains which prevent the development of the African continent may be broken." The prayer of the Church is bearing fruit (see also pp. 121, 122).

Medjugorje's Krizevac in Malawi

Bronze plaques of the Way of the Cross in Malawi are identical to
the ones in Medjugorje.

St. James Church in Malawi

St. James Church in Panama

A REPLICA OF MEDJUGORJE'S ST. JAMES CHURCH IN PANAMA & A NEW RELIGIOUS ORDER: THE SISTERS OF MARY QUEEN OF PEACE

(As noted in the testimony given previously by Archbishop Jose Dimas Cedeo, President of the Bishops Conference, Panama)

"I am an Archbishop in Panama, Central America, and President of the Bishops Conference. This is my first time to Medjugorje, but there are already many fruits of Medjugorje in Panama. For example, we have a parish community led by Fr. Francesco Verar. He often comes to Medjugorje and their church is identical to St. James Church in Medjugorje! Francesco has also founded a community that is called: The Sisters of Mary Queen of Peace. Every evening they have the same prayer program as here in Medjugorje! They are very active.

"The community has been given recognition by the Church. I recognized the community on the diocesan level when I sensed their spirituality, saw what they are doing and how they are living, and that their main work is to pray for peace.

"The community has already been in existence for several years. They are having good experiences. I recognized the community precisely on June 25, 1998. And that is exactly also the anniversary of the apparitions. I am fully conscious that this is a fruit of Medjugorje!" Archbishop Jose Dimas Cedeo, President of the Bishops Conference, Panama (Press Bulletin 117, May 19, 1999).

Fr. Verar posts the following at <www.mariamagnificat. org>:

"We, Comunidad de Jesús Eucaristía (Jesus Eucharistic Community), are a Catholic community of engagement, formed by priests, single and married lay people and consecrated; we have members inside the community and others that are external. We consider Mary Queen of Peace as our Mother and Teacher in our spiritual life, in order to follow up inner deliverance by the Holy Spirit to testify the peace of Christ risen to the world.

"Our spirituality is centered in Christ the Healer through the Holy Spirit, in the permanent intercession of Mary Queen of Peace and fraternal life.

"Virtues to cultivate: humility, abandonment, love and joy.

"Mission: testify altogether with Mary of the peace of Christ risen.

"Our greeting: Praised be Jesus Christ!

"Annual Feast: Solemnity of Maria Queen of Peace, June 25 [the anniversary date of Our Lady's apparitions in Medjugorje].

"Where are we? Our main house is in Medjugorje." [1]

A picture graces their web site of their own St. James Church – *a replica of St. James church in Medjugorje!*

---

1. Other new religious communities, for example, Kraljica Mira, have been founded in Medjugorje. And numerous religious communities have received and are receiving spiritual impulses in Medjugorje for their life and their work, for example the therapeutic community Cenacolo of Sister Elvira, where former drug and alcohol addicts are being healed. The Cenacolo Community, active throughout the world, has two houses in Medjugorje. Many other religious communities, those already established for many years, as as well as younger ones, continue to express a desire to start a branch of their community in Medjugorje. This fact is worth noting because religious communities are particularly sensitive in matters concerning spirituality.

Fr. Daniel Ange, whose youth ministry, *Jeunesse Lumiere,* is active in more than 35 countries, and is considered by many – As he was by the late Pope John Paul II – the foremost youth minister in the Church, often states: "Medjugorje is the Bethlehem of the new millennium!" Testimonies abound. One example: A Eucharistic Procession that hadn't taken place for more than 40 years at the University of Notre Dame began again in 2005 - at the instigation of Children of Mary, a student organization founded to live and spread the messages of Our Lady in Medjugorje.

THE LITTLE MEDJUGORJE OF KAZAKHSTAN

Archbishop Tomasz Peta, on pilgrimage to Medjugorje from Kazakhstan, was so inspired by the cross on Krizevac he built a cross – an exact replica – in Ozernoj in the district of Kodszetauskaj. Cardinal Glemp came from Poland and consecrated the cross and the Shrine to the Queen of Peace, "the little Medjugorje of Kazakhstan," in the presence of Mons. Jan Pawel Lenga, M.I.C., Archbishop of Karaganda, Kazakhstan (Press Bulletin 102, October 21, 1998).

Fr. Daniel Ange gives the following testimony regarding the Medjugorje Shrine of the Queen of Peace in Kazakhstan. Kazakhstan is in a strategic position, since it links Eastern Europe (freed of Communist ideology) to China (still under Marxist oppression). Fr. Daniel Ange had the grace of preparing the youth for the visit of Pope John Paul II which, he said, would be "decisive for Asia, *the continent of the Church's third millennium.*"

"After the immense joy of participating at the youth festival in Medjugorje I received the gift of leaving for the 'little Medjugorje' in Kazakhstan to prepare young Catholics for the Pope's visit.

"This oasis sprouted up from nothing in the middle of the desert in 1936 during the first wave of massive deportations under Stalin. [Their suffering was terrible. For Daniel Ange's complete testimony, go to <http://www.medjugorje.org//echo/e160.pdf>] ...I had the grace of meeting some of the survivors who had been torn away from their hometown of Galicia (west Ukraine, then Poland). The faces of these old men and their wives were deeply marked not so much by the torrid summers (+40 degrees) and freezing winters (-50 degrees), but by the dramatic events of their youthful years. They were between 5 and 15 years old when they arrived here...

"In 1941 a miracle answered their desperate prayers. Reduced to famine and dying by the day, the entire village was pleading with the Queen of Heaven to intercede, when on March 25 the big freeze was suddenly over. Never before had there been such an early and sudden thaw. And there before them lay a large lake (7 km long and 70 m deep) which had formed under the snow; full of big fish. The catch was so easy and abundant that aeroplanes from Karaganda (650 km) came to find food for the big city. (And the fish were tropical - never seen before in that region - and in such abundance a cannery was built providing jobs for the local inhabitants.) Over the years the lake diminished in size as living conditions improved; now it is a little more than a large pond. I met members of the delegation that in the '80's dared to go to Moscow to ask permission to build a church. It was denied; but in 1990 – at long last – a fisher of men arrived: a priest from

Poland [John Paul II]. This was a bigger miracle than the fish! Thomas Peta, the capital's young bishop for the past two years, had the joy of receiving his beloved Holy Father...

"Local authorities eventually gave way to the pressing demands of the inhabitants, and a church with two spires was built and dedicated to the Queen of Peace: the first Marian shrine in Kazakhstan.

"Fr. Thomas [Archbishop Tomasz Peta, Archbishop of Maria Santissima in Astana, Kazakhstan] was very surprised when he went to Medjugorje and discovered that the title was one she had given herself, and that his little church was strangely similar to the Marian shrine in Hercegovina. When he went back home he had a copy of the great cross on Krizevac erected on a little volcanic hill and dedicated it to the martyrs of Kazakhstan. He also called Ojiorne the 'little Medjugorje of Kazakhstan'.

"Four years ago Fr. Thomas asked the Beatitudes Community to organize a national youth festival for the Feast of the Assumption. This year I was invited to prepare the youth for the Pope's visit; and I had the immense grace of attending the international festival in Medjugorje (12,000 youth from 25 countries) first, then this one here with 300 young people from Kazakhstan. The event had to be limited in size because of the heat and the complete lack of shade; hence it was essential that everyone could fit in the church. In any case, it is a huge number, considering the overall number of Catholics, and the distances which separate them.
" 'Do not fear my little flock!' Who knows how much this handful of young people from this tiny Catholic Church is in need of consolation, encouragement and, above all, of love! 'The kingdom is for you!' Yes, the kingdom was reflected in their transfigured faces at the end of the meeting, after the long hours spent contemplating the King in all His Eucharistic humility – in this village the Most Blessed Sacrament is exposed day and night all year long! This, plus confession, was what it took to make them shine anew with the divine beauty which comes from being God's children. An intense moment was the 14 km march to the great cross while praying, singing and confessing. The sight of their heads bobbing up and down over the top of the grain crop which was ready for harvest made me think: they are the crop of the martyrs! They would not have grown if the seeds (parents and grandparents) had not resisted beneath the thick icy layer in that endless winter of persecution. In fact, the majority of these young people were the grandchildren of deportees...Few let themselves be contaminated by the ideology which churned out slogans all day long. With us was Fr. Marcin Babraj, a Polish Dominican who had been deported in '39 when he was only six. "I thought freedom lay just the other side of that distant volcanic hill. I dreamt of going there to see, but it was severely forbidden to leave the village." When he returned many years later he saw the big cross of martyrs on the hill. 'It is a visible sign of that freedom, and it tells us that freedom is here amongst us now.' "

140

Our Lady Queen of Peace church in Kazakhstan

The little rotunda of Our Lady Queen of Peace Church
in Kazakhstan.

After Archbishop Peta erected a replica of Medjugorje's cross in Kazakhstan, Cardinal Glemp came from Poland and consecrated the Shrine to the Queen of Peace.

MEDJUGORJE SHRINES IN ARGENTINA
www.mensajerosdelareinadelapaz.org

Upon returning to Argentina from Medjugorje, a pilgrm[1] began holding prayer meetings in her house – which soon became too small to hold all the people coming to pray. Now a Medjugorje Shrine is being constructed in Achachay (Catamarca), Argentina, to accommodate the large numbers.... A meeting room, where Masses are presently being celebrated, has already been constructed. A picture of the June 25, 2005, procession of dedication, led by the bishop, can be found on their Queen of Peace web site. The faithful processed with the Pilgrim Image of the Queen of Peace to the site of the future shrine dedicated to Our Lady of Peace, in Achachay, Catamarca.

Note the caption to the top picture at right (p. 145) showing the bishop laying the corner stone to a new church in his diocese that will be built in the likeness of St. James Church in Medjugorje.

Bishop Juan Aberto Puigari of Mar del Plata, Argentina, has also authorized the construction of a Church in his diocese, identical to St. James Church in Medjugorje!

---

1.   Alica Veron, who began the prayer group after returning from a pilgrimage to Medjugorje, works for *Radio Maria*, Argentina. *Radio Maria*, active now all over the world, began in Medjugorje! In La Paz (Peace) in Entre Rios, the Church has built a Medjugorje Prayer Corner recreating the Blue Cross. In 2005 a picture of Our Lady of Medjugorje wept 58 times in the Church in Canals, Cordoba.

     After growing up a Protestant, Stephen Camilli converted to Catholicism (Medjugorje played a role in his conversion). After attending a talk given by one of the visionaries from Medjugorje he began fasting on Wednesdays and Fridays. One day in Argentina, while fasting, he asked God to show him what he should do with his life. On that day he saw someone on the street rummaging through a trash can looking for food. He had his answer! He began Fundacion Banco de Alimentos, which now has 11 food banks up and running in Argentina distributing 350,000 kilos (770,000 pounds) of food per month reaching 800 organizations that feed 110,000 people.

     After a pilgrimage to Medjugorje in 1987, the Smith / Scurlock family (California, USA) begain One Family, a humanitarian outreach to the poor living in Bosnia, Afganistan, Peru, Nicaragua and El Salvador, Pakistan (after the earthquake), Mississippi (after the hurricane), etc., etc. Trusting in Providence – with no advertising – One Amercia has delivered over 100 tons of relief supplies to the needy, see < www. onefamily.org >. *The list goes on....*

Bishop Elmer Miani, hands a box containing rocks from Podbrdo and Krizevac and dirt, water and leaves from Medjugorje to the Mayor, Dr. Ricardo Guzman, who assists the bishop placing them in the cornerstone of the new church, which will be a replica of St. James Church in Medjugorje.

Mass at St. James Church in Medjugorje celebrating the 25th Anniversary of Our Lady's apparitions.

Information "Mir" Medjugorje, <www.medjugorje.hr>)

145

CATHOLIC UNIVERSITY MARIA REINA DE LA PAZ
(OUR LADY QUEEN OF PEACE) <www.unicah.edu>

The Catholic University of Our Lady Queen of Peace was founded in Honduras in response to an appeal from Our Lady during an apparition to Marija Pavlovic Lunetti when she was visiting Honduras along with her spiritual director, Fr. Slavko Barbaric, in early March, 1992.

Later that same year, Archbishop Enricque Santos laid the cornerstone and commisioned Bishop Oscar Rodriguez to found the university. (Later named the first cardinal of Honduras, Cardinal Rodriguez, President of the Episcopal Conference until 2002, was often mentioned by the media as a likely succesor to Pope John Paul II). Today the university has 10 campuses.... A life-sized statue of Our Lady of Medjugorje is placed at the entrance of each campus.... Another identical statue is located in each of the 10 campus chapels.... (One of the statues, the one in Santa Rosa de Copan, is crying and the local bishop has declared it a miracle.) A picture of Our Lady's statue – popularly identified as Our Lady of Medjugorje – is highlighted on the university's web page <unicah.edu>. On the campus in the city of Danli the university constructed an exact replica of St. James Church, just as it is in Medjugorje (soon to be designated St. James Parish). At the university's retreat house in the Valley of Los Angeles there is a replica of the same cross that is on the top of Mt. Krizavec in Medjugorje...

The university belongs to the Church – the Bishops of the dioceses where the university has campuses make up its governing body "Claustro Universitario"...though the Gospa is acclaimed the over all "Rectora" of the University. Dr. Elio Alvarenga, President of the University, states: *"Most of those in positions of authority, teachers and students, traveled to Medjugorje and experienced the spirituality there. As they came back they wanted to live the spirituality that they had experienced. Now, through the life of the university, this is happening, and also being transmitted to the students who were not able to travel to Medjugorje. Living the messages of the Gospa at the university is natural for everybody!"*

St. James Church on the Danli campus of the Catholic Univeristy of Honduras, "Our Lady Queen of Peace"

St. James Church in Medjugorje.

A statue of Our Lady of Medjugorje stands at the entrance of each of the 10 campuses of the Catholic University of Honduras, "Our Lady Queen of Peace" .... (the same Medjugorje statue of Our Lady is in the chapel at each of the university's 10 campuses). The statue at the Santa Rosa campus (left) is weeping and the Bishop, who reports that many healings are taking place there, has declared it a miracle. A replica of the cross on Mt. Krizevac in Medjugorje has been constructed at the university's retreat house in the Valley of Los Angeles. "Living the messages of the Gospa at the university is natural for everybody!" (Dr. Elio David Alvarenga Amador, President of the University).

A replica of the Medjugorje cross at the Catholic University of Honduras, Maria Reina de la Paz (Our Lady Queen of Peace)

Curacao's replica of the original Medjugorje cross on Mt. Krizevac.

Appendix 1.

Transcripts of Pope John Paul II's Letters on Medjugorje

John Paul II:
I Send You Greetings and Bless You
The Pope's Private letters

The author was given permission by Marek Skwarnicki to include in this book letters he had received from the Holy Father making reference to Medjugorje. Mr. Skwarnicki's book containing the Pope's letters was published in Polish in October, 2005, by Swiat Ksiazki-Bertelsman Media Sp. z.o.o., Warszawa, Poland, 2000.

His comments on sections of the Holy Father's letters referring to Medjugorje are reproduced in italics at the end of each translation (along with the page number where they can be found in *John Paul II: I Send You Greetings and Bless You The Pope's Private letters*).

Mr. Skwarnicki was nominated a member of the Pontifical Council for the Laity by Pope Paul VI. The nomination was again conferred by Pope John Paul II.

8.12.

+ Drodzy Państwo!

Otrzymałem życzenia, opłatek i dwa listy, jeden od Andrzeja, drugi od Ciebie. Dziękuję za to wszystko, pragnę odwzajemnić się na Boże Narodzenie i Nowy Rok. Wśród wspomnień tego roku [illegible] opłatek [illegible].

Panu Profesorowi dziękuję za wszystko, co łączy się z [illegible]. Ja też codziennie podejmuję [illegible] w modlitwie: łączę się z modlitwą i wszystkimi, którzy tam się modlą - albo stamtąd czerpią wezwanie do modlitwy. [illegible] wezwanie zrozumiałbym lepiej. Cieszę się, że mamy [illegible] ludzi modlitwy i apostołów

Panu Marianowi dziękuję za obie [illegible] - ten z Włoch i ten dla Tygodnika. Polecam troskę o Tygodnik. Codziennie polecam Bogu to środowisko. Panu Marianowi życzę dalej siły i zdrowia

[signature]

NATIVITA
WAWEL (1475)
CATTEDRALE DI CRACOVIA

TIPOGRAFIA VATICANA

Christus natus est nobis!

Venite, adoremus!

Jan Paweł II papież

Z życzeniami i błogosławieństwem na Boże Narodzenie 1992.

December 8, 1992

+ Dear Marek and Sophia,

I have received your greetings, the wafer and two letters, one from you, Marek, and one from you, Sophia. Thank You for everything. I wish to return the greeting for Christmas and New Years. May the Christmas Eve wafer express this as well.

I thank Sophia for everything concerning Medjugorje. I, too, go there every day as a pilgrim in my prayers: I unite in my prayers with all those who pray there or receive a calling for prayer from there. Today we have understood this call better. I rejoice that our time does not lack people of prayer and apostles.

I thank Marek for both poems (songs) – The one from Huta and this one for Lagiewniki. I share your concern for "The Weekly" and every day I entrust this name to God. I wish Marek the gift of courage and health.

J Paul II

Christus natus est nobis!

Venite, adoremus!

John Paul II, Pope

Marek comments: *"All that the Pope writes here about Medjugorje is of great value. It does not concern the long-term controversies regarding the authenticity of apparitions. For the Catholic Church, only one revelation is certain – the Scriptures of the Old and New Testaments. After all, the Pope participates in the faith of God's people, as the Highest Priest of the Church, so he joins the poor people of Medjugorje through prayers, having become convinced about a special plan of God in that very place regarding a growing devotion to the Blessed Mother. Because the main concern in the Medjugorje messages was the Mother's warning about upcoming confusion and war, the Pope in 1992, while the Balkans were still at war, writes, "Today we have understood this call better. I rejoice that our time does not lack people of prayer and apostles"* (p. 107, lines 1-11).

+ Drogi Panie Marku!

Bóg zapłać za "Misterium!"
Aby wiedzieć, co w sobie kryje,
muszę naprzód przeczytać, ale
już z Pańskiego listu można coś
przeczuć. Rychło postaram się
przeczytać.

Na razie dziękuję za tekst
(jeszcze nie przeczytany) i za
dobre słowo od Autora. Niech
Matka Boska stale czuwa nad
Markiem i Zofią, oraz Ich Rodziną.

A teraz codziennie wracamy
modlitwą do Medjugorii.

Watykan 28 maja 1992 r.

154

+ Dear Marek,

May God reward you for the "Misterium [Mystery]." To know what it contains, I will have to read it but I can feel something in my bones from reading the letter only. I will make sure to have it read promptly.

Meanwhile, I thank you for the text (still unread) and for the kind words from its author. May Our Lady always protect Marek and Sophia, and their family.

And now we every day return to Medjugorje in prayer.

John Paul II

Vatican, May 28*th*, *1992*

(in handwriting)

"Christ is Risen, My Lord and my hope"
/an Easter passage/

With my (best) wishes and blessing

John Paul II, the Pope

Easter, 1992

   Marek comments: *"Reference to Medjugorje is a sign of how deeply the Holy Father felt over the Balkan fratricidal war and be-lieved more and more in the sanctity of the Medjugorje sanctuary"* (p. 102, lines 21-23).

Watykan, 25 lutego 1994 r.

+ Drodzy Państwo!

Bardzo dziękuję za oba listy. Pani Zofia pisze o Bałkanach. Teraz chyba lepiej rozumie się Medjugorie. To jakieś „naleganie" Matki rozumie się dziś lepiej, mając przed oczyma wielkość zagrożenia. Równocześnie odpowiedź szczególnej modlitwy – i to ludzi z całego świata – napawa nadzieją, że i tutaj dobro zwycięży. Pokój jest możliwy – taka była myśl wiodąca dnia modlitw 23-go stycznia, przygotowanego przez specjalną sesję w Watykanie, w której brał też udział T. Mazowiecki.

Może też dzięki temu Europa trzeźwieje. W Polsce też ludzie trzeźwieją, jak wynika z tego, co Państwo piszecie. Może będzie im łatwiej pogodzić się teraz z Papieżem, który nie głosił „zwycięstwa demokracji", ale przypominał Dekalog.

Dziękuję też za przypomnienie Kalwarii („polska Umbria"). Dziękuję, bo sam byłem z nią bardzo związany. To może jedyne takie sanktuarium na świecie. Co do „Tygodnika", to Bogu dzięki i za to, co Pan Marek pisze. Byłaby przecież straszliwa szkoda, gdyby to znakomite pismo miało przepaść. Szkoda tylko, że nie „wytrzymali" na etapie przejścia do demokracji. Teraz była tutaj tzw. „młoda redakcja" z p. Ziutą i ks. Adamem. Z tego, co czytam w liście, wynika, że odwiedziny te były pożyteczne.

Jeszcze w sprawie przyjazdu grupy z Wilna. Może byłoby dobrze zadzwonić do o. Konrada, a także do ks. Stanisława. Myślę, że jakieś środki się znajdą. Będę się również bardzo cieszył, jeżeli Państwo kiedyś tu się zjawicie. Powiedziałem „Tygodnikowi", że bardzo brak tych „Podróży po Kościele", czyli tego, co wnosił Pan Marek. Proszę też powiedzieć Leszkowi Nowosielskiemu, że będę pamiętał o jego śp. Matce.

To tyle. Piszę to z początkiem W. Postu. Niech Bóg błogosławi w tym świętym czasie, abyśmy wszyscy pełniej przeżyli zwycięstwo Chrystusa.

Z błogosławieństwem

Jan Paweł II

+ Dear Marek and Sophia:

I thank you very much for both letters. Sophia is writing me about the Balkans. I guess Medjugorje is better understood these days. This kind of "insisting" of our Mother is better understood today when we see with our very eyes the enormousness of the danger. At the same time, the response in the way of a special prayer – and that coming from people all around the world – fills us with hope that here, too, the good will prevail. Peace is possible – such was the motto of the day of prayers of January 23rd, prepared by a special session at the Vatican in which Mr. T. Mazowiecki also participated.

Perhaps it is thanks to this as well that Europe is coming back to its senses. People in Poland are getting back to their senses, too, as follows from your writing. Maybe it will become easier for them to come to terms with the Pope who has not preached "the victory of democracy" but has instead reminded them of the Decalogue.

I thank you because I myself am very much attached to that place. It can be that there is only one such sanctuary in the world. Regarding Tygodnik, thanks be to God for what Marek has written me. After all, it would do terrible harm if this superb magazine were to be lost. It is only too bad that they "did not hold out" on the transitional stage to democracy. These days I was visited here by the so-called "young editorial board" including Mrs. Ziuta [Josephine] and Fr. Adam. From what I read in the letter, it follows that the visit was helpful.

Also, on the issue of the arrival of the group from Vilnius. Perhaps it would do well to call Fr. Conrad [Hejmo] and Fr. Stanislaus [Dziwisz]. I think that some means will be found. I will also be very glad if you show up here one day. I told Tygodnik that I missed very much those "Travels around the Church," i.e. what Marek was bringing in. Please also say to Leszek Nowosielski that I will keep in mind his late mother.

That's that. I am writing this at the beginning of the Lent. May God bless us in this holy period of time so that we all live out the victory of Christ.

With my blessing,

John Paul II

Marek comments: " ' *This kind of "insisting" of our Mother' refers to years of consistent messages, repeated through Medjugorje apparitions, which some adversaries deemed impossible"* (p. 119, lines 1-3).

Castel Gandolfo, 3 września 1994 r.

+ Drodzy Państwo,

Bardzo dziękuję za ten list po 40-tej rocznicy Waszego Ślubu.
Cieszę się, że tak pięknie uczczona została przez samych Jubilatów
i innych uczestników modlitw u ss. Dominikanek.
Druga część listu podaje wiele cennych informacji z pielgrzymki
do Medziugorje na 15 sierpnia, w której uczestniczyła P. Zofia.
Są to więc wrażenia bezpośredniego Świadka, czyli wiarygodne
pod każdym względem. Bóg zapłać! Trudno nie czytać tych słów
bez serdecznego współczucia dla owych biednych sierotek i wszystkich
mieszkańców tamtejszej krainy. Nic dziwnego, że ludność pokłada
nadzieję tylko w Bogu, gdy tutaj nie widzi oparcia w najbliższym
otoczeniu.
Polecam Bożej Matce Panią Zofię, Pana Marka i całą Ich
Rodzinę. Życzę zdrowia.
Z serdecznym błogosławieństwem

Jan Paweł II

Castel Gandolfo, September 3, 1994

+ Dear Marek and Sophia:

I thank you very much for this letter following the 40th anniversary of your marriage. I am glad that it was celebrated so beautifully by the celebrators of the jubilee themselves and other participants of the prayers at the Dominican nuns' priory.

The second part of the letter provides many valuable pieces of information concerning the pilgrimage to Medjugorje on August 15 in which Sophia participated. These are then the impressions of a first-hand witness, that is to say, they are reliable in every respect. May God reward you! It is difficult not to read those words without heartfelt compassion for those poor little orphans and all the local inhabitants of that land. No wonder that the people put their hope only in God as, there, they do not get any support from their nearest community.

I commend to the Mother of God Sophia, Marek and their whole family. I wish you to stay healthy.

With a blessing from my heart,

Jan Paul II

Nota Bene: *Marek informed the author that in the Polish edition of his book he did not include any comment at the end of this letter, because the Holy Father's words are clear and speak for themselves. Sophia's information about her pilgrimage is the account of a first-hand witness, and therefore needs no further certification. And it is hard for the Holy Father to read what she wrote about the refugees without experiencing very deep sorrow for all the poor orphans and inhabitants of that unhappy country, recognizing the people's only hope was in God.*

Watykan, 26 lutego 1997 r.

+ Drodzy Państwo,

Bardzo dziękuję Panu Markowi i Jego Małżonce za list, z dołączonym do nich polskim wydaniem 10 dróg krzyżowych z Koloseum "Via Crucis", które jak słyszę, zostało dobrze przyjęte przez wiernych. Cieszę się, że wśród Autorów figuruje też Pan Marek, który wycofał się z "Tygodnika Powszechnego", ale nie odkłada pióra, wykorzystując "dar"swego powołania na kartach innej publicystyki formacyjno-katolickiej. Okazuje się, że zmiana mieszkania daje okazję do nowych natchnień i przemyśleń, kierując wzrok ku "świątyni cierpienia", jakim jest Klinika Kardiologiczna, znana Mu z własnego doświadczenia. Jeśli Pan Bóg pozwoli, poświęcenie gmachu będzie stanowić jeden z programów mojej wizyty w Krakowie. Wielkimi krokami zbliżamy się już do tych dni. Dobrze, że są one przedmiotem modlitw moich Rodaków, jak również bliska podróż do Sarajewa, która w specjalny sposób angażuje do modlitwy Panią Zofię, myśląc o Medziugorje. Dobrze, że napisała recenzję do książki S.Emilii o Apokalipsie, może wzbudzi zainteresowanie nią.

Wgłębiamy się w czas Wielkiego Postu więc życzę Łask Bożych na ten okres tak ściśle związany z Tajemnicą Cierpienia Zbawiciela.

Pozdrawiam serdecznie Panią Zofię, Pana Marka i "Dzieci" z Pawełkiem. Z błogosławieństwem

Jan Paweł II

Vatican City, February 26, 1997

+ Dear Marek and Sophia:

I thank you very much, Marek and your wife, for the letters and the attached Polish edition of *10 Ways of the Cross from the Coliseum "Via Crucis"* which, as I hear, was well received by the faithful. I am glad that, among its authors, there also figures Marek who has opted out of Tygodnik Powszechny but has not put aside his pen, using the "gift" of his calling on other pages of Catholic formational journalism. It turns out that changing apartments gave him an opportunity for new inspirations and considerations by directing his eyesight to "the temple of suffering," meaning the Cardiological Clinic, so well-known to him from his own experience. If the Lord permits, the dedication of the building will be part of the program of my visit to Krakow. We are already approaching these days in great strides. It is good that they are an object of my countrymen's prayers, as much as my immediate trip to Sarajevo which, in a special way, involves Sophia in her prayers when thinking about Medjugorje. It is good that she wrote a review to the book by S. Emily on the Apocalypse, perhaps to arouse interest in it.

As we delve into the Lenten season, I wish you divine mercies for this period of time so tightly connected to the secret of the suffering of Our Savior.

I greet heartily Sophia, Marek and the Kids, together with little Paul.

Blessings,

John Paul II

Marek comments: *"...[the Holy Father] was planning to leave for Sarajevo. Medjugorje, nearby, was not included in his itinerary during his visit to Bosnia Hercegovina"* (p. 146. lines 6,7).[1]

---

[1] *See page 181*

+ Drodzy Państwo!

Serdecznie dziękuję za wspólny list Skwarnickich: Zofii i Marka. Dziękuję też za życzenia wielkanocne. Z całego serca je odwzajemniam pod adresem Państwa i Młodego Pokolenia (Dzieci i Wnuków), wreszcie pod adresem "Tygodnika" i całego Społeczeństwa. Ufam, że Matka z Jasnej Góry pomoże mi na szlaku czerwcowej pielgrzymki. Wszystkich bardzo proszę o modlitwę. W modlitwie też pamiętam codziennie o Ks.Andrzeju B. A dla Moniki szczególne błogosławieństwo na dzień I Komunii św. I niech wszystko dobrze się układa na szlaku Medziugorje-Rzym. Z serdecznym błogosławieństwem
Watykan 30 marca 1991 r.

Jan Paweł

Pokój Chrystusowy niech panuje w sercach waszych kol 3,15 Alleluja

Z błogosławieństwem

Jan Paweł II papież

Watykan 1991

+ Dear Marek and Sophia,

I cordially thank you for the joint letter from the Skwarnickis, Sophia and Marek. I also thank you for the Easter wishes. I return them with all my heart to you and the younger generation (the children and grandchildren), and, eventually, to the "Weekly" and the whole Society. I trust that our Mother of Jasna Góra (the Bright Hill) will help me on the route of my pilgrimage in June. I do ask you for your prayers. I also remember in my daily prayers Father Andrew B. And I am sending a special blessing for Monica on the occasion of her First Holy Communion. And may everything work out fine on the Medjugorje to Rome journey.

With a heartfelt blessing,

John Paul II

Vatican, March 30th, *1991*

(in handwriting)

May the Peace of Christ reign in your hearts (Colossians 3, 15) Halleluiah!

With Blessings,

John Paul II, the Pope

Easter 1991

Marek comments: *"The phrase, 'on the Medjugorje to Rome journey' was not an allusion to any journey. It meant a relationship between the Medjugorje sanctuary and the Vatican, because controveries regarding the Medjugorje apparitions were still persisting as was the conflict between the Medjugorje Franciscans and the Bishop of Mostar. It was the time when Medjugorje matters were referred to Yugoslavian episcopal authorities for consideration," [who had sought the Vatican's intervention].*   (p. 95, lines 4-8).

Regarding the Holy Father's hope concering Medjugorje's journey to Rome, its worth noting that a statue of Our Lady of Medugorje bleeding in Civitavecchia would later be declared a miracle (see pp. 26, 27 and endnote #5 on p. 32). Civitavecchia is identified in Italian tourist brochures as "the doorway to Rome." As noted earlier, Pope Benedict XVI made reference to the statue of Our Lady of Medjugorje in Civitavecchia when he spoke to the Italian Bishops Conference on June 1, 2005.

The Bishop of Civitavecchia, Mons. Grillo, has shared that one evening at the end of February, 1995, he carried the miraculous statuette to the Vatican to John Paul II, who venerated it, prayed in front of it and, at the end, placed on the head of the Virgin a crown which he had brought himself.

Watykan, 6 grudnia 1993 r.

+ Drogi Panie Marku,

Dziękuję serdecznie za „Intensywną terapię". Właśnie znajduję się na ostatnim etapie lektury. Myślę, że tom jest znakomity, bardzo oryginalny. Chyba niewielu poetów uczyniło przedmiotem poezji klinikę kardiologiczną. Jest to bardzo nowoczesne. Nie wiem, co tutaj powiedzą największe wyrocznie typu Miłosz i Barańczak – ale myślę, że Pański tom jest znakomity. Jest znakomity również dlatego, że pod temat kliniki podłącza się temat „podróży po Kościele". W ten sposób tom ma charakter całościowy i poniekąd biograficzny. Dowiadujemy się, że ten, który trafił na klinikę kardiologiczną, jest tym samym człowiekiem, który jeździł z Papieżem do Australii, a przedtem jeszcze do Meksyku i gdzie indziej.

Szkoda, że takich doświadczeń nie mają młodsi członkowie redakcji TP. Może wówczas nie pisaliby takich rzeczy (jak np. młodszy Woźniakowski) o naszym Millenium czy o papieskich odwiedzinach w Polsce. W gruncie rzeczy nic złego i w jakiś sposób prawdziwe, ale równocześnie bardzo jednostronne, a przez to nieprawdziwe. Ma Pan rację, gdy pisze w ostatnim liście, że wszystko poniekąd kończy się na Jerzym Turowiczu oraz ks. Tischnerze, który ostatnio napisał doskonały artykuł o „Veritatis splendor" oraz na M. Ziębie, który jest nowym nabytkiem – niestety jedynym tego rodzaju w TP. I dobrze, że go drukują także w Tablet'cie. Dobrze, że w TP drukują M. Novaka, J. Neuhausa, czy Weigla, a także czasem wspomną A. Frossarda. Ale poza tym, wszystko urywa się na Jerzym Turowiczu. Może czasem jeszcze z jakim „wypadem" P. Hennelowej, a także T. Żychiewicza (poniekąd Pańskiego kolegi z kliniki kardiologicznej). Redakcja TP nie chce być więcej, jak to mawiał Kard. Kominek: retro-oculata, chce być koniecznie ante-oculata, tzn. wpatrzona w przyszłość. Zapomina tylko, że bez tego „retro" nie ma także tego „ante". A poza tym sprawa asystenta kościelnego – o ile wiem – stoi w martwym punkcie. Kard. Macharski zajął słuszne stanowisko, że asystent nie może być tylko do „kiwania głową".

Czytając Pański list, wyczuwam, że obaj walczymy poniekąd o to samo dziedzictwo. Jeśli Pan widzi, że Tygodnik zaczyna nawiązywać do tego dziedzictwa, to jest to dla mnie – rzecz jasna – wielka pociecha. Równocześnie jednak i Pan stwierdza, że nie ma bardzo komu kontynuować tego dziedzictwa i powstaje nieodzowne pytanie o to, kto miałby je konserwować w sposób twórczy, patrząc na tzw. „młody skład". Ci panowie napisali kiedyś do mnie list, na który im odpowiedziałem. Jerzy zawiózł tę odpowiedź, ale to nie zmienia faktu, że Kościoła wciąż trzeba się uczyć, tak jak Chrystusa i Ewangelii, a nie można się go nauczyć bez jakiegoś zaczynu.

Ten zaczyn to jest miłość Kościoła, a nie może nim być nigdy żadna liberalna krytyka Kościoła, choćby powoływała się na najgłośniejsze nazwiska posoborowych teologów.

Dziękuję Panu, Panie Marku, za Jego ostatni list. Widzę, że Autor listu martwi się nie tyle tym, co napisał, ale tym, że tak dużo napisał. Ja natomiast cieszę się z tego, że napisał i że tak napisał, bo jest to wyrazem troski, a troska z kolei jest zawsze wyrazem miłości i nie zawaham się powiedzieć, że takiej miłości potrzebuje TP w obecnej koniunkturze. Nie wiem, czy znajduje ją w dostatecznej mierze w polskim Kościele. Ale przede wszystkim musi ją znajdować we własnym domu. Zacytuję tu słowa Św. Jana od Krzyża: „Tam gdzie nie ma miłości, zaszczep miłość – a znajdziesz miłość".

Jak Pan widzi i ja się rozpisałem wbrew moim obyczajom. Nie mogę jednak – tak jak Pan – przestać tego pragnąć, żeby Tygodnik był pismem katolickim, tzn. pismem dla katolików, którzy dzisiaj w inny jeszcze sposób niż w przeszłości poszukują i chcą w tym piśmie odnaleźć Kościół i siebie.

Panie Marku, stąd też moje życzenia dla Pana i Jego Małżonki oraz młodszego pokolenia w rodzinie Skwarnickich. Wiem, że Pani Zofia patrzy bardzo w stronę Medjugorie, a ostatnio również w stronę Ostrej Bramy, na podstawie całej swojej przeszłości. Ja, jak wiadomo, byłem w Ostrej Bramie, nawet cytowałem tam Mickiewicza. Nie byłem natomiast w Medjugorie, lecz również patrzę w tamtą stronę. Niech Pan powie o tym Żonie. Patrzę w tamtą stronę i zdaje mi się, że nie można zrozumieć dzisiejszych strasznych wypadków na

Bałkanach bez Medjugorie. To jeszcze jeden dodatek na zakończenie mojego listu, w którym przesyłam opłatek wigilijny, aby się nim połamał przy stole wigilijnym z Małżonką i Rodziną, a także z TP, jeżeli jeszcze do Pana zachodzą – z listu wynikało, że nie za bardzo... Ale co zrobić... To nie tylko Św. Jan od Krzyża napisał, że Pan Jezus nam w noc betlejemską ukazał, że tam, gdzie nie ma miłości, „trzeba zaszczepić miłość, ażeby miłość znaleźć". I to są moje życzenia dla Pana i dla całego tego środowiska, z którym wciąż staram się nie rozstawać, także na modlitwie. Jest to bowiem w jakimś sensie nasze wspólne dziedzictwo.

Vatican City, December 6, 1993

+ Dear Marek,
My heartfelt thanks to you for *Intensive Care*. I am right now at
the last stage of the reading. I think that the volume is superb, very
unique. Surely there have not been many poets who made a cardiological clinic an object of their poetry. This is very modern. I do
not know what such great oracles as Milosz and Baranczak might
say, but I think that your volume is excellent. It is also excellent
because, under the theme of the clinic, it links up with the theme
of "travel around the Church." This way the volume has a general
character and is, in a way, biographical. We find out that the man
who happened upon the cardiological clinic is, consequently, the
man who drove along with the Pope over to Australia and, even
before that, to Mexico and elsewhere.

It is too bad that the younger members of TP [the liberal
Catholic *"Tygodnik Powszechny"* weekly] have not had such
experiences. Maybe they would not then write such things (like the
younger Wozniakowski did) on our Millennium or the Papal visit
in Poland. In fact, what he writes is not all bad or untrue, but very
one-sided and therefore not the whole truth. You are right when
you write in the last letter that, in a way, everything ends up with
Jerzy [George] Turowicz and Fr. Tischner who has lately written
an excellent article about *"Veritatis Splendor"* and M. Ziebie who
is a new acquisition at TP – one of a kind, unfortunately. And it is
good that they print him also in the "Tablet." It is good they print
in TP M. Novak, J. Neuhaus or Weigel, and sometimes mention
A. Frossard. Apart from that, however, everything breaks off with
Jerzy Turowicz. Sometimes, maybe, with some sort of a "sneak
attack" by Madam J. Hennel and T. Zychiewicz (in a way, your
friend from the cardiological clinic). The editors of TP do not want
to be, as Card. Kominek used to say: more retro-oculata, they want
to be necessarily ante-oculata, i.e. gazing intently into the future.
They only forget that, without this "retro," there is also none of this
"ante." And, besides, the matter of the church assistant – for what

I know – remains in a deadlock. Card. Macharski took the right position that the role of the assistant may not be only to "nod in approval."

When reading your letter, I feel that, in a way, we both fight for the same heritage. If you see that *Tygodnik* (Weekly) begins to make references to this heritage, then this is for me – obviously – a great consolation. Concurrently, however, you ascertain that there is hardly anyone to continue this heritage and there comes into being an essential question regarding who would have to preserve it in a creative way, when looking at the so-called "young personal composition." Those gentlemen once wrote me a letter to which I replied. Jerzy delivered that reply but that does not change the fact that it is necessary to learn from the Church continually, just like Christ and the Gospel, and one cannot learn from it without some kind of leaven.

This leaven is the love of the Church and it can never be any liberal critique of the Church, even if it referred to the most loudly acclaimed names of the postconciliar theologians.

Thank you, Marek, for your last letter. I see that the author of the letter worries not so much about what he wrote but that he wrote so much. I am glad, however, that he wrote and that he wrote this way because an expression of his concern, and the concern, in turn, is always an expression of love: and I will not hesitate to say that *TP* needs such love in the present situation. I do not know whether they find it in the sufficient measure in the Polish church. But, first of all, they must find it in their own house. I quote here the words of St. John of the Cross: "Where there is no love, graft love – and you will find love."

As you see I, too, have written at length against my custom. I cannot, however – just like you – cease to desire for the *Tygodnik* weekly to be a Catholic magazine, i.e., a magazine for Catholics who, today, search otherwise than in the past and want to find the Church and themselves in this magazine.

Hence, Marek, are also my wishes to you and your wife and the younger generation in the Skwarnicki family. I know that Sophia looks very much towards Medjugorje and, of late, towards Ostra Brama for the reason of her entire past. I, actually, was in Ostra Brama, I even quoted from Mickiewicz there. I was not in Medjugorje but I also look in that direction. Please tell your wife about it. I look in that direction and it seems to me that one cannot understand today's terrible events in the Balkans without Medjugorje. This is another postscript to my letter in which I am sending you the Christmas Eve wafer so that you break it at the Christmas Eve table and share it with your wife, your family and the *TP* editors if they still come to you for it – it followed from the letter they do not do it too much... But what can we do... It is Saint John of the Cross who wrote that our Lord Jesus showed us in the night of Bethlehem that, where there is no love, "it is necessary to graft love, in order to find love." And these are my wishes for you and for your entire community with which I continually try to remain a part of, also in prayer. For this is, in some sense, our common heritage.

John Paul II

Marek comments: *"And again about Medjugorje. 'It seems to me that one cannot understand today's terrible events in the Balkans without Medjugorje,' writes the Holy Father at the time when the Balkan war intensifies... Over the years, the Blessed Mother had warned against hatred and sins of people leading to human calamity"* (p. 117, lines 15-24).

Watykan, 15 kwietnia 1986 r.

Droga Pani Zofio i Panie Marku,

Dziękuję za podzielenie się ze mną obserwacjami, spowodowanymi
ukazaniem się tłumaczonej przez Panią Zofię książeczki, którą
i mnie obdarzyła. Dziękuję Jej za to serdecznie, jak i Panu Markowi za
dopisek do Jej listu. Pociesza wiadomość o reakcji ludu Bożego
i wprowadzaniu w życie tego, co najistotniejsze w całym tym
wydarzeniu, co pobudza do gorliwości, pojednania serc, do uwielbienia
Miłosiernego Ojca, do otwarcia serc na przyjęcie łaski Bożej.
       Zbliżamy się do dni poświęconych czci św. Marka
i św. Zofii – czyli Drogim Solenizantom należy przesłać także
serdeczne życzenia imieninowe, a wraz z nimi zapewnienie o pamięci
w modlitwie i serdeczne pozdrowienia

   JP II

   Zmartwychwstał
   Dobry Pasterz
   Alleluja!

   Z błogosławieństwem
   Jan Paweł II papież
   Wielkanoc 1986

Vatican City, April 15th, 1986

Dear Sophia and Marek:

Thank you for sharing with me your observations prompted by the issuance of a little book translated by Sophia, a copy of which she sent me as a gift. I thank her for this cordially, as well as you, Marek, for your postscript to her letter. It is comforting to hear the news about the reaction of God's people – and the implementation of what is the most essential in all this event, which stimulates the zeal, the reconciliation of hearts, to worshiping the Merciful Father, to opening up hearts to the acceptance of Divine Mercy.

We are getting close to the celebration of the feast days in honor of St. Mark and St. Sophia – so it is time to also send the dear Name-bearers my best wishes on the occasion of their Patron saints' days and, along with them, the assurance of their memory in my prayers and heartfelt greetings.

JPII
The Good Shepherd
is risen, Alleluia!
     With blessing,
Jan Paul II, the Pope, Easter
1986

Marek comments: *"'a little book' mentioned by the Pope was the very first Polish publication regarding the Medjugorje apparitions. It was translated from German into Polish by our friend, Maria Balewicz. Because the Pope received it from my wife he mistakenly assumed that Sophia had been a translator of that book. The Pope's interpretation of the apparitions is interesting. At this early time the controversies within the Church were significant. Moreover, an increasing interest in the Medjugorje events, among faithful in both the former Yugoslavia and other countries, was an impediment for the local government, because Yugoslavia was a state of athiestic communism. The Medjugorje pastor was arrested. The Bishop of Mostar, who had an ecclesiastical governance over that area, was against acceptance of the authenticity of the apparitions. Local Franciscans were of a different opinion. Monastic orders are not subject to the Bishop's authority; so the controversies kept growing... Those who believed in the apparitions (which themselves were revealing nothing contrary to the Church's doctrines) and some respected French and Italian mariologists, supported the local Franciscans. John Paul's reply to my wife's letter and to my note was written during that very period...* (p. 43, lines 1-2).

Appendix 2.
Yugoslav Bishops Conference Declaration on Medjugorje

At the ordinary session of the Bishops Conference of Yugoslavia in Zadar, Croatia, April 9-11, 1991, the following was adopted:

Declaration

"The Bishops, from the very beginning, have been following the events of Medjugorje through the Bishop of the diocese (Mostar), the Commission of the Bishop (Mostar) and the Commission of the Yugoslav Bishops Conference on Medjugorje.

"On the basis of the investigations so far, it cannot be affirmed that one is dealing with supernatural apparitions and revelations.

"However, the numerous gatherings of great numbers of the faithful from different parts of the world, who are coming to Medjugorje prompted both by motives of belief and various other motives, do require attention and pastoral care – in the first place by the Bishop of the diocese and with him also of the other Bishops, so that both in Medjugorje and in everything connected with it a healthy devotion to the Blessed Virgin Mary may be promoted in accordance with the teaching of the Church.

"For this purpose the Bishops will issue specially suitable liturgical-pastoral directives. Likewise, through their Commissions they will continue to keep up with and investigate the entire event in Medjugorje."

> The Bishops of Yugoslavia
> In Zadar, April 10, 1991
> (Published in *Glas Koncila* [Zagreb] May 5, 1991)[1]

"non constat de supernaturalitate"

"It is not true that from the document summarized by the bishops at the end of November It expressly follows nothing supernatural is happening in Medjugorje. The bishops wrote: 'non constat de supernaturalitate' (supernaturality is not established) and not: 'constat de non supernaturalitate' (it is established that there is nothing supernatural). This is an enormous difference. The first formulation does not permit itself to be interpreted in a definitive way; it is open to further developments."

> **Msgr. Franc Perko**
> **Archbishop of Belgrade**
> *(30 Days,* **February 2, 1991)**

---

[1] see last paragraph, p. 183

On Medjugorje – *Something More Definite*
Editorial Commentary in *Glas Koncila,*
(Newspaper of the Croatian Bishops Conference)
Zagreb, May 5, 1991

The latest declaration on Medjugorje from the Catholic Bishops of the Socialist Federal Republics of Yugoslavia is a classic example of the centuries old practice of authentic ecclesiastical prudence. It demonstrates that the Church respects facts above all, that it carefully measures its competency and that in all matters it is mostly concerned for the spiritual welfare of the faithful.

"It is a fact known to the whole world that, because of news about Our Lady's apparitions already for a full ten years, both believing and inquisitive people have been gathering in Medjugorje. Is it a fact that the Mother of God is really appearing there and giving messages? The Bishops, carefully holding to their competency, declare that, 'On the basis of investigations so far it can not be affirmed.'

"The content and the sense of that declaration have to be considered on two levels. In this case the first and the essential level is that the contents of such possible so-called private revelations cannot be added to the revealed and obligatory contents of the faith. Therefore, neither the bishops nor the Pope himself have the authority either to conclude infallibly that Our Lady has really appeared somewhere or the authority to impose on the faithful to believe that she has appeared. The magisterium of the Church is infallible under well known conditions only when it affirms that something is contained or not contained in that Revelation which the Church received up to the end of the apostolic age and which is preserved in Scripture and Tradition. Whatever is included neither in Scripture nor in Tradition the magisterium cannot proclaim as a doctrine of the faith nor as content to be believed under obligation. Accordingly, only the uninstructed could expect the bishops to resolve the question of the Medjugorje apparitions for us so as then to know exactly what we are allowed or not allowed to believe about them.

"But on the other hand, then why are they so carefully investigating that report? Because they do have the obligation to establish whether that which is taking place there and is being proclaimed from there is in accordance with the entirety of the revealed truth of the faith and or moral doctrine. If it is established that there is nothing contrary, that the revelations and messages are in accordance with Catholic faith and morals, they, as the most responsible in the Church, could proclaim that there is neither any objection to gatherings of the faithful in that place nor to the development of the spiritual life according to the sense of those messages. On the contrary, it would be their obligation to expose errors and prevent abuses. The pertinent expressions in the new Declaration show that the investigations are also continuing in that sense.

"But the main force of the Declaration shows that our bishops are above all taking notice of the factual gathering of a large number of the faithful and of the inquisitive in Medjugorje and they consider it their duty to insure that such a large number of gatherings there receive a correct proclamation of the faith, an orthodox and up-to-date catechesis, so that the holy sacraments are correctly and worthily administered there and especially that the Medjugorje Marian devotion develops in accord with Christian orthodoxy.

"Surely, as the document itself states, one should expect suitable liturgical-pastoral directives for the solemn celebrations in Medjugorje. A proposal made long ago, which was also emphasized in *Glas Koncila,* would also thereby be realized, namely, that the bishops' care for Medjugorje be divided between two commissions. One would continue investigating whether there are or are not supernatural apparitions or revelations, and the other would take care of the proper and healthy ecclesiastical conduct of the Medjugorje gatherings. This is because it is really possible that the first of these commissions would still be investigating for a long time and maybe even decide not to publish its final opinion, whereas care for the gatherings cannot be postponed because they are continuously taking place.

"For many devout people around the world this Declaration will serve as a valuable relief in the area of conscience. Those, namely, who come to Medjugorje motivated by belief, will from now on know that those gatherings are covered by the ordinary and responsible care of the successors of the Apostles. This position is the real news of this document."

Appendix 3.

Critics of Medjugorje

Medjugorje does, of course, have its detractors. The ancient Bosnian antagonism between secular clergy and Franciscans has something to do with this.[1]

The spiritual warfare which attaches itself to all centers of grace also has a part to play in the cloud of controversy surrounding Medjugorje. In America the leading opponent is E. Michael Jones, editor of *Culture Wars* (formerly *Fidelity Magazine*).[2] At the conclusion of one of his last public attacks against Medjugorje (a 16 - page pamphlet distributed throughout the world in March, 1990), Bishop Pavao Zanic mentioned Jones's book, requesting that everyone read it in order to learn the truth about Medjugorje.[3] It is worth noting however, that Fr. Robert Fox, who authored the foreword to that book and had been among Jones's strongest supporters, later stated in *The Fatima Family Messenger:* "Some time ago I wrote Michael Jones and asked him to discontinue using my name in the advertisement of *Medjugorje: The Untold Story*... I would like to ask you to join me in praying for Michael Jones. In the past couple of years I have come more and more to question the integrity of methodology and journalistic responsibility [he has] exercised... publish[ing] without facts and too often with misinformation... The uncharitableness in false accusations is most serious" (*The Fatima Family Messenger*, July/September, 1992).[4]

A recent attack on Medjugorje is Donal Anthony Foley's misnamed *Understanding Medjugorje*. Foley is already notorious for writing an article on Marian apparitions in the magazine *The Voice of Padre Pio* and slipping in his pet peeves about Medjugorje. The subsequent protests from readership of the magazine led its editors to apologize for this abuse of authorial privilege. Foley's book is in some ways an extended version of the article. It deploys a *Da Vinci Code* strategy in its polemics, creating a mosaic of half-truths and outright falsehoods that appears plausible to the ignorant and the innocent. There are no new facts, discoveries or insights in the book. It is a rerun of previous devious assaults. For detailed responses to these frequently reincarnated charges, see *Medjugorje – A Time for Truth and a Time for Action.*

Opposition in Europe to Medjugorje has been led by the Counter-Reformation movement with the Abbot of Nantes in France. Monsieur l'abbe Georges de Nantes, who wrote the first public pronouncement against the authenticity of Medjugorje for theological reasons, had for years been publicly accusing Popes Paul VI and John Paul II of formal heresy, at one point presenting to the Vatican a *Book of Accusation against Pope John Paul II for Heresy, Schism and Scandal*, in which he officially requested the Church to hold a trial against the Holy Father, before his own tribunal, as "Supreme Judge of the Faith."[5]

With the Balkan war having destroyed 80% of his diocese, Bishop Zanic requested that his assistant be named Coadjator.[6] Msgr. Ratko Peric succeeded him as the Bishop of Mostar. But since Msgr. Zanic had been relieved of the dossier in 1986 by the Prefect for the Congregation of the Doctrine of the Faith (at the time Cardinal Ratzinger), the local bishop no longer enjoys the same discretionary powers over "the Medjugorje events." In 1986 the dossier had been entrusted to the Commission of Inquiry of the Episcopal Conference with Bishop Komarica as president. This Conference consisted of the three bishops of Bosnia-Hercegovina. As noted earlier, an official directive from the Congregation for the Doctrine of the Faith later clarified that Bishop Peric's negative view of the reported apparitions "should be considered the expression of the personal conviction of the Bishop of Mostar which he has the right to express as Ordinary of the place, but which is and remains his personal opinion," (CDF, Pr. No 154/81-06419, 5/26/98, see p. 19).[7]

The Bishop of Banja Luka, **Mons. Franjo Komarica, President of the Commission**, clarified in the April 25, 2006, issue of the Croatian newsdaily, *Veãernji list*: "Before the war, I paid several official visits to Medjugorje. For a considerable time now, Medjugorje is a world phenomenon that has outgrown the limits of the local diocese. Responsibility for the judgment of the Medjugorje phenomenon must rest with the Holy See, while the local bishop has the right and the duty to take care of the correct liturgical and pastoral life of his diocese as a whole, which includes the parish of Medjugorje."

> ### *"I also wish to come to Medjugorje!"*
> ### Pope John Paul II

In a remarkable dimension of the Vatican's de facto recognition of Medjugorje as a Marian shrine, Fr. Raniero Cantalamessa, OFM Cap, Preacher to the Papal Household from 1980 to the present, was the keynote speaker at the 12th International Seminar for Priests in Medjugorje July 2 - 7, 2007. The theme of the conference was, "With Mary Waiting for the Holy Spirit."

It was no secret that throughout his pontificate the Pope of the Secret of Fatima wanted to go to Medjugorje. As previously cited, the Holy Father had often expressed this desire, and not only privately.

Pope John Paul II, however, would not impose his visit to Medjugorje without first being invited into the diocese by the local Ordinary. The Bishop of Mostar would never extend the invitation.[8]

Finding himself in Sarajevo (April 12 - 13, 1997), the Holy Father wanted to discretely give a sign of his attachment to Medjugorje. At the Cathedral, as at Kosovo stadium, he added these words to his

> ### *"Our Lady of Medjugorje, pray for me!"*
> ### Pope John Paul II

written text: "Kraljice Mira, moli za nas!" ("Queen of Peace, pray for us!") Back in Rome at his Wednesday General Audience (April 16th) he declared: "During the war the pilgrimages of the faithful to the Bosnia - Hercegovina Marian Shrines did not cease [...], to ask the Mother of Nations and the Queen of Peace to intercede for peace to come back to this martyred region." [9]

The Pope's own letters now confirm his belief in the authenticity of Our Lady's apparitions in Medjugorje. And it can be verified by those responsible for helping to draft his regular Angelus Address that Pope John Paul II would conlcude his own daily private rosary while walking in the Vatican gardens,**"Our Lady of Medjugorje, pray for me!"**

Several months before the Holy Father's June 22, 2003, trip to Banja Luka in Bosnia, Zenit made public a report from the Holy See that he also wished to visit Mostar. Though the government had extended an invitation, local media reported the Bishop of Mostar's response that it would be a mistake for the Pope to come into his diocese (as he told the media every time Pope John Paul II traveled to Croatia or Bosnia).

> *"I thank Sophia for everything concerning Medjugorje. I, too, go there everyday as a pilgrim in my prayers: I unite in my prayers with all those who pray there or receive a calling for prayer from there. Today we have understood this call better."*
>
> Pope John Paul II

And so the Holy Father had to content himself on that trip – his last to the country – with only visiting Banja Luka,[10] the Serbian captial of Bosnia. Previously he had visited the Muslim capital, Sarajevo, twice. He was never able to visit Mostar, the Catholic capital of Bosnia. Bishop Ratko Peric, the Ordinary of the diocese that incorporates St. James Parish in Medjguorje (20 miles from Mostar) would not invite him into his diocese.

On March 25, 2005, looking up at the window of his papal apartment overlooking St. Peter's Square, where exactly twenty-one years before Pope John Paul II had encouraged Bishop Hnilica to go to

> *"Medjugorje is better understood these days. This kind of 'insisting' of our Mother is better understood today when we see with our very eyes the enormousness of the danger."*
>
> Pope John Paul II

181

Medjugorje, saying, "Medjugorje is the fulfillment and continuation of Fatima," Pope Benedict XVI said that throughout the 26 years Pope John Paul II served as pontiff, "everyone was quite aware of the presence of the Virgin Mary as Mother and Queen of the Church during his spirituality and his untiring ministry. This presence was most obvious during the attack on his life in St. Peter's Square on May 13, 1981. In memory of that tragic event, Pope John Paul II wanted a mosaic of the Virgin to be placed high above the Apostolic Palace, overlooking St. Peter's Square. It would be there as a reminder of both the highlights and the more everyday moments of his long papacy, which entered its final phase precisely a year ago, a phase that was simultaneously painful and triumphant..."

Let us remember that during his papacy the Pope of the Secret of Fatima was going every day to Medjugorje as a pilgrim in his prayers, uniting in his prayer with all those praying there or receiving a call for prayer from there. "Today we have understood this call better," he wrote (p. 152). *Testimonies from Cardinals and Bishops throughout the world attest that today the whole Church understands this call better!*

We are challenged now to set aside giving priority to our own personal agendas – our individual "miserable interest"[11] – and heed the warning of the late Cardinal Hans Urs von Balthasar, Pope John Paul II's favorite theologian and the director of Pope Benedict XVI's doctoral thesis (his acknowledged mentor and guide): **"The theology of Medjugorje rings true. I am convinced of its truth. Everything concerning Medjugorje is authentic from the Catholic point of view. All that happens there is so evident, so convincing! ...There is only one danger alone for Medjugorje – that people will pass it by!"** [12]

Appendix 3 End Notes

1. *(text on p. 178)* A senior European leader had a private meeting with Bishop Ratko Peric and other witnesses in 1998 and has given his sworn testimony on the meeting. In the course of this meeting the Bishop denied that any supernatural events were occurring in Medjugorje. The Bishop went so far as to deny that supernatural events had taken place at Lourdes or Fatima and said he did not believe in *any* apparitions. With regard to Lourdes he said he believed in the dogma of the Immaculate Conception but this was pronounced before the event. When a tribute was paid to the dedication of the Franciscans in Medjugorje, the bishop was visibly incensed and, according to the interviewer, became completely incoherent. He also said that the only resolution to the problem was "that the Franciscans must submit and Medjugorje must be abolished." While denouncing the Medjugorje apparitions, he said he had never met or spoken with the six visionaries.

Bishop Peric's predecessor, Bishop Zanic, had a similar attitude to Medjugorje as shown in a published interview with Gabriel Meyer (*National Catholic Register*, April 1, 1990):

"'What do you as bishop want to have happen in Medjugorje? What could the Franciscans and the parishioners there do to work with you?' Zanic leaned back in his chair. 'Simple. I want Medjugorje destroyed.'"

The reporter later told the author that he was so surprised with the bishop's words that to be sure he had understood the question correctly he had repeated it three times (this can be verified by the tape recording of the inverview as well as by the translator, Slavinca Marincic, who still resides in the area and is willing to be contacted). Looking directly into his tape recorder the Bishop repeated those same words each time. (Out of charity, Mr. Meyer added "as a phenomenon" in parenthesis, when quoting the Bishop's statement.)

Regarding the 1991 Declaration of the Yugoslav Bishops Conference (BYC) on Medjugorje (see p 175), an article quoting the President of the Doctrinal Commission of the BYC, Archbishop Frane Franic, in the January 6, 1991 issue of *Slobodna Dalmacija* (following their preliminary meeting - see below) was not reported to the English - speaking world: "The bishops used this ambiguous sentence because they did not want to humiliate Bishop Pavao Zanic of Mostar who constantly claimed that Our Lady did not appear to the seers. When the Yugoslav bishops discussed the Medjugorje issue, they told Bishop Zanic that the Church was not giving a final decision on Medjugorje and consequently his opposition was without any foundation. Hearing this, Bishop Zanic began to cry and to shout, and the rest of the bishops then quit any further discussion." Worth noting is Our Lady's subsequent message from Medjugorje following the worldwide dissemination of the resulting press release, "Yugoslav Bishops Say Medjugorje Not Supernatural": "I stay among you as long as it is God's will. Thank you that you will not betray my presence here and I thank you because your response is serving God and peace," (1/25/91). (Archbishop Franic's Jan. 6, 1991, article was in regard to a Nov. 27, 28, 1990, meeting of the Bishops of the former BYC gathered at Zagreb in special session, preliminary to the Zadar meeting of April 10, 1991.)

Bishop Zanic orchestrated the 1990 press release, "Yugoslav Bishops Say Medjugorje Not Supernatural" by sending his version of the bishops' meeting to the Italian Catholic News Service in much the same way as his succesor, Bishop Peric, went to the media in June, 2006, with his homily calling for an end to the apparitions and the visionaries giving messages. In 1990 a correction by the Secretary of the Bishops Conference that "no definitive judgment" had been made was ignored by the Catholic media: "The Secretariat of the Bishops Conference has taken no position on the events in Medjugorje. It is astonished that the Italian news agency, 'ASCA' could have come by such information," (*Gebatsaktion*, 1990, & O'Carroll, Ibid, p. 38). Though the Catholic media in America spread widely Bishop Peric's June 15, 2006 demand for obedience and an end to the events of Medjugorje, it gave little notice to the July 15, 2006, public rebuke he received from Cardinal Pulic, the President of the Bishops' Conference.

2. *(text on p. 178)* The March 26, 1998, edition of *The Wanderer* (USA) reported that Jones "lost nearly 50% of his readers" because of his attacks against Medjugorje. It is this attrition that led him to change the name of his magazine. In its story, *The Wanderer*, a traditionalist Catholic paper, championed Jones's scathing attacks against Medjugorje, crediting, for example, the dissolution of a man's marriage to the apparitions (see endnote #3 below). Although most of the paper's sources have since admitted their charges were fabricated - and it has become widely acknowledged that Jones's reporting was simply a continuation of his personal crusade (as of this writing, according to the July 13, 2006 *The Birmingham News*, the ex-husband has been jailed for contempt of court and released on a quarter of a million dollar bond) the paper has never printed a retraction.

3. *(text on p. 178)* At the conclusion of the author's meeting with the Bishop of Mostar in February, 1989 (see the third paragraph in footnote #7, below), Msgr. Zanic handed him Jones's book, saying, "Here, read this. This is a good book. It will tell you the truth about Medjugorje!" The bishop had lamented, "There are hundreds of books in favor of Medjugorje and only three against. But nobody wants to read the ones against!"

Jones included this book, *Medjugorje: The Untold Story*, in its entirety in the second book he wrote attacking Medjugorje. The first chapter of that second book credits the dissolution of a man's marriage to Medjugorje (Jones erroneously writes that if this man "went back to Bosnia, the Franciscans were going to have him killed," because he had discovered the Franciscans of Medjugorje had actually turned the parish into a center for drug laundering and pedophilia)!

What Jones does not tell his readers is that the court issued a 30 - year restraining order against this man when his wife separated from him on the advice of her spiritual director because of a 39 - year abusive marriage - that had nothing at all to do with Medjugorje. Moreover, it is not only asserted that his adult children will see him only in the presence of a psychiatrist but that he funded publication of Jones' second book, allegedly telling his wife that if she didn't return to him, he would destroy the thing closest to her heart: Medjugorje. Towards this end he himself published that he has devoted millions of dollars employing, journalists, film crews and a legal system. For example, he kept alive for two years a story in the Muslim *Feral Tribune* that all money collected by the Medjugorje parish during the Bosnian War for refugee aid was actually used by the Franciscans for ethnic cleansing of Muslims, and in *Ljiljan* (The Lily), a Muslim-oriented weekly, a series accusing Our Lady in Medjugorje of brain washing and destroying marriages in America. His campaign became so perverse, according to Croatia's news weekly *Nedjeljna Dalmacija*, that the newspaper felt it necessary to publish a long rebuttal by the Franciscan Provincial (April 17, 1998). The month before, the paper had published an interview with this man's wife: "Behind this whole affair stands her ex- husband's revenge because of their divorce... she prayed in Medjugorje, together with her friends for her, as she says, 'disturbed' husband who, because of her, wants to 'destroy' Medjugorje... 'My whole family is united in trying to help my disturbed ex-husband, all of our three adult children, my sister, my mother, as well as his three sisters. His family prays for him... those who are constantly working against Medjugorje are using him, and he is using them." The newspaper went on to report that he "gave to Network 5 and to the journalist E. Michael Jones $1.7 million to compromise and defame Medjugorje," (*Nedjeljna Dalmacija* March 27, 1998, p. 43). The ex-husband posted on the internet his correspondence with Msgr. Peric, the Bishop of Mostar. Jones regularly featured on the backcover of his magazine a picture of himself walking arm in arm with Bishop Peric.

4. *(text on p. 178)* The May 10, 1992, edition of the *South Bend Tribune* quoted Fr. Robert Fox (after he spoke at the 1992 National Conference on Medjugorje at the University of Notre Dame): "Although Medjugorje has not been authenticated by the Vatican, the fruits of the transformation of souls and the conversions are great. This cannot be the work of the Devil... What we have at Medjugorje are not new prophecies, but Our Lady in a motherly way reaching out to her children. The messages are so simple that the youngest child could understand it... Medjugorje is fulfillling what Fatima promised."

5. *(text on p. 179)* The Catholic Counter Reformation's argument against Medjugorje turns out in fact to be the best case for its authenticity! Under the heading, "MAY THE END OF MEDJUGORJE SOUND THE DEATH KNELL OF THE REFORM," Brother Michael of the Holy Trinity concludes his publication *Apparitions at Medjugorje?*: "Sooner or later, Rome will have to allow the truth to triumph. It will then be recognized – all the more clearly for having been so long delayed – where lay good faith in the service of the truth and where hypocrisy and lies for the propagation of heresy. It will then be clear that the keenest supporters of Vatican II's novelties concerning ecumenism and religious liberty were also the most fanatical propagandists of this diabolical Apparition, impudently preaching the same doctrine – to the point of unmasking and compromising it beyond repair. Then will dawn the first light of the Catholic Counter Reformation, miraculously victorious through the all-powerful grace of Our Lady of Fatima. May the end of Medjugorje sound the death knell of the Reform [i.e., Vatican II] at the same time

as the triumph of the Immaculate Heart of Mary!"

6. *(text on p. 179)* Fr. Rupcic notes that Fr. Peric was Bishop Zanic's right hand throughout his tenure as Bishop, referring to himself in parish documents as "Bishop Zanic's clerk" (below, Rupcic, p. 233). In 1981, it was Fr. Peric (who in 1993 succeeded Zanic as bishop) who led a delegation of 12 priests demanding that Bishop Zanic change his mind and turn against the apparitions or there would be a rebellion from the priests in his diocese. Prior to that demand, after a meeting in Rome, Bishop Zanic "visited St. Jerome's Croatian Pontifical Institute and in front of everyone, including some students, with exaltation spoke about the Medjuguorje apparitions. The principal of the Institute, Dr. Ratko Peric was angered by this speach and protested by thumping his hand against the table! This was testified by one of the people who was present, now high in the Church hierarchy." *(Once Again the Truth About Medjugorje,* Fr. Ljudevit Rupcic, K. Kresimir, Zagreb, 2002, p. 235).

In his earlier book *"The Truth About Medjugorje"* 1990, Fr. Rubpcic (a respected theologian who, for instance, had translated the New Testament into Croatian) quotes Bishop Zanic's explanation to Fr. Jozo as to why he hadn't said a word in his defense during the trial that had sent Fr. Jozo to a Communist prison: the secular priests of his diocese would revolt and he was too old to take the chance of facing prison himself! "In such a situation, the bishop 'had' to think of his own interests, he told F.r Jozo. 'How could I have acted differently?' the bishop asked. 'I could not have gone to prison for Medjugorje,' he said, thinking of the U.D.B.A. [secret police] threat, 'nor did I wish to go from being bishop to assistant pastor of a village,' referring to pressure from his diocesan priests. He feared the U.D.B.A because they could imprison him, and his preists because he was a newcomer to the diocese and the clergy had threatened him with some sort of boycott if he had continued to support Medjugorje" (Rupcic, p. 73).

7. *(text on p. 179)* Thirteen years before, in an official note from the office of the Vatican Secretary of State, No 150.458, 04/01/85, Cardinal Casaroli had made known to Msgr. Peric's predecessor, Bishop Zanic, to: "suspend the diffusion of his personal declarations." Indeed, he had spread his reports (not official) throughout the world. For example, on March 15, 1988, Bishop Zanic wrote Michael Jones, editor of *Fidelity Magazine:* "At the feast of St. Jacob I celebrated the Sacrament of Confirmation at Medjugorje and among others by myself I pronounced the speech which is enclosed with this letter. I ask you to publish this speech in all newspapers. You can do it with my authority and responsibility. Thank you!" In that speech, Bishop Zanic had condemned all who purported that Our Lady was giving messages in Medjugorje "to the lowest place in hell!" ("He expected to see the parishioners revolt, but they silently listened to him with respect, in spite of the deep hurt they felt in their hearts," Fr. Rene Laurentin, *Seven Years of Apparitions,* pp 72-77).

Bishop Zanic had told Fr. Milan Mikulich, a native of Croatia and editor of *Orthodoxy of Catholic Doctrine* – one of the first priests to visit Medjugorje from

America after the report of apparitions in June, 1981 – that if the Vatican didn't accept his condemnation of the apparitions "there will be a war in the Church!" Fr. Mikulich responded, "Bishop, I think you are fighting against Our Lady and not against the seers or the Franciscans in Medjugorje." He replied, "If I lose, there will be a war." (Fr. Mikulich's testimony was presented at the 1991 Medjugorje Conference at Notre Dame). His succesor, Bishop Peric, continues this same war. For example, when the Franciscan parish in Capljina was to be turned over to diocesan clergy, the bishop was advised to take several weeks changing the priests gradually in order to make the change easier for parishoners. Instead, he removed all the Franciscans and staffed the parish with his diocesan clergy on the same day fanning the flames of an already tense situation. As he had been warned before hand would happen, the parishioners revolted giving the example of disorder in his diocese that he wanted and has since been able to refer to. Pope Benedict XVI's address to Bishp Peric during his 2006 "ad limina" visit – contrary to how the bishop had spread it to the media – can be taken as an admonition (endnote #3 on page 32). The testimony of a bishop visiting Medjugojre comes to mind: "I came to the conclusion that the problems that exist in the Church are not solved and perhaps the pastors in the Church are responsible for that...We need more holy priests and pastors who are disposed to live according to Jesus Christ the Good Shepherd." Bishop Lazaro Perez, De Autlan Jalisco, Mexico (Press Bulletin no. 82, January 14, 1998).

During a filmed interview in February, 1989, with Bishop Pavo Zanic, the author appealed: "It would show great openness on the part of Your Excellency if you would go to Medjugorje and pray during a reported apparition." The bishop's response: "I don't need to go to Medjugorje. I've seen them on video tape." In response to his question, "Who is the pastor in Medjugorje?," the bishop replied, "I don't know. I think it's the fat one." As previously noted, not only has his successor, Bishop Ratko Peric, never been present at an apparition, he's gone on record stating (during a formal meeting in his episcopal residence on October 9, 1998, before witnesses who have given sworn testimony) that *he's never met any of the visionaries, and he doesn't believe in the authenticity of any apparitions, specifically naming Fatima and Lourdes!* "I believe only in what I have to believe, the Immaculate Conception!" A priest present at this meeting, who had been sent by the cardinal primate of his country with a formal letter of introduction to the bishop in order to carry out a private investigation of the events of Medjugorje, has felt constrained all these years never to make the bishop's answers public for fear of incurring his retaliation! This gives some picture of what the Franciscans of St. James Parish in Medjugorje have had to live with all these years.

The present Bishop of Mostar has forbidden religious of the parish from accepting speaking invitations abroad. One Francsican advertised as a speaker at a Marian Conference in America where the local Ordinary of the diocese was also speaking – as well as another archbishop – was called to Mostar (the bishop is careful not to put all his demands in writing) and told that if he went and spoke at the conference he would be banished to a far corner of Bosnia and never set foot again in Medjugorje. The day another Franciscan was named pastor he was called to the chancellery in Mostar where the Bishop drew three circles on a piece of paper, to demonstrate, the priest was told, the situation of the Church: the first circle represented God, the second the Pope and the third circle represented the Bishop... As pastor of the parish he was the bishop's representative - and no converstation could take place in the village that wasn't under his authority, i.e., could take place without his approval....even a family sitting around their dinner table at night could not have a converation that wasn't authorized by the Bishop! When Zenit reported some time ago that new directives were being prepared by the CDF to help bishops deal with the reports of apparitions in their dioceses, Bishop Peric was quoted saying finally the church would be able to stop the laity from using the internet to spread reports of apparitions without first receiving the local bishop's approval.

In 1988 a diocesan priest from the vicinity of Zagreb wrote "Kralijica Mira u Medjugorje," ("Queen of Peace in Medjugorje") but felt it necessary to use the pseudonym, Jacov Marin, because of recriminations for having written a positive book on Medjugorje.

8. *(text on p. 180)* Fr. Rene Laurentin had given his explanation in 1997: "I do not think that the Pope's desire can be realized, given the opposition of the local bishop, for even if the Pope is theoretically all – powerful, he shows maximum respect for the established authorities in the Church according to the principle of subsidiarity that: the higher level must avoid interference with the lower level, while maintaining its freedom to confirm its convictions privately." Having been invited to have breakfast with Pope John Paul II, "to submit an important question to him," Fr. Rene Laurentin wrote, "when I finished, he spent the rest of the breakfast asking me questions about Medjugorje." Fr. Laurentin, author of more than 150 books, is the foremost Mariologist in the Church.... (*René Laurentin - The Position of Medjugorje in the Church*, was originally published in July, 1997, and then republished by the "Information Centre 'Mir' Medjugorje" on July 20, 2005.)

9. *(text on p. 180)* Croatia's main news daily, *Slobodna Dalmacija,* carried the headline in its April 18, 1997 issue: **"The Pope Confirms Medjugorje!"** The front page of Mostar's May 2, 1997 issue of *Horizont* carried the same headline.

10. *(text on p. 181)* Parish Bulletin 189 (2003) reports: "On July 14, an official reception was held in the diocesan house in Banja Luka, at the occasion of the conclusion of all the work linked to the Holy Father's visit, which took place on June 22. For this reception, which was initiated and organized by Msgr. Franjo Komarica, Bishop of Banja Luka, the highest representatives of Church, as well as civil authorities that were involved in the organization of the Holy Father's visit, gathered. Awards and acknowledgements were given to organizations and individuals who were involved in this event. Msgr. Komarica gave an award and an acknowledgement to *Radio "Mir" Medjugorje,* whose broadcasting accompanied the preparation for the Holy Father's visit, and the visit itself, to Bosnia and Hercegovina. Msgr. Komarica gave the award and the acknowledgement to Fr. Mario Knezovic, the chief editor of *Radio 'Mir' Medjugorje.*"

Apparently Fr. Mario was doing too good a job. The Bishop of Mostar, Msgr. Peric, later banished him from living in St. James Parish in Medjugorje. Fr. Mario continues running *Radio 'Mir' Medjugorje*, but now has to commute to Medjugorje every day from Posusje. This had also been the case for Fr. Slavko Barbaric, the spiritual director to the visionaries, who for years had been forced to commute from Humac.

As previously noted, though Bishop Ratko Peric has been the Ordinary of the diocese since 1993, he has never met any of the Medjugorje visionaries. But this doesn't keep him from writing articles and going on speaking tours (Ireland in 2002) publicly defaming them. Like his predecessor, Bishop Zanic, he has never attended an appariton. He went to Medjugorje in August, 1981, but left in disgust just before an apparition on the mountian after listening to an account from village girls, telling his friend Fr. Luka Pavlovic (presently his Vicar General who was then the parish priest in Hrasno) "'Don Luka, we could leave now. There is nothing authentic here!' This is his final position that he has not changed to this day" (*Once Again the Truth About Medjugorje*, Fr. Ljudevit Rupcic, K. Kresimir, Zagreb, 2002, p. 229).

11. *(text on p. 182)* As the war in the Balkans began spreading Our Lady warned in her message: **"You have gone away from God and from me because of your miserable interest... Satan is playing with you and with your souls and I cannot help you because you are far away from my heart. Therefore, pray, live my messages and then you will see the miracles of God's love in your everyday life. Thank you for having responded to my call"** (March 25, 1992).

12. *(text on p. 182)* Interview with Fr. Richard Foley, S.J., November, 1985. Eight years after the cardinal's warning the visionary Ivanka was shown horrible scenes of black people killing black people – rivers filled with dead bodies (June 25, 1993, apparition). Our Lady explained this wasn't inevitable, it could be averted if she received more of a response to her call for prayer and fasting. Who doesn't still shutter at the memory of what took place in Rwanda the following April? Our Lady's presence with us, and her messages, incur great responsibility. On June 26, 1981, she pleaded with tears, **"Peace, Peace, Peace! Be reconciled! Make peace with God and with each other!"** Ten years later to the day the war in the Balkans began (see p. 110). Her presence with us today is a grace not to be passed by: "Today (1950) the hatred of the Moslem countries against the West is becoming hatred against Christianity itself. Although statesmen have not yet taken it into account, there is still grave danger that the temporal power of Islam may return and, with it, the menace that it may shake off a West which has ceased to be Christian, and affirm itself as a great anti-Christian world power. It is our firm belief that the fears some entertain concerning the Moslems are not to be realized, but that *Moslemism*, instead, will eventually be converted to Christianity, through a summoning of the Moslems to a veneration of the Mother of God" (Archbishop Fulton J. Sheen, *The World's First Love,* 1952, McGraw-Hill, NY). It is for this reason that the weekly TV program, "Medjugorje: Our Mother's Last Call," produced by the author, continues being aired by Tele Lumiere, the TV station sponsored by the Bishops and Patriarchs of Lebanon, in Arabic, to every Arabic speaking country in the world.

Appendix 3 Conclusion:
In Remembrance of the 25th Anniversary of the Events in Medjugorje
Fr. Tomislav Pervan, OFM [1]

For the past twenty-five years, Medjugorje has been an actuality on the world scene. Today, it has its zealous advocates; however, it also has its fierce opponents. Opposing front lines in the battle are not likely to sue for peace any time soon. Advocates are tireless in their visits to Medjugorje, all the while believing the authentic voice of Heaven is the starting point, namely, the appearance of the Gospa—Our Lady. Meanwhile, the opponents are fierce in their opposition and seek out elements of contention surrounding the entire set of events.

In the meantime, the ever-increasing daily flow of pilgrims to this place does not allow us to be indifferent. Facts and numbers speak for themselves. The number of pilgrims is ever increasing. They come from all corners of the earth, are of all colors of skin, and from all nations and nationalities. While other places of pilgrimage mark a decrease in pilgrims and pilgrimages despite being advertised widely, the number of pilgrims and faithful of all languages and locales constantly increases. As a phenomenon, Medjugorje does not have an active propaganda machine: individuals spread its fame by word of mouth, witness, and personal experience.

On the one hand, the priests who work in Medjugorje feel they are overburdened in their daily work and that they are stretched to their physical limits. They are faced with innumerable calls for personal counseling, endless confessions, and constant evangelization. On the other hand, they are also faced with the suspicion that they are teetering at the edge of heterodoxy. The constant criticism is hurled at them that they are fostering something that is contrary to the Church, namely, the nonexistent apparitions and the like. We, on

---

1   Fr. Tomislav Pervan, OFM, was the Pastor of St. James Parish in Medjugorje from 1982-1988, and the Franciscan Provincial in Hercegovina from 1994-2001. Presently living in Medjugorje, Fr. Pervan's reflection was originally published by the parish's Information Mir Center on July 13, 2006.

the other hand, cannot fail to speak, fail to give witness about that which we have heard or seen, or that which we experience daily by way of our senses (cf. Acts 4:20). Hence, we invite all to come and see. So many bishops and priests had their doubts; however, after many hours of hearing confessions, they changed their minds and the doubts vanished.

The voice of conscience forces upon us the obligation to be of assistance to those who are in misery and who come here. We wish to be in harmony with the Church to the very end, and not to sin against the Church's teachings or practice. Meanwhile, the accusations and reproaches hurt. Quite frequently, questions are raised that ask: What need did we have of all of this? Were we not able to be like every other parish, that is, carry out the well-entrenched pastoral patterns within the usual norms of the Church and Gospels? Who was it that cooked this stew, such that, to this very day, the river of pilgrims has not dried up, but, to the contrary, continues to grow greater and more dynamic?

For this reason, and as a friend and participant of these events from their beginnings in 1981, I give consideration to what must be done to change the present situations to escape the entrenched position of persistent denial, constant disputation, or, in fact, indifference and silence on the part of the Church's media, all of this while the flow of thousands of pilgrims to this place continues. It is obvious that all the denials, disputations, and silence find no acceptance on the part of the faithful. Meanwhile, Church circles continue to be deaf, and the prohibition against this activity on the part the faithful persists on the part of the media.

It is the inner voice of conscience and the experience of faith that motivate the faithful. I am convinced that the Holy Spirit Himself is the initiator of all these events. I am further convinced that, after twenty-five years have passed, the principle of the locus theologicus (the theological position), according to the notion of the sensus fidelium (understanding on the part of the faithful) and the consensus fidelium (unanimity of the faithful), applies as offered for acceptance by the documents of Vatican II and post-Vatican II, and by statements of Popes following the Council. Things we read about in the Acts of the Apostles are happening here. I am convinced that the Church is being gathered in this place from the four winds and every corner of the earth into the one Kingdom as what took place in Jerusalem at Pentecost. In this place, we find mirrored the universal —"Catholic"— Church in miniature.

It is in this sense that I believe the instruction of the Congregation for the Faith entitled, "The Criteria for Judging and Differentiating Revelations and Apparitions," dated the 27th of February, 1978, and signed by the then Prefect, Cardinal Franjo Seper, should serve as the "vade mecum" (that is, the constant companion, the manual) when considering, passing judgment upon, and making decisions about Medjugorje and the Medjugorje phenomenon. The text has lost nothing of its immediacy and value to this very day. It can be fully applied to the events of Medjugorje with all its implications. It can examine the events of Medjugorje from the positive or negative side with all the arguments presented pro and con.

The Congregation for the Faith in its instructions reduces to three levels, or degrees, the norms that relate to reactions to alleged apparitions.

The seers must be examined to determine if, perhaps, it is a question of self-styled visions. Then, all the messages must be gathered and examined and viewed from the point of view of the degree of education of the seers. The mental and physical state of the seers must be examined thoroughly, as well as their moral integrity. All that is explainable from the purely human point of view must be taken into consideration; however, by the same token, all that cannot be explained in purely human terms and with the aid of the most contemporary psychological or physical sciences, and which, in the end, has no cause within human power, must also be taken into consideration.

Following the first phase, if the matter has not died on its own, has not come to a halt or fallen into oblivion, the principle ad experimentum (for the purpose of experiment) comes into play. At the same time, of course, it must be emphasized that the employment of this principle in no way suggests or recognizes the authenticity of the alleged apparitions. It simply channels events to proper and healthy Church routine: practices regarding prayer, devotions, the sacraments, constant spiritual growth and holiness.

When an appropriate period of the ad experimentum phase has elapsed, and in the light of experiences, especially after a close examination of the spiritual fruits occasioned by the alleged apparitions, and of the devotional practices surrounding them, a competent judgment of the events must be given if circumstances demand it.

As regards the first point, everything can be reduced to a simple conclusion: To the present day, in the entire history of the Church, no Marian apparitions were so intensively and extensively investigated (from 1984-2005) on the part of numerous and independent qualified, international experts in the fields of medicine and psychology, or whose investigations and their results were found to correspond to and complement each other. All of the experts concluded that the subjects investigated were found to be spiritually, psychologically, and physically healthy individuals. They were found not to be hallucinating, subject to confabulation, (auto) suggestion, hysteria, hypnotic or other loss of consciousness, deceit, suggestion or exterior inducement of any sort. Hence, it is irresponsible to publicly proclaim them to be liars or inventors of false visions and messages.

Many experts from the fields of medicine, psychology, and parapsychology have occupied themselves with the Medjugorje seers. They failed to uncover any sort of pathological deviation from the norm in their lives. The scientific experts are capable of reaching the full limit of their tests. However, once they have arrived at that limit, their ability to explain ceases. They are able to discern what does or does not pertain to medicine and pathology and what must be excluded from a medico-psychological perspective. The experts have done so and have left behind a record of their findings. Because of that, and because of intellectual honesty, we, who have regard for the truth, must take their investigations and judgments as to the phenomena of Medjugorje into serious account.

The convergent proofs in favor of the authenticity of the Medjugorje phenomenon are perceptible when one takes into consideration the theological, sociological and scientific experiments carried out upon the seers by French, Italian, and Austrian teams of experts from 1984 through 2005. According to the theologian and Mariologist, R. Laurentin, who has published works of capital value (17 books) on Lourdes, and has thoroughly investigated the apparitions in Medjugorje, the latter give evidence of being more powerful as regards the proof of their authenticity than those in Lourdes, to which the Church gave its formal approval.

According to the teaching of St. Ignatius on discernment of spirits, the causes of those or similar manifestations can be determined to be purely human, divine, or demonic. Effects must always be judged by their cause. In all that took place in Medjugorje, one must ask what the cause was, or where the causal beginnings had their roots. If we take into consideration the first days of the events that took place in Bijakovici in June and July of 1981, the experts who thoroughly examined the seers concluded that the seers had some sort of fundamental and key experience, some initial encounter that put them into the center of something that they could not begin to imagine or foresee, something against their will or inclinations, something they were scarcely able to predict.

Science as such can neither confirm nor deny whether the Gospa is, or is not, appearing, (just as it would not have been able to utilize scientific instruments to register the resurrection of Christ were they to have been present alongside the Roman guards at the tomb of Jesus). All that science can say after twenty-five years is that the seers are physically and psychologically healthy, and that the seers had a deep-seated and far-reaching experience which continues to affect them to this very day, one that it is impossible to deduce from their biographies. All of that is, for the visionaries, a holy treasure. For that reason one must exclude a purely human cause, and, by the same token, one that is demonic, inasmuch as the Devil is unable to yield good fruit that is constant and so long-lasting.

Since twenty-five years have elapsed, a review 'sine ira et studio' (without rancor and [with] diligent attention) would be expedient, both in the local Church and the Church at large, as to the fruits which have been given and continue to be given through Mary's apparitions beyond all ideological suppositions and prejudices. When observed from the purely statistical point of view as a whole, close to some fifty thousand priests have passed through Medjugorje, hundreds of bishops, cardinals, and millions upon millions of the faithful. The Una Sancta et Catholica (the One Holy and Catholic [Church]) in miniature comes to pass here every day. Were there something to be found heretical, schismatic, or contrary to Church teaching, the Church would be obliged to undertake measures against such abuse. That has not resulted up to the present. Therefore, a fifteen-year ad experimentum period since the Zadar Pronouncement in 1991 is a suf-ficient amount of time so as to allow to conclude that no straying from official Church teaching and practice is taking place in Medjugorje. The Liturgy and devotions celebrated there are fully Christological, Marian, Eucharistic, sacramental, and in full harmony with Church regulations.

It cannot be asserted that the particular fruits of Medjugorje are those of intensive prayer and administration of the sacraments. To do so would be to create a "circulus vitiosus" (vicious circle): there are other places in the world where prayer and the sacraments are a fixed practice; however, what is lacking there are the efficacious effects that we note as attributable to Medjugorje. It is clear that prayer and the sacraments bear copious fruits for the entire Church throughout the world; however, from where and why do so many people come pre-cisely to Medjugorje? Why do they come to this remote place where they have a concrete experience of God and grace, are converted, learn to pray, and subsequently carry the fruits of Medjugorje to their homes, give witness to what they have experienced, and become missionaries? It simply is not possible to separate the assertions of the seers regarding the apparitions from the fruits of the apparitions which we see in the Church.

The "consensus fidei et fidelium" can be seen by the fact that all levels of God's people, all classes in society and the Church, all peoples, and all races are represented in Medjugorje, and by the fact that Church life is sustained by all of this in the form of witness, divine worship, sincere service, charity, (*martyria, liturgia, et diakonia*), and, by the fact that all grow in holiness. Medjugorje is a worldwide phenomenon. Its fruits can be seen in all parts of the world. In essence, Medjugorje is a laymen's movement, a movement of faithful laymen, laden with spirituality, devotion, and sincerity toward the Lord and Our Lady. The seers themselves are ordinary lay people and, as such, are able more readily to touch the hearts of plain folks who easily identify with them.

Medjugorje is a peace and pilgrimage movement inasmuch as people come here for the sake of inner peace. It is also a renewal movement within the Church—"Ecclesia semper reformanda" (the Church ever to be renewed), as well as a humanitarian movement, inasmuch as it has accomplished tremendous charitable and Samaritan works throughout the world (a point made by the present Pope in his encyclical on the God of Love). *Lumen Gentium* (The Vatican II Document: *Light of the Nations*) clearly states: "Be they most illustrious, be they simple and more widespread, Charisms are useful and are especially suited to the needs of the Church and must be received with gratitude and consolidation" (LG 12:2). Meanwhile, *Apostolicam Actuositatem (Apostolic Activity)* states even more explicitly: "The receipt of Charisms, even those that are humble, give rise to the right and duty for each of the faithful to make use of them in the Church and in the world and for the good of mankind and the growth of the Church in the freedom of the Holy Ghost" (AA 3:3).

After the past quarter of a century, it can be asserted that Medjugorje is about a prophetic Charism—a prophetic revelation that calls for repentance. These Charisms are able to be found in all similar phenomena within the Church. Prophetic revelations and apparitions are about an imperative under the impetus of the Holy Spirit as to how one is to behave here and now, and what it is that the People of God must do in a specific situation. Accordingly, the Church must not relate to such phenomena indifferently. She is duty-bound to investigate such an imperative with openness and, congruently, to act if she recognizes the Will of God in the said phenomenon. It is obvious that the "Ecclesia orans" (the praying Church) has recognized God's Will and Mary's presence in this instance, of which our dearly departed Pope spoke in his homily in Zadar (!) three years prior, on the feast of Mary, the Mother of the Church (Pentecost Monday, 2003). On that occasion, the Pope specifically mentioned the above cited "sensus fidei fidelium" (the understanding of faith of the faithful).

If, as is the case with ordinary beatifications and canonizations, the process begins with the local Church, and, after an appropriate interval of time, investigation, and conclusions based on the materials offered in favor of beatification or canonization, the matter is transferred to Rome, I think that would be appropriate in this case. After all has been investigated at the local level, the entire case of the Medjugorje phenomenon should be transferred to the appropriate Roman dicastery, especially in light of the fact that it has outgrown the local Church's boundaries and has become widespread so as to encompass the entire Church. The countless prayer groups throughout the entire world have come into existence because of the events in Medjugorje. They carry the mark of authenticity and veracity. The entire phenomenon is caught up in the very being of the Church and, as such, carries more weight than does a beatification of one of God's chosen ones. If, as is the case for beatification, the People of God are asked their approval, why shouldn't we do so in this case as well, especially in light of Mary's efficacious presence in specific places (John Paul II, in Zadar!), and in light of the personal experiences and miracles that individuals experienced precisely here in Medjugorje?

Throughout the entire history of Salvation, God has established communication with his creatures through apparitions. This form of communication is especially suitable for man's physico-spiritual structure: it immerses man's senses, especially his sight and hearing. The Medjugorje phenomenon can be explained in this manner or that manner; however, intellectual honesty demands that the entire affair engage us in light of revelation, mysticism, supernatural experiences and so many other similar experiences in other cases, and, for that matter, in other faiths.

If God has truly spoken throughout history, why should we be exempted from such a manner of communication wherein the Holy Spirit makes use of apparitions for the sake of the many needs of the contemporary world? The greater the misery in the world, so much the greater is the need for God's voice and communication. Hence, we might well conclude as did Paul: "Do not extinguish the Spirit. Do not disdain prophetic communications. Investigate all and hold on to what is good!"(1 Thess. 5:19-21).

Noting in 1996 that ever-increasing numbers of pilgrims from throughout the world were coming to Medjugorje, Fr. Tomislav Pervan presented the following observation.[2]

Thousands of Polish people are coming these days to Medjugorje, even though they have their own "Madonna Nera," and at Easter there were over two thousand Czech people and there are even more than that now. Among them, a large representation of youth and some very devoted priests. It was really the evil spirit of Communism which spread decay and diluted the fervor of the Czech people. It gradually ripped the seams of the Czech church and took God out of their everyday life. Today we witness the renaissance of the faith of that people. Their deceased Cardinal Tomasek, who was something like a symbol of resistance to the Communist dragon in former Czechoslovakia, was very pro-Medjugorje. He welcomed the visionaries as well as the Franciscans. Clearly his position had an influence on the faithful who visit Medjugorje. I suppose every human being is a little like the migrating bird, always looking for a warmer place, especially for the heart and the soul. If countless millions hadn't found exactly that, the warmth of the mother, her heart, if they hadn't experienced a glimpse of heaven being given, graces inducing conversion, others wouldn't have received the strength to undertake such a long journey, with so many sacrifices and renunciations. Just as the migrating bird has a built-in urge to long for warmer regions when it begins to freeze, so too man, surrounded by indifferent hearts and a non-caring society, in a cold atmosphere of cities with all its technology and computerization, also seeks a refuge where he can nourish his heart and soul. He requires a heavenly purification where he can wash away his whole past and unburden himself of what he has been carrying. Then he is no longer Sisyphus or Prometheus. He is already a follower of Jesus Christ and it is Mother Mary who has led him to her Son.

---

2   An interview with Fr. Tomislav Pervan, *"Medjugorje, the New Emmaus,"* published in *GLAS MIRA* No. 7. 1996, pages 9/13. Fr. Pervan was the Franciscan provincial at the time.

It is not coincidental that Our Lady's Magnificat became something like a manifest among the oppressed and the homeless of Latin America. Mary's prayer is like an overture to Jesus' Sermon on the Mount, which revolutionizes relationships between people. In this way the "little ones" and the oppressed become aware of their important role and their responsibility for the destiny of the world. Jesus, and Mary too, with their lives give measure and perspective how to responsibly approach the world and change it. And it really is those "little ones" who are most open towards what's new in the Gospel and to heaven's message.

Examining the history of the world retrospectively – over the last century and a half in the light of the history of salvation, if we just try and highlight where it converges with the history of philosophical thought and its development – there we find the phenomenon of Mary's apparitions, beginning in 1830, ten years after the famous Marxist "Communist Manifest." At Lourdes in 1858, Mary reveals herself as the Immaculate Conception, who crushes the head of the Serpent (which might well be the Communist Serpent, too). On the eve of the October Revolution we have the apparitions at Fatima. A huge sign, an appeal to conversion, and an appeal to pray for Russia who will bring an atheistic ideology to the world. In the middle of this century, Pope Pius XII proclaims the doctrinal truth of Mary's assumption into heaven as a response to the vast slaughtering in the Second World War, where one hundred million people lost their lives. These numerous wars were the result of all these new philosophies and existentialism having underestimated, invalidated and distorted the truth about the human condition. It was amid all ungodliness and turmoil that faith in the "resurrection of the body" was proclaimed, with Mary as the model and heralder. Medjugorje was something like Jericho's triumphant trumpet blast, a seven-year-long prayer overture, a torch-lit march in prayer to break down the Communist atheist and antihuman reign of terror. [3] As far as I know, no one has written about

---

3   Responding to the allegations of Bishop Peric, the present Bishop of Mostar, that the messages of the Gospa ("Our Lady") are being written by the Franciscans and the visionaries are pretending to have apparitions, Fr. Rupcic writes:

"Who could possibly believe that a Communist regime – the fifth most this event treating it as a big occurrence, in the light of philosophical history. But we can be sure that, without the prayer and sacrifices of those "little ones," the deprived, who day by day fasted, prayed and cried out to God to save us and to deliver us from evil and the evil one, this important event would never have taken place. It may even be the most important event since the dawn of Christianity.

I think it was C.G. Jung who said that the Gospel is the remedy for the whole world. So, the words of Jesus of Nazareth stand out with authority for all peoples of all times. They give bearing and proportion, true perspective and direction for human life and the future of humanity. If we were even in a small measure to accept Jesus' authority, I believe that the face of this earth would look different. It was the saints and the mystics who greatly helped this world, not by

powerful in all of Europe, armed with the most modern weapons – could not have forced out a children's 'phantom' from Medjugorje but that she forced them out of Yugoslavia and Europe? That several ordinary village children with their game can initiate an avalanche of facts, shake up the world and motivate millions and millions of people from all over the world to think what they think, to accept what they say and to do what is asked of them? That these more illiterate than literate children can convince world experts and scientists of their 'imaginations' and 'lies' and pass this on to them as the truth?

"Who can believe that hundreds and hundreds of sick people – among whom were those with incurable diseases – who could not be healed by the best experts in the world, were healed with a trick by irresponsible children? Who could believe that millions of people were tricked by mischievous children and converted, left alcohol, drugs, swearing, returned to their families and became new people? That thousands of young people were motivated by immature children from Medjugorje to cast off hedonsism, debauched sexual lives, and consciously chose self denial, fasting and a life in keeping with the Gospel. Some after leaving behind drugs and debauchery headed off into the missions. That millions of people who for years had not been to confession, nor peeked into a church, at the advice of immature children, approached substantial confession and accepted the practice of Sunday Mass? That thousands upon thousands of families, who did not make the sign of the cross, at the mere hint of some children decided to pray the Rosary every day?

"Whoever believes that any of this comes from hallucinations and sick children in particular, and whoever believes that this comes from the Devil, has incredibly 'strong faith,' but it is not reasonable or acceptable belief because it does not respect a basic principle of reason which says that no thing can happen without sufficient cause, and no repercussion can be greater than its cause" (*Once Again the Truth About Medjugorje*, K. Kresimir, Zagreb, 2002, pp. 329, 330).

delving into the depths and expanses of space, but by going into the depths of their hearts. There, they uncovered an image of God within themselves which they were then able to pass on to others as a fount of wisdom for life. How they differ from all those intellectuals and scientists who with their discoveries only led man to his downfall and to hell. Life without technology and technological advances is hardly imaginable, but what if all of it moves out of control? That really is the path that we are on, because modern man is Prometheus or Camus's man in revolt, against every authority, trying to dominate whatever is most out of his control. We ourselves don't even know where these chariots of fire are leading us. That is why Medjugorje in all its simplicity (and simplicity is always perfection!) is essentially an invitation to live the Gospel. There is no new teaching, just an accentuation of truths known, written and lived for centuries. It is a clear contemporary proof of how possible it is to live by the Gospel today. People are open to these messages, many prayer groups have been formed, inspired by the events, which is a clear message of how this can happen. It is not on the surface, but deep in the heart of the Church, centering around the Eucharist...

"Right from the beginning I have been tightly linked with Medjugorje, and after fifteen years I am convinced that it is not a meeting place for the inquisitive, the sensationalists and the fanatics. It is already known as a place of prayer, conversion and for celebrating the sacred mysteries of our faith, especially the Holy Mass. Medjugorje began with the laity, with ordinary children, it was brought to the laity and it was they who first believed and only then was it passed on to the priests. And today it is the laity who bring the Medjugorje movement to the whole world. It is really the laity who hundreds of times cross even oceans to come to Medjugorje. When I ask them why they come so often to Medjugorje, and why they bring pilgrims to these parts which aren't safe, they reply that they do it because they see changes in people. Spiritual changes. Just like the change in the apostles before and after Jesus' Resurrection and after the descent of the Holy Spirit. People change and that becomes a motive for a return visit, for the establishment of prayer groups, and then we have a renewal of the Church from the base upwards. Note that neither

Mary nor Jesus and certainly not the apostles nor the first disciples came from the priesthood, but rather from the laity. Jesus Christ is clearly the Son of God, but he wasn't brought up in the Temple and among the priests and hierarchy of his time. Because of Herod and the Roman government they even tended to hide Him from the world.

"... Just this Monday and Tuesday (the 15th anniversary), over fifty thousand Holy Communions were distributed, there were many occasions of grace and of reconciliation, of interior and physical healing. On the 25th of June at Holy Mass, there were 250 concelebrants and at least 50 tireless confessors worked in the confessionals throughout the day.

"There, where Holy Mass is celebrated, it breaks the power of Satan and the dragon, and there, where Mary is loved and esteemed and sung to with raised hearts and hands which cry up to the heavens, the hellish violence which was shackling and still chains us will disappear. Let's allow the Spirit of God to work through us. Even today the Pope in his foreword to the new Code of Canon Law says " it appears sufficiently clear that the Code is in no way intended as a substitute for faith, grace, charisms and especially charity in the life of the Church and of the faithful. On the contrary, its purpose is rather to create such an order in the ecclesial society that, while assigning the primacy to love, grace and charisms, it at the same time renders their organic development easier in the life of both the ecclesial society and the individual persons who belong to it." The important question is whether it's this love and grace which are a driving force in our lives or just mere rules We should all ask ourselves that question. It is a simple question, but the most difficult one to face.

Appendix 4

Postscript

In November, 2004, **Bishop J. Faber MacDonald** (St. John, New Brunswick, Canada) went on pilgrimage to Medjugorje to celebrate 25 years of ordination as a bishop (May, 1981). Upon returning home he wrote "Medjugorje, My Personal Experience," a Pastoral Directive that he published from his episcopal office: [1]

After Our Lady started appearing in Medjugorje on June 24, 1981, "the local Bishop, at the beginning, after visiting the visionaries, made a statement based on what is known as the Gamaliel principle which is recorded in Acts 5:38-39. Gamaliel said, 'If this movement is of human origin, it will destroy itself. If, on the other hand, it comes from God, you will not be able to destroy it without fighting God Himself.' Not long after declaring himself in this way, the local bishop changed his mind and his position completely, going against the principle. The speculation of those close to the situation and aware of the history is that his change is situated in a long-standing tension between the diocesan clergy and the Franciscans. The present bishop has continued in the same position, without even speaking with the visionaries. The other Yugoslav bishops have an open attitude. There have been a large number of bishops and cardinals who have come from all over the world on pilgrimage to Medjugorje...

"The Medjugorje event, especially the negative attacks, are situated in the context of God's Word to the serpent from the first pages of the Bible. This Word has been played out in human history, and is being played out in a unique way in relation to Medjugorje. The text: 'I will put enmity between you and the woman, between your offspring and hers; he will strike at your head, while you strike at his heel" (Gen. 3:15).

"The appearance of Our Lady in Medjugorje saw all hell break loose, in the division between the Bishop and the Franciscans; the Bishop contradicting himself; the Bosnian war with its layers of suppressed religious and ethnic hatreds exploding with unspeakable cruelty; the cynicism and rejection of vast numbers of clergy worldwide, without ever having gone to experience the event, now 24 years old; ignoring the huge number of pilgrims, over 30,000,000, and ignoring, as well, the huge number of converts with dramatic stories of grace and conversion...

"It is events like Medjugorje that remind us that God is not indifferent nor is He 'way out there in space.' God is concerned about each one of us. He expresses this in sending His mother. He reminds us of the role of the Church – to keep people awake; to keep us aware of His love and His concern for us. This destruction of Jerusalem happened as Jesus said it would.

" As he came near and saw the city, he wept over it, saying, 'If you, even you, had only recognized on this day the things that make for peace! But now they are hidden from your eyes. Indeed, the days will come upon you, when your enemies will set up ramparts around you and surround you, and hem you in on every side. They will crush you to the ground, you and your children within you, and they will not leave within you one stone upon another; because you did not recognize the time of your visitation from God'" (Luke 19:41-44).

"In our time Jesus is weeping over the New Jerusalem, His Church. In Medjugorje, through His mother, He has revealed the things that make for peace. Isn't it time to recognize this visitation from God?"

1. In August, 1988, the same month Bishop Michael Pfeifer, Ordinary of San Angelo, Texas (USA) published a Pastoral Letter to his diocese, *The Gospel, Mary and Medjugorje*, E. Michael Jones began his attacks in *Fidelity Magazine* (see Appendix 3, p. 178). Though the bishop's Pastoral Directive was completely ignored by the Catholic media – much attention was given to Jones's attack. (See again footnote #3 on p. 20 and the last paragraph of endnote #7 on p. 35.)

Bishop Luigo Secco and the Prime Minister of the Netherlands Antilles, Mrs. Emily de Jongh-Elhage, after celebrating the first Mass in the shrine's adoration chapel (for Mary TV's project). Some see the shrine as an answer to prayer. Addressing the Prime Minister when visiting Curacao on May 13,1990, Pope John Paul II said, "I pray to Almighty God that the people of the Netherlands Antilles, with wise counsel and generous endeavor, will build a just and caring society, a place of peace and well-being for all the inhabitants of these islands."

The Netherlands Choir sang during a special outdoor Mass (offered for the success of Mary TV's satellite project, see pp. 208- 214). Such a facility could connect Medjugorje shrines with the mother shrine in Bosnia Hercegovina.

The orginal cross on Mt. Krizevac in Medjugorje.

Denis and Cathy Nolan and their 8 children (and 12 grandchildren) live in South Bend, Indiana. Cathy writes a daily reflection on one of Our Lady's messages from Medjugorje that is posted on **MARY TV**'s web page: <http://www.marytv.tv> Those wishing to receive it by email (and/or be on **MARY TV**'s email list) can email their email address to:

<dnolan@marytv.tv>

Denis directs **MARY TV**, a lay apostolate responding to Pope John Paul II's last appeal to the Church, his Apostolic Exhortation, "The Rapid Development," made public on February 22, 2005. (For more information, go to **MARY TV**'s web site or write: **MARY TV** • PO Box 899 • Notre Dame, IN 46556 (USA) Tel: (574) 255 - 0209).

MARY TV's television satellite project - which has the potential of bringing Medjugorje, live, directly into family living rooms throughout the world and allowing live teleconferencing worldwide to Medju-gorje Shrines and conferences, will only become a reality if the laity join together in response to the Holy Father's appeal. **MARY TV**'s most important need right now is for committed spiritual intercessors who will join Cardinal Sin and Mother Angelica in praying for its success (see pp. 213, 214).

MARY TV also needs monetary donations. Consider becoming a regular monthly donor (all donations are tax-exempt). **MARY TV** brochures, "This Time Is My Time" (see pp. 209 - 212) are available upon request. For brochures, copies of this book and/or CD's & DVD's, go to:

http://marytv.tv/Store/

IMPORTANT: The Chapter on "Good Fruit" (Chapter X, pp. 116 - 150) was not originally intended to be part of this book. When beginning research, however, the testimonies included in Chapter 10 were unavoid-able – and are no doubt just the tip of an iceberg. Please send to **MARY TV** – for possible future edtions of this book – testimonies of the good fruit of Medjugorje that you have witnessed or are aware of. *Send to:*

MARY TV • PO Box 899 • Notre Dame, IN 46556 (USA)
or email to: **<dnolan@marytv.tv>)**

Dear Children!
You are responsible for the messages.
The source of grace is here, but you,
dear children, are the vehicles
transmitting the gifts. Therefore,
dear children, I am calling you
to work responsibly. Everyone will
be responsible according to his own measure.
Dear children, I am calling you to give the gift
to others with love and not to keep it for yourselves.
Thank you for having responded to my call."

(May 8, 1986)

"We've got to do this for Our Lady!
We've got to do this for Our Lady!
We've got to do this for Our Lady!

"We've got to put the advanced communications technologies
at HER disposal and not just complain about how its being used
by others to spread pornography!"

Denis Nolan addressing the
2004 National Conference on Medjugorje
at the University of Notre Dame

The pastoral ministry vested in me, the councilor outlook I have
o often spoken about and encouraged; my personal experience
ind convictions about humanity, about Christianity and about
*:he role of bishop, **all lead me to emphasize the possibilities***
for good, the richness, the timeliness of the media!"

Pope John Paul II, May 10, 1981

IN HIS FINAL APOSTOLIC LETTER, *The Rapid Development,* released by the Vatican on 2/21/05, **Pope John Paul II** told us the use of modern communications technologies "is the responsibility of each and every one…an integral part of the Church's mission in the third millennium…

"The first Areopagus of modern times is the world of communications, which is capable of unifying humanity and transforming it into—as it is commonly referred to—'a global village.'…**Do not be afraid of the new technologies!** These rank 'among the marvelous things'—'inter mirifica'—which God has placed at our disposal…To Mary, who gave us the Word of life, and who kept his unchanging words in her heart, do I entrust the journey of the Church in today's world."

WHAT?   a TV Satellite Uplink Facility in Medjugorje

WHERE?   Adjacent to St. James Church.

WHEN?   Construction has already begun. Several Networks have said they will broadcast whatever we uplink to Satellite. *We will begin right away streaming on the internet the prayers and liturgies in St. James Church.*

WHO IS DOING THIS?   "Mary TV", a lay apostolate founded by Denis Nolan.

HOW YOU CAN JOIN & HELP: Two ways…

#1) Spiritual: Intercessors — people willing to offer up their sufferings in prayer for it's spiritual protection. To become an intercessor, email <dnolan@marytv.tv> or write to "Mary TV" (address below).

#2) Material: Begin today sending your monthly donation (tax exempt) to "Mary TV" for the cost of construction, TV equipment, programming preparation, satellite time, etc.

Checks can be made out   **"Mary TV"**
to "Mary TV" & sent to: P.O. Box 899
                           Notre Dame, IN 46556 (USA)
                           www.marytv.tv

This is a private lay appeal,
not an appeal coming from the parish of Medjugorje.

THE LAITY ARE BEING CALLED!

"Public opinion has been shocked at how easily the advanced communication technologies can be exploited by those whose intentions are evil. At the same time, can we not observe a relative slowness on the part of those who wish to do good to use the same opportunities?...It is not easy to remain optimistic...

"It would be a significant achievement if Christians could cooperate more closely with one another in the media..."

Pope John Paul II, May 11, 1997

The Holy Father taught in *Christifideles Laici:* "First of all, the *freedom for lay people in the Church to form such groups* is to be acknowledged. Such liberty is a true and proper right that is not derived from any kind of 'concession' by authority, but flows from the Sacrament of Baptism which calls the lay faithful to participate actively in the Church's communion and mission....A citation from the recently published Code of Canon Law affirms it as well: 'The Christian faithful are at liberty to found and govern associations for charitable and religious purposes or for the promotion of the Christian vocation in the world...,' (sec. 29)... Pastors of the Church, even if faced with possible and understandable difficulties as a result of such associations and the process of employing new forms, cannot renounce the service provided by their authority, not simply for the well-being of the Church, but also for the well-being of the lay associations themselves..." (Sec. 31).

Mary TV is a lay apostolate in communion with the Church that has been established to respond to Our Lady's call and the Holy Father's appeal. On May 28, 2004, the Pope told visiting bishops from the United States: **"Now is above all the hour of the lay faithful!"**

When News of Our Lady's Presence with Us
in Medjugorje Reaches People through the Media...

LIVES ARE CHANGED.

As a young boy **Don Calloway** was taking heroin, crack, opium
— every day! By the age of 14 he had committed felonies. His was a life
cycle of death! And then one night his whole life changed when he saw
pictures of Medjugorje in a book and read about Our Lady's apparitions!
*(The testimony of Fr. Donald Calloway, MIC., Vocations Director for the
Marians of the Immaculate Conception, is available from Mary TV on DVD.)*

Lola Falana, the highest paid female entertainer in Las Vegas history,
happened to see scenes of Medjugorje on TV one night in 1987 when
she was lying in bed suffering from MS. She found herself praying
that she'd gladly give up all her fame if she could just go there, climb
that mountain and pray before that cross! Within the year she went
to Medjugorje, was healed and became a Catholic. She has centered
her life ever since around adoration of Jesus in the Blessed Sacrament!

Fr. James Wiley, of Pittsburgh, left the priesthood in 1974. He no longer
believed in the existence of God. As a favor he tape-recorded a TV
program one night for a friend: "After seeing a program on TV about
Medjugorje I suddenly believed. I went from unbelief to belief overnight.
I was given the grace of conversion by seeing that one program on TV!"
Fr. Wiley has been reinstated by his bishop to active ministry in his diocese.

A Prime Minister who happened to hear Medjugorje being spoken
about over the radio in his country decided to give his life to Our Lady
and consecrate his county to her Immaculate Heart! He officially did
the consecration (and continues receiving Our Lady's monthly messages)
though he and his wife, and 85% of his country, are Hindu!

After seeing a program on TV about Medjugorje, the founder of the
Congressional Human Rights Caucus (not a baptized Christian)
organized a Congressional briefing in Washington, DC, on the
importance of the messages of peace being given to the world today
by Our Lady in Medjugorje!

The incredible grace experienced by these people could happen for
the whole world—overnight—if we joined together and responded to
the Holy Father's last Apostolic Letter, *The Rapid Development.* Soon after
its release he told us in his will, **"Victory, when it will come, will
be a victory through Maria!"**

His Eminence Jaime L. Cardinal Sin, D.D.

06 June 2005

DENIS NOLAN
President
Mary TV
Notre Dame, Indiana

Dear Mr. Nolan,

Peace in Christ!

Thank you for the letter and copies of the brochure, *"This time is my time!"*, that you gave me. Your thoughtfulness is a source of joy and consolation. I want you to know that I gladly suppot your project.

You are a true friend, so priceless and valuable in life. God is so good for sending friends like you. Let us together praise and give thanks to the Lord!

I will offer my prayers and sacrifices for your intentions.

Thank you for remembering me in your prayers.

With every best wish, I remain,

Devotedly in Christ,

+ JAIME L. CARDINAL SIN, D.D.
Archbishop Emeritus of Manila

    Cardinal Sin is no doubt continuing his intercession from Heaven (see p. 128). Mother Angelica, foundress of EWTN and the nuns of Our Lady of the Angels Monastery are also interceding. Their vicar, Sr. Catherine, writes (see p. 214): "Dear Denis, Thank you so much for your letter, the CD – Listen to My Messages, DVD of Fr. Donald Calloway's incredible testimony and a copy of your booklet! Mother and I are most grateful for these special gifts as well as your fidelity to the great mission Mary has entrusted you with. Be assured that you have our prayers as well as the prayers of the whole Community..."

A Day of Prayer

will be offered by

The Nuns of Our Lady of the Angels Monastery

for

The Special Intentions of Denis Nolan

on

April 28, 2006

~Feast of St. Louis Marie de Monfort~

at the request of

Sister M. Catherine

Dear Denis, Thank you so much for your letter, the CD - Listen to My Messages, DVD of Fr. Donald Calloway's incredible testimony and copy of your booklet! Mother and I are most grateful for these special gifts as well as your fidelity to the great mission Mary has entrusted you with. Be assured that you have our prayers as well as the prayers of the whole Community before Jesus our Eucharistic King! May you receive an abundance of graces and blessings flowing from His glorious Resurrection!

Remembrance at Mass · Divine Office · Rosary · Adoration Hour · Prayerful Good Works

Adoremus in Aeternum Sanctissimum Sacramentum

214

Suggested Reading:

The parish of Medjugorje has the best library on these events. Fr. Slavko Barbaric's books and the most up to date information can be found on the web site of *Information Center "Mir" Medjugorje:* <http://www.medjugorje.hr>.

The Apparitions of Our Lady at Medjugorje, by Fr. Svetozar Kraljevic, Franciscan Herald Press, Chicago, IL, (1984).

The Queen of Peace Visits Medjugorje, Fr. Joseph A. Pelletier, Assumption Publ, 50 Old English Road, Worcester, MA 01609 (1985).

A Thousand Encounters With the Blessed Virgin, by Fr. Janko Bubalo, Friends of Medjugorje, 4851 So. Drexel Blvd, Chicago, IL, 60615, (1987). (The Italian edition of this extensive interview with the visionary Vicka was awarded the 1985 "Sapienze Award" by Cardinal Angelo Rossi, dean of the College of Cardinals.

God Sent — A History of Accredited Apparitions of Mary, Roy Abraham Varghese, Crossroads Publishing Company, 370 Lexington Ave., NY, NY 10017 (2000).

Medjugorje: The 90's — The Triumph of the Heart, by Sr. Emmanuel, Queenship Publishing, PO Box 220 Goleta, CA 93116; Tel: (800) 647-9882 www,queenship.org.

Is the Virgin Mary Appearing at Medjugorje? by Fr. Rene Laurentin & Fr. Ljudevit Rupcic, The Word Among Us Press, Box 3646, Washington, D.C., 20037 (1984).

Echo of Mary Queen of Peace, Casella Postale 27, I - 31030, Bessica (TV) Italy

Medjugorje Gebetsaktion (Quarterly) Postfach 18, A-1153 (Vienna) Austria.

Medjugorje, The Message, Wayne Weible, Paraclete Press, Orleans, Mass.

Medjugorje: A Time for Truth and a Time for Action, Denis Nolan (published by Queenship Publishing Co., PO Box 220, Goleta, CA 93116; www.queenship.org. Tel: (800) 647-9882). This book is also available from MARY TV, PO Box 899, Notre Dame, IN 46556, Tel: (574) 255-0209 (www.marytv.tv).

Our lady Speaks form Medjugorje, by Andrew Yeung, Ave Maria Center of Peace, Box 489, Station U, Tornoto, Ontario, M8Z 5Y8, Canada

My Sweet Angels is the best DVD on Medjugorje...available from Parish House in Medjugorje, or in the U.S. from Medjugorje Web, <www.medjugorje.org>